Vorstufen des Exils / Early Stages of Exile

Amsterdamer Beiträge zur neueren Germanistik

STUDIES IN GERMAN LITERATURE AND CULTURAL STUDIES

Founding Editor

Gerd Labroisse

Series Editors

William Collins Donahue
Norbert Otto Eke
Sven Kramer
Elizabeth Loentz

VOLUME 91

The titles published in this series are listed at *brill.com/abng*

Vorstufen des Exils / Early Stages of Exile

Herausgegeben von / Edited by

Reinhard Andress

Egon Schwarz gewidmet

BRILL

RODOPI

LEIDEN | BOSTON

Cover illustration: Ernst Barlach, Lesender Mann im Wind. Source: Lempertz Auction House: https://www.lempertz.com/de/kataloge/lot/1059-1/321-ernst-barlach.html

Library of Congress Cataloging-in-Publication Data

Names: Andress, Reinhard, 1957- editor. | North American Society for Exile Studies.
Title: Vorstufen des Exils = early stages of exile / herausgegeben von, edited by Reinhard Andress.
Other titles: Early stages of exile
Description: Leiden ; Boston : Brill Rodopi, [2020] | Series: Amsterdamer Beiträge zur neueren Germanistik, 0304-6257 ; volume 91 | Includes bibliographical references and index. | Contributions in German and in English.
Identifiers: LCCN 2020023500 (print) | LCCN 2020023501 (ebook) | ISBN 9789004424708 (hardback ; acid-free paper) | ISBN 9789004424715 (ebook)
Subjects: LCSH: Exiles in literature--Congresses. | Authors, Exiled--Congresses. | Exiles--Congresses.
Classification: LCC PN56.5.E96 V67 2020 (print) | LCC PN56.5.E96 (ebook) | DDC 809/.8920691--dc23
LC record available at https://lccn.loc.gov/2020023500
LC ebook record available at https://lccn.loc.gov/2020023501

Typeface for the Latin, Greek, and Cyrillic scripts: "Brill". See and download: brill.com/brill-typeface.

ISSN 0304-6257
ISBN 978-90-04-42470-8 (hardback)
ISBN 978-90-04-42471-5 (e-book)

Inhaltsverzeichnis / Contents

Vorstufen des Exils: ein unterbeleuchtetes Kapitel in der Exilforschung

Reinhard Andress

In den Worten des bekannten deutschen Historikers Claus-Dieter Krohn war „die Vertreibung aus dem nationalsozialistischen Deutschland einzigartig, denn keine der anderen zu der Zeit erzwungenen Fluchtbewegungen beruhte auf so einseitig begründeter Gewalt, Brutalität, Ausschließung und schließlich physischer Vernichtung" (1). Insgesamt wurden 500.000 Menschen aus Deutschland, dem 1938 „angeschlossenen" Österreich und dem annektierten Sudetenland verjagt, unter ihnen ungefähr 10.000 Literaten und Künstler (vgl. Krohn 1–2). Viel hat die in den 1960er-Jahren in Gang gekommene Exilforschung schon geleistet, um dieses traurige Kapitel aufzuarbeiten. Das dreibändige, von Herbert A. Strauss und Werner Röder herausgegebene *Biographische Handbuch der deutschsprachigen Emigration nach 1933* (1980–83) ist nur eines der vielen, umfangreichen Publikationen, die hier angeführt werden könnten.

Inzwischen ist die Exilforschung im Zusammenhang mit dem Nationalsozialismus so weit vorangeschritten, dass es Ansätze zur Perspektivenerweiterung gibt. Im Jahre 2012 auf einer Tagung der Gesellschaft für Exilforschung unter dem Titel „Quo vadis, Exilforschung? Stand und Perspektiven. Die Herausforderung der Globalisierung" forderte der Sozialhistoriker Marcel van der Linden, „das Exilthema weiter zu fassen und es als einen Bestandteil der weltweiten Flüchtlingsproblematik zu behandeln. Exilanten sind ja auch Flüchtlinge, und ihr Schicksal kann deshalb wenigstens teilweise auch aus der allgemeineren Perspektive der Flucht betrachtet werden" (6). Das ist eine groß angelegte Aufgabe, bei der multidisziplinäre und interdisziplinäre Ansätze zum Tragen kommen, die das Phänomen global, geschichtlich und bis hin zu den aktuellen Migrationsbewegungen erfassen. Allerdings wurde diese Aufforderung der Perspektivenerweiterung nicht völlig in einem Vakuum ausgesprochen, wie das etwa zur selben Zeit erschienene *Handbuch der deutschsprachigen Exilliteratur* (2013) beweist. Im Vorwort umreißen die Herausgeberinnen Bettina Bannasch und Gerhild Rochus ihr Ziel, anhand von sechzig exemplarischen Werken zu zeigen, „dass und inwiefern transnationale, transkulturelle und transhistorische Ansätze der aktuellen Exilforschung verständlich gemacht und gewinnbringend auf literarische Texte angewendet werden können" (XI). Wie der Untertitel des Handbuchs „Von Heinrich Heine bis Herta Müller" verdeutlicht, beschränkt sich die Auswahl der Werke keineswegs auf die Zeit des Nationalsozialismus, wenn auch dieser im Zentrum der Aufmerksamkeit bleibt.

Eine andere Perspektivierung wird mit dem vorliegenden Band angestrebt, die in der zeitlichen Erweiterung des Exilbegriffs an sich liegt. Denn gewöhnlich wird Exil als die Zeit definiert, in der man getrennt von der Heimat im Ausland als Zufluchtsort aus einer Vielzahl von Verfolgungsgründen lebt, eventuell freiwillig, doch eher gezwungenermaßen oder verbannt. Exil kann aber weiter gefasst auch als Prozess begriffen werden, der bereits in der Heimat, unterwegs und/oder vor der Ankunft im Exilland anfängt. Es sind Vorstufen des Exils. Die Zeichnung von Ernst Barlach, „Lesender Mann im Wind" (1922), die auf dem Banddeckel wiedergegeben wird, stellt vielleicht diesen Zustand in künstlerisch gedrängter Form dar. Sitzend mit einem aufgeschlagenen Buch auf den Knien ist ein leicht androgyn wirkender Mensch – somit alle Geschlechter umfassend – einem starken Wind ausgesetzt, symbolisch den Stürmen der Zeit, denen er lesend und denkend als Zeichen seines intellektuellen Daseins trotzt, doch nicht ohne eine Andeutung des möglichen Aufbruchs: Im Hintergrund ist ein großes Wasser zu sehen, das es vielleicht im Exilgang zu überqueren gilt.

An sich waren die Vorstufen des Exils schon lange in der Exilforschung wenigstens indirekt vorhanden. Der Historiker Peter Gay, dessen Buch *Weimar Culture: the Outsider as Insider* (1968) federführend in der Auseinandersetzung mit der intellektuellen Migration als Folge des Nationalsozialismus wurde, schrieb 1969 in seinem Essay „Weimar Culture":

> The excitement that characterized Weimar culture stemmed in part from exuberant creativity and experimentation; but much of it was anxiety, fear, a rising sense of doom. With some justice, Karl Mannheim, one of its survivors, boasted not long before its demise that future years would look back on Weimar as a new Periclean age. But it was a precarious glory, a dance on the edge of a volcano. Weimar culture was the creation of outsiders, propelled by history into the inside, for a short, dizzying, fragile moment. (12)

Indem Gay solche Zustände wie Angst erwähnt und von einem schwindelerregenden, fragilen Moment, einem steigenden Gefühl des Untergangs oder einem Tanz am Rande des Vulkans spricht, geht es um die zunehmende Marginalisierung, die die später vertriebenen Literaten und Künstler schon vor 1933 empfanden (vgl. Krohn 10), also um Vorstufen des Exils. Schließlich wurden ja die Insider der Weimarer Kultur mit dem aufkommenden Nationalsozialismus wieder zu Outsidern. Zwar sprach Gay die Vorstufen des Exils implizit an, doch soll es hier um deren explizite Auslotung gehen, wobei auch andere geschichtliche Exilkontexte im Sinne der oben zitierten Aufforderung eingeschlossen werden.

Auch der vorliegende Band ist nicht in einem Vakuum entstanden. Zu er-
wähnen ist z.B. die im Dezember 2016 an der LMU München organisierte Tagung unter dem Titel „Passagen des Exils / Passages of Exile", die mit einer Vor-
tragsreihe des *Center for Advanced Studies* der LMU von Oktober 2016 bis
Februar 2017 verbunden war (vgl. „Passagen der Migration"). Die umgearbei-
teten Vorträge zusammen mit anderen Essays wurden dann unter demselben
Titel der Tagung im *Jahrbuch der Gesellschaft für Exilforschung* herausgegeben
(vgl. Dogramaci u. Otto). Wie der Bandtitel schon andeutet, ging es dabei angesichts der aktuellen Fluchtbewegungen um einen bestimmten Aspekt der
Exilvorstufen, nämlich um einen „Schwellenzustand", bzw. den Weg, „der zwischen Ausgangspunkt, Zwischenzielen und Endpunkt von Migration liegt"
(Dogramaci u. Otto 7). In zwanzig Beiträgen aus interdisziplinärer Perspektive
und in drei Kurzgeschichten werden die Momente des Übergangs ins Exil als
Resultat der Russischen Revolution, der NS-Zeit, des Kalten Krieges sowie in
der Gegenwart behandelt. Der Band bietet dann vielfältige Antworten zu den
folgenden Fragen:

> Wie werden Wegstrecken des Exils – auch jenseits eigener Fluchterfah-
> rungen – von Künstler*innen und Literat*innen reflektiert? Welche Tech-
> niken der Aufzeichnungen sind bereits auf der Flucht möglich, wie werden
> diese später ausformuliert? Wie prägen Reisewege und auch Transport-
> mittel – Schiff, Eisenbahn, Flugzeug oder Automobil – die spezifischen
> Fluchterfahrungen, und welche Bedeutung haben die (auch geschlechtss-
> pezifischen) Machtverhältnisse auf den verschiedenen Routen? Inwie-
> fern werden Flucht, Transit und Passage später autobiographisch gedeu-
> tet, umgedeutet oder verdrängt? Wie werden Sprachwechsel im Transit
> zwischen Herkunfts- und Zielland wahrgenommen? Und wie lässt sich
> der Zwischenraum dort und hier, der Heimat und der Fremde, der Vergan-
> genheit und Zukunft, dem „Bereits" und „Noch nicht" in Bilder, Filme, Ob-
> jekte und Texte fassen?
>   DOGRAMACI U. OTTO 13–14

Ebenfalls widerspiegelt sich das Thema der Vorstufen in der neuen Dauerausstellung des Deutschen Exilarchivs 1933–1945 (Frankfurt), „Exil. Erfahrung
und Zeugnis", die sich dreiteilig in „Auf der Flucht", „Im Exil" und „Nach dem
Exil" gliedert, deren erster Teil sich also bewusst den Vorstufen des Exils widmet. Eine der Kernfragen der Ausstellung lautet entsprechend: „Was bedeutet
es, ins Exil gehen zu müssen?" (vgl. „Exil"). Zu den Exilvorstufen in der Ausstellung gibt es einen Beitrag von Sylvia Asmus im vorliegenden Band. Dabei
geht es um direkte Zeugenschaft, zu der die hier abgedruckten persönlichen

Texte von Guy Stern und Egon Schwarz zu ihrem eigenen Exilgang ebenfalls beitragen.

Damit wären wir beim eigentlichen Anlass des vorliegenden Bandes angekommen. Um nämlich auf das oben von van der Linden formulierte Desiderat im Kontext der Exilvorstufen weiter einzugehen – gewissermaßen als Fortführung der LMU-Tagung und der erwähnten Ausstellung –, trafen sich im Mai 2018 internationale Wissenschaftler aus mehreren Disziplinen an der Loyola University Chicago, um im Rahmen einer Tagung der *North American Society for Exil Studies* (*NASES*) die Vorstufen des Exils intensiver zu erforschen. Die Vorträge wurden zum größten Teil für diesen Band umgearbeitet; weitere Beiträge kamen ergänzend hinzu. Dabei fand die Tagung zu Ehren von Egon Schwarz (1922–2017) statt, der selbst ein NS-Opfer und Exilant aus Österreich war, die Vorstufen des Exils am eigenen Leibe erfuhr, als Literaturwissenschaftler auf vielfältige Weise zur Exilforschung während seiner langen akademischen Karriere beitrug und uns ein äußerst angenehmer, menschlicher Zeitgenosse war. Deswegen ist ihm hier auch ein Nachruf gewidmet. Mit dem Essay aus seinem Nachlass, „Dank an die Emigration", kommt Schwarz autobiographisch als Zeuge zu den Vorstufen des Exils zu Worte, wie oben erwähnt, abgesehen von der Analyse dieses Textes im Zusammenhang mit seiner Autobiographie *Unfreiwillige Wanderjahre* (2005) im Beitrag von Helga Schreckenberger.

Wie die in diesem Band enthaltenen Aufsätze noch weiter aufweisen, ist der Ausgangspunkt für die Vorstufen des Exils zunächst das allgemeine Gefühl einer tiefen Entfremdung von der Heimat, deren politische, kulturelle und intellektuelle Ursachen vielfältig sein können. In diesem Zusammenhang vgl. die Ausführungen von Gregor Thuswaldner zu Stefan Zweig oder Thomas Pekar im Zusammenhang mit Thomas Mann. Zum Gefühl der Entfremdung kommen gesetzlich untermauerte Diskriminierungen verschiedenster Formen (politisch, rassisch, religiös, sexuell, sprachlich) hinzu, ebenfalls andere repressive Maßnahmen eines diktatorischen Regimes wie z.B. die Einschränkung der Redefreiheit oder Zensur, Vermögensentzug, die Entfernung aus dem Berufsleben, Einschüchterung, Korruption oder das Empfinden einer Atomisierung des Lebens durch ungewohnt rasante, moralisch-ethisch fragwürdige Entwicklungen in der Gesellschaft. Der Beitrag von Helmut G. Asper zur „Affäre Ophüls" in der Theaterwelt kann hier als Beispiel angeführt werden.

Die emotionalen und psychischen Folgen der Entfremdung sind ebenfalls vielförmig. Verzweiflung und Hoffnung wechseln einander ab. Verunsicherungen, Unentschiedenheit, Beklemmungen, Angst, das Gefühl vom Verlust der heimatlichen und kulturellen Zugehörigkeit und sonstige Desillusionierungen können eintreten. Die Entfremdung vom eigenen biologischen Geschlecht hat scheinbar wenig mit traditionellem Exil zu tun, doch können deren Folgen, erschwert durch äußere Diskriminierung, durchaus analog zu den Vorstufen des Exils verlaufen, wie der Beitrag von Pamela Caughie zu Lili Elbe einleuchtend aufweist und unser traditionelles Verständnis von Exilforschung sprengt.

Trotz der vielfältigen Aspekte der Entfremdung will man vielleicht noch nicht unbedingt ins Exil. Eventuell sucht man weitere Formen der eigenen Arbeit und des Einkommens. Andere politische, pädagogische und sonstige Netzwerke können vielleicht aufgebaut, dann aber auch verworfen oder unterdrückt werden. Hierzu vgl. die Beiträge von Swen Steinberg zur Situation in der deutsch-tschechoslowakischen Grenzregion und von Inge Hansen-Schaberg zur politischen und pädagogischen Arbeit Ernst Papaneks als Vorstufen seines Exils.

Exil als Ausweg wird dann vielleicht immer realer, was auch die gedankliche Auseinandersetzung mit einem inneren Exil einschließen kann. Rückt ein tatsächlicher Exilgang näher, gibt es praktische Vorbereitungen: anderes Fachkönnen muss vielleicht angeeignet, zusätzliche Fähigkeiten gelernt werden, um die neue Existenz im Ausland zu erleichtern, was Jutta Vinzent im vorliegenden Band schlüssig mit den Begriffen „motility" vs. „mobility" in ihrem Beitrag zu institutionellen Vorbereitungen auf den Exilgang nach Kenya umreißt. In diesem Zusammenfang vgl. auch den Beitrag von Robert Kelz, der zum Schluss kommt, dass die Vorbereitungen aufs Exil nicht so viel anders als auf die allgemeine Emigration sein müssen, wie er uns anhand von zwei Fallbeispielen aus der Theaterwelt vorführt.

Der Gang ins Exil an sich hat dann auch eine bürokratische Seite: Die nötigen Papiere müssen beschaffen und Visa gewährt werden, oft für mehr als ein Land, denn der Exilweg kann mit Grenzüberquerungen und abenteuerlichen Stationen und Aufenthalten in Zwischenländern verbunden sein. Kommt es zur eigentlichen Trennung von der Heimat, wird diese oft als gewaltsam empfunden. Die Vorstufen des Exils setzen sich dann im eigentlichen Gang ins Exil fort. Eine neue Sprache muss gelernt werden. Gefühle der Wurzellosigkeit, des Dazwischens, der Dualität und des Heimwehs sind hier emotional-psychische Wegzeichen, die noch lange nachwirken können, wie Sarah Voke in ihrem Aufsatz zur türkisch-österreichischen Dichterin Seher Çakır ausführt, somit nicht als Beispiel aus der Nazizeit, was wiederum die Beständigkeit der Exilerfahrung und ihre Vorstufen hervorhebt.

Der Weg durch die Vorstufen zum eigentlichen Exil wird durch aufbewahrte Gegenstände und verschiedene Formen der Dokumentation markiert, die später als Erinnerung dienen und z.B. die Basis der erwähnten Ausstellung „Exil. Erfahrung und Zeugnis" bilden kann. Dazu gehört auch, dass vielfache Versuche unternommen werden, die Vorstufen des Exils geistig zu verarbeiten. Angesichts der Radikalität des eigenen Erlebens steht Autobiographisches und

eigene Zeugenschaft zumeist im Vordergrund. Zur literarischen Auseinandersetzung mit den Vorstufen des Exils vgl. die bereits erwähnten persönlichen
Texte von Schwarz und Stern, ebenfalls die Aufsätze von Friederike Heimann
zum Tagebuch von Hertha Nathorff oder von Olena Komarnicka zu den Auswirkungen der Exilvorstufen im Werk von Stella Hershan.

Eventuell sucht man auch nach ähnlichen Erfahrungsmustern in anderen
Kulturen und Literaturen und übersetzt sie emotional für sich oder auch buch-
stäblich in die eigene Sprache, um irgendwie besser zurechtzukommen, wie
uns Julie Elsky in ihrem Beitrag zu Arthur Adamov aufzeigt. Es finden also
Einordnungen statt: Man sieht sich eventuell als Wanderer, Tourist, Flüchtling
oder als eine Art Odysseus, um dann schließlich Emigrant und Exilant zu
werden, was die Vorstufen des Exils gewissermaßen abschließt, wenn auch die
Übergänge keineswegs klar definiert, sondern eher fließend sind. Insofern es
zu einer Reemigration kommt, kann neue Entfremdung das Durchleben er-
neuter Vorstufen des Exils bedingen, wie uns Krisztina Kaltenecker in ihrem
Beitrag zu Thomas Bernhards Theaterstück *Heldenplatz* vorführt.

Die Wikinger sollen einmal gesagt haben: „Über den Wind können wir nicht
bestimmen, aber wir können die Segel richten" (*Auswanderermuseum* 36). Das
metaphorische Bild bringt die Exilproblematik als Teil der Migration auf den
Punkt: Es wird wohl immer den *homo migrans* geben, offensichtlich verschärft
im 21. Jahrhundert. Diesbezüglich schreibt Elizabeth Otto im Zusammenhang
mit der LMU-Tagung: „[...] it seems *the refugee* has already become the paradig-
matic figure of the twenty-first century" (Dogramaci u. Otto 15). Ist Exil nun in
unserem Zeitalter unabdingbar, gilt der zweite Teil der Wind- und Segel-
metapher der Wikinger, nämlich, wie wir uns produktiv damit auseinanderset-
zen können. In der Neuausgabe seiner Autobiographie *Unfreiwillige Wanderjahre* (2005) stellt Egon Schwarz, dem ja die NASES-Tagung gewidmet war, die
indirekte Frage, „warum man sich immer noch mit so alten Geschichten beschäftigen soll, wo doch schon wieder eine neue Völkerwanderung ausgebro-
chen ist und die Welt von Exilanten wimmelt" (8). Als Antwort betont er die
Wichtigkeit, solche Lebensgeschichten im Kontext der Historie zu lesen, um so
zu erfahren, „wie solchen Exilanten zumute ist und wie man mit ihnen umgehen bzw. nicht umgehen sollte" (8). Der bekannte Ausgangspunkt dafür ist die
Erinnerung, den die Kulturwissenschaftlerin Aleida Assmann auf den Punkt
gebracht hat: „[...] die gemeinsame Erinnerung an eine Gewaltgeschichte ist
die wirksamste Methode, um die Voraussetzungen, die sie möglich gemacht
haben, zu überwinden" (68).

So sieht sich der vorliegende Band als multidisziplinären Versuch, zur ebenfalls von Assmann heraufbeschworenen „Gedächtniskultur" (54) beizutragen,
wobei der engere Konstrukt von Exil und Auswanderung gesprengt wird, d.h.

bewusst auch deren Vorstufen eingeschlossen und in einigen Fällen über den Nationalsozialismus hinaus analysiert werden, um ansatzweise zu einem umfassenderen Bild des Phänomens zu kommen. Damit trägt der Band zu einem unterbeleuchteten Kapitel in der Exilforschung bei. In der Zusammenstellung der Beiträge ergaben sich bestimmte thematische Schwerpunkte, die keineswegs den Anspruch auf Vollständigkeit erheben, die sich aber in der Kapitelaufteilung folgendermaßen zeigen: direkte Zeugenschaft; politische, kulturelle und intellektuelle Entfremdung; praktische, politische und pädagogische Arbeit; Dazwischen und Übergang; Diskriminierung in der Theaterwelt und schauspielerische Überlebensfähigkeiten; literarische Prozesse.

Wie die Ursachen der Migrationsbewegungen besser in den Griff zu bekommen sind, so dass es weniger zu den Vorstufen des Exils und Exil überhaupt kommt, kann endlos diskutiert werden und ist in der letzten Instanz eine Frage des politischen und gesellschaftlichen Willens. Es sollte jedoch eine wesentliche Diskussion unseres Zeitalters sein. Schließlich geht es um solche grundlegenden Werte wie Menschlichkeit, Toleranz, Würde, Freiheit, Solidarität und politischen Pluralismus.

Zitierte Literatur

Assmann, Aleida. *Auf dem Wege zu einer europäischen Gedächtniskultur?* Wiener Vorlesungen. Picus, 2012.

Das Auswanderermuseum Ballinstadt. Betriebsgesellschaft BallinStadt mbH, o. J.

Bannasch, Bettina und Gerhild Rochus (Hg.). *Handbuch der deutschsprachigen Exilliteratur. Von Heinrich Heine bis Herta Müller.* De Gruyter, 2013.

Dogramaci, Burcu und Elizabeth Otto (Hg.). *Passagen des Exils / Passages of Exile. Exilforschung. Ein internationals Jahrbuch* 35/2017. edition text + kritik, 2017.

„Exil. Erfahrung und Zeugnis. Dauerausstellung des Deutschen Exilarchivs 1933–1945": http://www.dnb.de/DE/Ausstellungen/Frankfurt/dauerausstellungDEA2.html.

Gay, Peter. *Weimar Culture: the Outsider as Insider.* Harper and Row, 1968.

Gay, Peter. "Weimar Culture". *The Intellectual Migration. Europe and America, 1930–1960.* Donald Flemming und Bernard Bailyn (Hg.). Harvard UP, 1969.

Krohn, Claus-Dieter. „Exilforschung". *Docupedia-Zeitgeschichte,* 20.12.2012: http://docupedia.de/zg/Exilforschung?oldid=125452.

van der Linden, Marcel. „Globale Arbeitsgeschichte, Flüchtlinge und andere MigrantInnen". Momentaufnahme der Exilforschung / Proceedings of Exile Studies. Dokumentation der Tagung der Gesellschaft für Exilforschung e.V. in Zusammenarbeit mit dem Internationaal Instituut voor Sociale Geschiedenis, Amsterdam, 23.–25.

März 2012, S. 5–10: http://www.exilforschung.de/_dateien/tagungen/Doku_2012 -GfE-Combi-neu.pdf.

„Passagen der Migration". LMU, München, 21.10.2016: https://www.uni-muenchen.de/ forschung/news/2016/cas_passage.html.

Schwarz, Egon. *Unfreiwillige Wanderjahre. Auf der Flucht vor Hitler durch drei Konti-nente.* Mit einem Nachwort von Uwe Timm. C.H. Beck, 2005.

Strauss, Herbert A. und Werner Röder (Hg.). *Biographische Handbuch der deutschspra-chigen Emigration nach 1933* (3 Bde.). Institut für Zeitgeschichte. De Gruyter, 1980–83.

In Memoriam Egon Schwarz: Exile, Literary Scholar and Human Being

Reinhard Andress

Egon Schwarz passed away on February 11, 2017. It was a fascinating life that he captured in his autobiography, first published in 1979 as *Keine Zeit für Eichendorff* (No Time for Eichendorff). In 2005, a new edition appeared under the changed title of *Unfreiwillige Wanderjahre* (Involuntary Years of Travel), which was awarded the prestigious Johann Friedrich von Cotta Literary Prize of the city of Stuttgart in 2008. Translations exist into English as *Refuge. Chronicle of a Flight from Hitler* (2002) and into Spanish as *Años de vagabundo forzado. Huyendo de Hitler a través de tres continentes* (2012).

That autobiography tells of how Egon, born in 1922 in Vienna as a Jew, was forced to leave his homeland soon after the National Socialist *Anschluss*. His exile first led him and his parents to Bratislava (Pressburg), then on to a no-man's land between Slovakia and Hungary before further flight took them to Prague, Paris, and finally South America where he spent ten years in Bolivia, Chile, and Ecuador under adventurous and adverse conditions. Aside from the early stages of exile in his autobiography and the impact they had on his subsequent development, which are explored in an contribution by Helga Schreckenberger to this volume, Egon himself outlines those early stages in the essay "Dank an die Emigration," also included in this volume.

Regarding his actual exile in Latin America, the strong social consciousness he gained there never left him, likewise the desire to educate himself further that led to voraciously consuming everything readable he came across. It was that unstinting will combined with fortunate circumstances that brought him to the US after the end of the war where he completed a Ph.D. in German Philology at the University of Washington in 1954, followed by a seven-year appointment at Harvard University, laying the groundwork for his distinguished career at Washington University in St. Louis. Interrupted by guest appointments all around the world, he taught there for thirty-two years, the latter part of them as the "Rosa May Distinguished Professor in the Humanities in Arts and Sciences." He wrote or edited over twenty books and penned hundreds of scholarly articles and journalistic essays. Over the years he became a very well-known literary historian and co-founder of the field of German Exile Studies, for example, with his book *Verbannung* (Bannishment, 1964), which documents a kind of phenomenology of the exile Hitler caused. Other noteworthy monographs Egon published are *Joseph von Eichendorff* (1972) or

EGON SCHWARZ, 1922–2017

Das verschluckte Schluchzen. Poesie und Politik bei Rainer Maria Rilke (Swallowed Sobbing. Poetics and Politics in the Works of Rainer Maria Rilke, 1972). His last major publication was *Wien und die Juden* (Vienna and the Jews, 2014), a collection of his best essays on the topic. He received many awards: honorary doctorates from the Universität Wien, Örebro Universitet or his own Washington University, the Joseph von Eichendorff Medaillon or the Österreichisches Ehrenzeichen für Wissenschaft und Kunst (Austrian Decoration for Science and Art).

It was not until the year 2000 that I met this unique individual and soon regretted that it had taken so long. Of course I knew of Egon Schwarz before that—how could that have been any different as a graduate student in German Studies at the University of Illinois in the '80s? Back then I read his scholarly articles on Hesse, Rilke, Thomas Mann, Schnitzler, or, more generally, on exile. And I thought to myself that's the way I wanted to write: not esoterically over the top and over-theoretically, but rather elegantly, comprehensibly, and insightfully embedded in socio-historical contexts. I don't know whether I ever achieved that goal, but I do know that Egon's scholarly writing always remained a model for me and still is.

In 1993, I joined the faculty as an assistant professor at Saint Louis University, while Egon was a highly venerated professor at neighboring Washington University, which, of course, I also knew. But I hesitated—also regrettably—to establish contact with him. Too great was probably my awe as a young Germanist of one of the international luminaries in our field. By chance it was Frank Baron of the University of Kansas who brought us together. He had organized a NASES meeting, both Egon and I were giving papers, and Frank asked whether I could drive him to Lawrence, Kansas for the conference. I remember well the drive through the expanses of Missouri into the prairie of Kansas, which Egon filled with tales from the fascinating world of his life that went so far beyond his literary scholarship and that I later read about in his autobiography as well. Soon a friendship developed that was so very intellectually enriching and always will be—whether it was in connection with the projects we undertook; the countless entertaining conversations or wonderful meals we had; whether in St. Louis in his cozily magical home with the luxurious garden his wife Dorle had lovingly created; whether in Mexico, Berlin, or here in Chicago. Our topics of conversation were wide-ranging: Austria's *fin-de-siècle* to all periods of German literature, exile, world travels, philosophy, or politics. When we last saw each other in October 2016 a month before the US presidential elections, I read to him from the *New York Times*, suffering in his old age as he did from partial blindness. We were, of course, appalled by Trump, and at least Egon has been spared the endlessly ensuing embarrassments and disasters of his administration.

I believe I speak on behalf of many when I say that on the one hand it was Egon's charmingly witty and entertaining way of conversing in a lightly tinged Viennese accent that made you a mesmerized listener. Sure, he could hold forth with the fascinating tales from his life but, on the other hand, he also possessed the gift, very unusual for older people, of also being able to listen to you seriously. In a friendly and calm way he always made the effort to understand you, engage you further, vehemently opposing everything that could be seen as an injustice. He was a human being of high integrity. That, also, made so many of us his fans.

During one of our many conversations, we debated the question of what might actually remain of all our literary scholarship. In the longer run very little, he thought, but he did harbor the hope that his autobiography might survive. One reason is perhaps contained one of the final passages that I've always found astounding:

> Zu verkünden, daß Hitler für mich gut war, wäre eine Verhöhnung der Millionen, die er auf dem Gewissen hat und zu denen ich, in jeder

Phase des faschistischen Vernichtungszuges durch die Welt, leicht hätte gehören können. Dennoch ist es eine Tatsache, daß ich durch die explosionsartigen Ausbrüche des Hitlerismus in die freie Luft geschleudert wurde, wo ich einen längeren Atem und einen weiteren Ausblick gewonnen habe, als wenn ich in der heimatlichen Enge geblieben wäre. Manche Menschen werden, wenn sie ihnen widerfährt, von der Durchtrennung der Wurzeln, die sie an ihr Fleckchen Umwelt binden, gefährdet oder gar zerstört. Mir hat sie zunächst auch nicht gerade wohlgetan, aber auf die Dauer hat sie Kräfte befreit, die sonst unerweckt für immer in mir geschlummert hätten. Anders als andere Emigranten, die der Heimat nachtrauern, heiße ich daher die Emigration gut und bekenne mich zu ihr, nicht weil sie mir just passierte und man für gewöhnlich sein Leben billigt, sondern beinah als Prinzip, als einen Prozeß, dem ich meine Befreiung und, so sonderbar das auch anmuten mag, die Gewinnung meines Gleichgewichts zu verdanken glaube.

SCHWARZ, *Unfreiwillige Wanderjahre* 233

The path to this take on exile was naturally not easy, ruthlessly exposed as Egon was without free will to the storms of history, but later fighting tirelessly for self-determination. Yet, what a courageously optimistic attitude pervades the quotation, in spite of everything, an attitude that so defined his life and that we wish for exiles and refugees once again in these troubling times.

When Egon died at the age of 94, it became clear to all of us who knew him that we had somehow hoped he would remain with us forever. In a certain sense that is possible. By that I mean the conversation I had with him about what remains. In that spirit let us read his *Unfreiwille Wanderjahre*, or let us read them again. Let us keep him alive in this way among us.

There is another thing I regretted about my relationship with Egon, namely a book tip he repeatedly gave me. Unfortunately, I didn't read it until after his death. Here's a quote from it:

Manchen stimmt schon das Wechseln seiner Wohnung traurig. Ein verlorenes Stück des eigenen Lebens bleibt immer zurück. Für jedermann ist es eine große Entscheidung, seine Stadt mit einer andern, sein Lebensland mit einem neuen zu vertauschen. Selbst der Gewohnheitsverbrecher legt den Weg in seine Gefangenschaft, ins Gefängnis schwer zurück. Aber rechtloser als ein Verbrecher sein, der doch noch den Schutz des Gesetzes genießt! Ausgetrieben werden von einem Tag zum andern, aus der Wohnstätte, von der Arbeit, aus dem im jahrelangen Fleiß Geschaffenen! Dem Haß überliefert! Ungerüstet auf asiatische Landstraßen geworfen, abertausende Meilen Staub, Stein und Morast vor sich! Zu wissen, man werde nie wieder ein menschwürdiges Nachtlager finden, nie

wieder an einem menschenwürdigen Tisch essen und trinken. Dies aber
ist noch nichts, unfreier sein als ein Sträfling! Zu den Verfemten, den Vo-
gelfreien gehören, die jeder ungestraft töten kann. Eingepfercht in ein
schleichendes Rudel von Elenden, in das wandernde Konzentrations-
lager, wo niemand ohne Erlaubnis auch nur seine Notdurft verrichten
darf.

WERFEL, *Die vierzig Tage des Musa Dagh* 117

Perhaps you recognize the passage. It comes from Franz Werfel's *Die vierzig
Tage des Musa Dagh* (*The Forty Days of Musa Dagh*), that novel the author
sketched out during a trip to the Near East in 1930, quickly wrote in 1932–1933,
published in 1933, and which tells the story of the Armenian Genocide from
1915 to 1917. On the basis of considerable research, Werfel describes the fate of
a kaleidoscope of Armenian figures who are increasingly alienated and persecuted, and who seek refuge on their local mountain, the Musa Dagh (today in
the Turkish province of Hatay). Under the leadership of the fictionalized protagonist, Gabriel Bagradian, they offer fierce resistance to the Ottoman government's forces until a miracle happens in the form of allied ships that rescue
them from the Mediterranean side of the mountain. In flowing, elegant language Werfel transforms the horrific historical events into a very noteworthy
epic piece of literature.

To return to the quote from the novel, were it not for the "Asiatic" rural roads,
the early stages of exile described there would fit for every exile situation. That,
too, makes the novel into a great piece of literature since Werfel succeeds in
describing exile transcendently. And it is no doubt the reason Egon saw his
own exile situation reflected in the novel in so many ways, why the book was so
important to him and worth recommending.

This volume of essays is dedicated to Egon and has taken on the task of a
closer look at those early stages of exile from many perspectives, including in
his own autobiography in the article in this volume by Helga Schreckenberger.
In the chapter on "Zeugenschaft / Witness," Egon himself speaks in a hitherto
unpublished autobiographical text, "Dank an die Emigration," in which he, in a
much more tighter format than the autobiography, outlines his path into exile
with the many early stages it entailed.

Works Cited

Schwarz, Egon. *Unfreiwillige Wanderjahre. Auf der Flucht vor Hitler durch drei Kontinente*. Verlag C.H. Beck, 2005.
Werfel, Franz. *Die vierzig Tage des Musa Dagh*. Fischer Taschenbuch 90362, 2011.

Illustrations

Notes on Contributors

Reinhard Andress
(Ph.D. 1988, University of Illinois) is Professor of German and Director of German Studies at Loyola University Chicago. He has published extensively in the areas of GDR literature, exile studies, Alexander von Humboldt studies, and German-American studies. He has co-edited several volumes, including, with Evelyn Meyer and Gregory Divers, *Weltanschauliche Orientierungsversuche im Exil / New Orientations of World View in Exile* (2010). More recently, he published a reedition of Fred Heller, *Das Leben beginnt noch einmal. Schicksale der Emigration* (2017).

Sylvia Asmus
(Promotion in Bibliothekswissenschaft, Humboldt-Universität Berlin) leitet das Deutsche Exilarchiv 1933–1945 der Deutschen Nationalbibliothek und ist Mitglied im wissenschaftlichen Beirat der Gesellschaft für Exilforschung und der Internationalen Joseph Roth Gesellschaft. Zu ihren Ausstellungen und Publikationen gehören: *„Meinem besten Porträtisten" – Porträtfotografien und -zeichnungen aus den Beständen des Deutschen Exilarchivs 1933–1945* (2005, zusammen mit Brita Eckert), *Rudolf Olden: Journalist gegen Hitler – Anwalt der Republik* (2010, zusammen mit Brita Eckert), *So wurde ihnen die Flucht zur Heimat. Soma Morgenstern und Joseph Roth. Eine Freundschaft* (2012, zusammen mit Heinz Lunzer und Victoria Lunzer-Talos) und *„... mehr vorwärts als rückwärts schauen ..." – Das deutschsprachige Exil in Brasilien 1933–1945* (2013, zusammen mit Marlen Eckl).

Helmut G. Asper
(Promotion 1970, Universität Köln) ist Theater- und Filmhistoriker. Bis 2010 lehrte er über Theater, Film, Fernsehen an der Fakultät für Linguistik und Literaturwissenschaft der Universität Bielefeld. Zu seinem Forschungsschwerpunkt Theater- und Filmexil 1933–1950 hat er zahlreiche Bücher und Zeitschriftenbeiträge veröffentlicht, u.a. *Max Ophüls. Eine Biographie mit zahlreichen Dokumenten, Texten und Bildern* (1998), *„Etwas Besseres als den Tod..." Filmexil in Hollywood. Porträts, Filme, Dokumente* (2002) und *Filmexilanten im Universal Studio 1933–1960* (2005).

Pamela L. Caughie
(Ph.D., University of Virginia) is Professor of English and Women's Studies and Gender Studies at Loyola University Chicago. A former president of the

Modernist Studies Association, she is a modernist scholar and a feminist and gender theorist whose research and teaching focus on the study of literature and culture of the early twentieth century. She is also the author of two books and fifty book chapters and articles, and editor or co-editor of four works, most recently, *Man into Woman: A Comparative Scholarly Edition* (2020), with its companion, the Lili Elbe Digital Archive (www.lilielbe.org).

Julia Elsky

(Ph.D. 2014, Yale University) is Assistant Professor of French at Loyola University Chicago. Her book, *Writing Occupation: Jewish Émigré Voices in Wartime France*, is forthcoming (2020). She co-edited (together with Lauren du Graf and Clémentine Fauré) a seventieth anniversary issue of *Yale French Studies* devoted to the subject of revisiting existentialism, the topic of the inaugural issue of the journal (Fall 2019). Her research has appeared in journals including *PMLA, La Nouvelle Revue Française, Archives Juives*, and *Diasporas: Circulations, migrations, histoire*.

Inge Hansen-Schaberg

(Promotion 1991, TU Berlin; Habil. 1998, Universität Potsdam) war Professorin an der TU Berlin für das Fach „Erziehungswissenschaft mit besonderer Berücksichtigung der Historischen Pädagogik" und in der Lehre der Georg-August-Universität Göttingen tätig, seit 2019 im Ruhestand. Sie hat zahlreiche Publikationen zur Pädagogik im 20. Jahrhundert, zu pädagogischen Biografien und zum Exil. Sie war Herausgeberin der elfbändigen Reihe *Frauen und Exil* in der *edition text+kritik* (2008–2019) und der sechsbändigen Ausgabe *Reformpädagogische Schulkonzepte* (Neuauflage 2012). Seit 2013 ist sie Vorsitzende der Gesellschaft für Exilforschung e.V. (www.exilforschung.de) und seit 2016 Vorsitzende des Fördervereins Cohn-Scheune e.V. (www.cohn-scheune.de).

Friederike Heimann

(Promotion 2012, Universität Basel). Sie studierte, Germanistik, Politologie und Soziologie an der FU-Berlin und machte dort ihr Erstes und Zweites Staatsexamen. Sie war Deutsche Sprachassistentin in Rom und studierte Italianistik in Hamburg. Zu ihren Veröffentlichungen gehört eine Monographie über *Beziehung und Bruch in der Poetik Gertrud Kolmars* (2013). Ihre Arbeitsschwerpunkte sind: deutsch-jüdische Literatur, Exilliteratur, literarische Gedächtnis- und Erinnerungskonzepte. Sie lebt als freiberufliche Autorin und Dozentin in Hamburg und arbeitet z.Z. an einem Buch über jüdische Dichterinnen im Berlin der ersten Hälfte des 20. Jahrhunderts. Seit 2010 ist sie auch Mitarbeiterin im Jüdischen Salon in Hamburg.

Krisztina Kaltenecker
(MA und Lehrerdiplom Geschichte und Ungarisch 1993, Loránd-Eötvös-Universität Budapest/Ungarn; Lehrerdiplom Deutsch 2015, Eberhard-Karls-Universität Tübingen/Deutschland) ist von Beruf Historikerin und Lehrerin für Geschichte, Deutsch und Ungarisch in der Sekundarschule. In ihren geschichts- und kulturwissenschaftlichen Studien untersucht sie die Konzepte und Maßnahmen des Social Engineerings, so in *Ungarndeutsche Geschichtskultur und bundesdeutsches Geschichtsbewusstsein* (2019)

Robert Kelz
(Ph.D. 2010, Vanderbilt University) is Associate Professor of German and Associate Director of International and Global Studies at The University of Memphis. He is the author of *Competing Germanies: Nazi, Antifascist, and Jewish Theater in German Argentina, 1933–1965* (2020) and, together with Silvia Glocer, co-author of *Paul Walter Jacob y las músicas prohibidas durante el nazismo* (2015).

Olena Komarnicka
(Promotion 2014, Adam Mickiewicz Universität in Poznan). Zu den Forschungsinteressen gehören deutschsprachige Exilliteratur nach 1933 und deutsch-polnische Beziehungen nach 1945. U.a. hat sie *„Man kann die Wohnung wechseln, aber nicht das Elternhaus". Österreichische Dichterinnen im New Yorker Exil zwischen 1938 und Beginn der 1980er Jahre* (2018) veröffentlicht.

Thomas Pekar
(Diss. 1988, Albert-Ludwigs-Universität Freiburg; Habil. 2003, LMU München) ist Professor für Neuere Deutsche Literaturwissenschaft und Kulturwissenschaften an der Gakushuin Universität Tokyo. Buch- und Aufsatzpublikationen hat er vor allem zu Autoren der klassischen Moderne (Musil, Thomas Mann, Kafka, Ernst Jünger, Hofmannsthal, Brecht) und der Exil- und Kulturkontakteforschung (insbes. in Hinsicht auf die deutschsprachige Japan-Rezeption). Er ist Mitherausgeber von verschiedenen Bänden, u.a. *Figuration – Defiguration. Beiträge zur transkulturellen Forschung* (2006), *Flucht und Rettung. Exil im japanischen Herrschaftsbereich (1933–1945)* (2011), *Kulturkontakte. Szenen und Modelle in deutsch-japanischen Kontexten* (2015) und *Wohnen und Unterwegssein. Interdisziplinäre Perspektiven auf west-östliche Raumfigurationen* (2019).

Helga Schreckenberger
(Ph.D. 1985, University of Kansas) is Professor of German at the University of Vermont. Her research interest focusses on contemporary Austrian literature,

and exile and migration studies. She has published on Arthur Schnitzler, Gerhard Roth, Lilian Faschinger, Ingeborg Bachmann, Erich Maria Remarque, Adrienne Thomas, Erika Mann, and Egon Schwarz. She has edited the following: *Ästhetiken des Exils* (2003), *Alchemie des Exils/Exil als schöpferischer Impuls* (2005), *Networks of Refugees from Nazi Germany: Continuities, Reorientations, and Collaborations in Exile* (2016).

Egon Schwarz

(Ph.D. 1954, University of Washington) gilt in der Germanistik als einer der wichtigsten Vermittler deutschsprachiger Literatur und Kultur in den USA. Er diente zuletzt als Rosa May Distinguished Professor in the Humanities an der Washington University (St. Louis). Er befasste sich mit deutschsprachiger Literatur des 19. and 20. Jahrhunderts und veröffentlichte bedeutende Beiträge zu Autoren wie Eichendorff, Rilke, Kafka, Thomas Mann und Hesse. Die von ihm mit Matthias Wegner herausgegebene Textsammlung *Verbannung* (1964) war das erste umfangreichere Buch über emigrierte Schriftsteller. In seiner Autobiographie *Keine Zeit für Eichendorff. Chronik unfreiwilliger Wanderjahre* (1979, Neuausgabe 2005 unter dem Titel *Unfreiwillige Wanderjahre. Auf der Flucht vor Hitler durch drei Kontinente*) beschrieb Schwarz seine eigene Exilzeit. Er verstarb 2017.

Swen Steinberg

(Ph.D. 2013, TU Dresden) is a Post-doctoral Researcher, Department of History at Queen's University in Kingston/Ontario. In addition, he is an Affiliated Scholar of the German Historical Institute in Washington/DC with its Pacific Regional Office at the University of California Berkeley. He also functions as editor of the international network/blog "Migrant Knowledge" and is a member of the Advisory Committee of the Austrian Archive for Exile Studies in Vienna. He has published several books, volumes and special issues, including, with Simone Lässig, *Migration and Knowledge* (2017) and *Knowledge and Young Migrants* (2019), as well as *Refugees from Nazi-occupied Europe in British Overseas Territories* (2020) with Anthony Grenville.

Gunter "Guy" Stern

(Ph.D. 1953, Columbia University) is a German scholar of literature, primarily German and comparative. He served at several institutions of higher learning, ending his academic career as a Distinguished Professor of German Literature and Cultural History at Wayne State University. He is currently the director of The Harry and Wanda Zekelman International Institute of the Righteous at the Holocaust Memorial Center in Farmington Hills (near Detroit). As author and editor, he has published extensively, including several books and compilations on German literary history, focusing mainly on literature on emigration and immigration, for example, *Literatur im Exil. Gesammelte Aufsätze 1959–1989* (1989) and *Literarische Kultur im Exil. Gesammelte Beiträge zur Exilforschung (1989–1997)* (1998).

Gregor Thuswaldner

(Ph.D. 2003, The University of North Carolina at Chapel Hill) is Provost and Executive Vice President at Whitworth University in Spokane, Washington. His recent book publications include the co-edited volumes, with Daniel Russ, *The Hermeneutics of Hell: Visions and Representations of the Devil in World Literature* (2017) and, with Stephen Dowden and Olaf Berwald, *Thomas Bernhard's Afterlives* (2020).

Jutta Vinzent

(Dr. Phil. 1996, Cologne; Ph.D. 2004, Cambridge) is Senior Lecturer in Modern and Contemporary Art at the University of Birmingham (UK). She has published widely on art in exile, particularly in relation to Britain, most recently an article on "The British Internment of Refugees from Nazi Germany in Kenya during WWII" (in *Yearbook of the Research Centre for German and Austrian Exile Studies*) and a monograph titled *From Space in Modern Art to a Spatial Art History. Reassessing Constructivism through the Publication* Circle (1937) (2020).

Sarah Voke

is a doctoral student in Comparative Literature at the University of Aix-Marseille (CIELAM). Her research focuses on the theme of exile in English, German, and French poetry. She is a member of the interdisciplinary collective of young researchers at the University of Aix-Marseille called "Migration et Altérité" and she teaches English at the Université Grenoble Alpes. In addition, she works as a translator.

PART 1

Zeugenschaft / Witness

∴

„In Gedanken reisen wir mit dir" – Vorstufen des Exils in der Dauerausstellung des Deutschen Exilarchivs 1933–1945

Sylvia Asmus

Abstract

For the first time in its almost 70-year history, the German Exile Archive 1933–1945 of the German National Library has mounted a permanent exhibit. Under the title of *Exile. Experience and Witness*, it is dedicated to German-speaking emigration as a result of National Socialist dictatorship. The exhibit presents a broad overview of and concentrates on the individual experiences of exile, whereby many of the exhibited items stand for the early stages of exile. They give witness to threshold conditions such as the time between discrimination, deprivation of rights, and persecution, and the resulting decision to leave Germany. They further document the time between that decision and its implementation, between departure and arrival. The memories of the early stages of exile are conserved in diverse material forms: in photos, tickets and schedules, in official documents and letters. Some of the exhibit items will be presented in greater detail in the following article. The focus is on Ernst Loewy's correspondence with his parents.

Am 21. März 1936 ist die aus Krefeld stammende Familie Loewy zu einem Fototermin zusammengekommen.[1] Angespannt schauen die Porträtierten Richard und Erna Loewy und ihr Sohn Ernst in die Kamera – zum Zeitpunkt der Fotoaufnahme war es ungewiss, ob sie sich je wiedersehen würden.

Das Foto ist eines von 250 Exponaten, die in der Dauerausstellung des Deutschen Exilarchivs 1933–1945 der Deutschen Nationalbibliothek gezeigt werden. Unter dem Titel *Exil. Erfahrung und Zeugnis* widmet sich die Ausstellung den Erfahrungen des Exils. Eingerahmt von einem Prolog und einem Epilog und strukturiert in die drei Themenkapitel *Auf der Flucht*, *Im Exil* und *Nach*

---

[1] Das Zitat im Titel aus: Loewy, Erna. Brief an Ernst Loewy. Krefeld, 28. März 1936. Nachlass Ernst Loewy, Deutsches Exilarchiv 1933–1945 der Deutschen Nationalbibliothek, Frankfurt am Main, EB 95/75.

© KONINKLIJKE BRILL NV, LEIDEN, 2020 | DOI:10.1163/9789004424715_002

dem Exil vermittelt die Ausstellung einen Überblick über das deutschsprachige
Exil aus dem Machtbereich der nationalsozialistischen Diktatur: Fluchtanläs-
se, Fluchtwege, Fluchthilfe, Alltag, Familie, Beruf, Sprache und Kultur, Widerstand, Rückkehr und Debatten des Exils werden in ihren unterschiedlichen
Ausprägungen dargestellt. Durch den Rückbezug auf individuelle Erfahrungen
des Exils lenkt die Ausstellung den Blick zugleich auf Details und wählt damit
eine multiperspektivische Annäherung an die Geschichte des deutschsprachigen Exils. Anhand von sehr disparaten Exponaten aus der Sammlung des
Deutschen Exilarchivs werden so individuelle Exilverläufe nachvollziehbar.
Dazu gehören Brüche, Verlust, sozialer Abstieg, Trennung von Familien,
Sprachbarrieren, aber auch gelungene Akkulturation, Neuanfänge und ergrif-
fene Chancen.

Die thematische Ausstellungsstruktur wird durch biografische Einstiege er-
weitert. Neben zweihundert aus den Exponaten abgeleiteten Kurzbiografien
werden acht Lebensverläufe, die für unterschiedliche Exil-Erfahrungen stehen, in der Ausstellung ausführlicher dargestellt. Auch Ernst Loewys Exilbio-
grafie zählt dazu.

Das eingangs erwähnte Foto der Familie Loewy wird im Kapitel *Auf der
Flucht* im Themenbereich *Fluchtwellen* präsentiert und damit in einem Ab-
schnitt, der fast ausnahmslos Exponate zeigt, die für Vorstufen des Exils stehen.

ILLUSTRATION 1.1   Blick in die Dauerausstellung des Deutschen Exilarchivs 1933–1945 in
Frankfurt

Die in diesem Themenabschnitt präsentierten Exponate zeugen zumeist von einem Schwellenzustand: Das Herkunftsland bot keine Perspektive mehr, ein neues Ziel aber war entweder noch nicht gefunden oder noch nicht erreicht worden. Der einschneidende Prozess zwischen Entscheidung und Umsetzung, zwischen Abreise und Ankunft wird an vielen Exponaten sichtbar. Den Auftakt des Kapitels bildet ein Formular für eine polizeiliche Abmeldung, ein sogenannter „Großer Meldeschein" vom 29. April 1933, mit dem der Jurist, Journalist und Politiker Prinz Hubertus zu Löwenstein und seine Frau Helga Prinzessin zu Löwenstein ihren Berliner Wohnsitz abmeldeten. Als künftige Adresse haben sie „auf Reisen" eingetragen. Das Formular markiert den Zeitraum zwischen dem Entschluss, aufgrund einer Warnung vor einer bevorstehenden Verhaftung Deutschland frühzeitig zu verlassen, und der erfolgten Exilierung. Die Löwensteins fanden vorübergehend in Österreich Zuflucht und ließen sich später in den USA nieder.

Der österreichische, in Berlin lebende Journalist und Reiseschriftsteller Richard A. Bermann dagegen begab sich im Frühjahr 1933 als Teilnehmer einer Expedition in die Libysche Wüste temporär in eine Vorstufe des Exils, um den politischen Ereignissen in Deutschland zu entfliehen. So leitet Richard A. Bermann sein Tagebuch ein:

> Was suche ich also in den unentdeckten Teilen der Libyschen Wüste? Ich habe eine Antwort darauf: den Kopf in den Sand stecken. Ich trete diese wildeste, abenteuerlichste meiner vielen Reisen an und weiß, daß es einfach eine Flucht ist, eine Flucht vor den unerträglich gewordenen politischen Verhältnissen in Mitteleuropa, vor den Nachrichten, vor den Ereignissen, vor der beruflichen Situation eines deutschen Schriftstellers, hinter dem die deutsche geistige Welt zusammenkracht wie ein morsches Gebäude. (1)

Die Expedition war für ihn ein Exil auf Zeit, aus dem er noch einmal zurückkehrte, bevor er nach der Annexion Österreichs endgültig aus Europa in die USA floh. Andere wurden durch Erlasse der neuen Machthaber an der Fortsetzung ihres Lebensentwurfs gehindert.

Dass die Phase zwischen Entscheidung zur Emigration und der konkreten Umsetzung oft von bürokratischen Hürden geprägt war, bezeugt eine Handgepäcksliste des Ehepaars Hermann und Josephine Marx, die in der Phase der Vorbereitung auf das Exil entstanden ist. Gezwungenermaßen klassifizierten sie in dem ebenfalls in der Ausstellung präsentierten Dokument ihr Handgepäck für die bevorstehende Ausreise nach Kuba im Hinblick auf die Ausfuhrbestimmungen. Einen anderen Zustand des „Dazwischen" stellen die

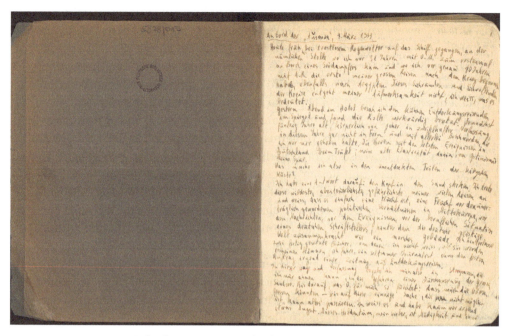

ILLUSTRATION 1.2   Richard A. Bermanns Tagebuch von der Saharafahrt

Schiffspassagen dar, von denen in der Ausstellung Exponate wie Fotografien, Mützenbänder, Schiffsprospekte und Routenbeschreibungen zeugen. Die Zeit auf dem Schiff war oft nicht eindeutig zuzuordnen. Es waren Schwellenzustände zwischen Reise und Flucht sowie Erfahrungen, die zwischen der Erleichterung über die gelungene Rettung und der Ungewissheit über das Bevorstehende hin und her wechselten.

Für die Familie Loewy hatte spätestens seit dem Erlass der sogenannten „Nürnberger Gesetze" und der Zuspitzung der Entrechtung der Jüdinnen und Juden eine Vorstufe des Exils begonnen, die maßgeblich von der Entscheidung geprägt war, den Sohn Ernst nach Palästina in Sicherheit zu bringen. Mit 15 Jahren hatte er das Mindestalter für die „Jugend-Alijah" erreicht. Für Loewy begann mit einem vierwöchigen Aufenthalt auf Gut Schniebinchen eine Zeit, die ganz konkret als Vorbereitung seiner bevorstehenden Auswanderung ausgewiesen war, denn der Aufenthalt diente dem Erwerb von Fähigkeiten, die den Jugendlichen in Palästina nützlich sein sollten.[2] Zusätzlich war die Zeit auf Gut Schniebinchen eine Bewährungsprobe, in der die Jugendlichen ihre

---

2   Vgl. den Beitrag von Jutta Vinzent in diesem Band über Groß-Breesen, eine 1936 gegründete Ausbildungsfarm, in der 370 nicht-zionistische Jugendliche landwirtschaftlichen Unterricht im Hinblick auf eine Auswanderung erhielten.

Tauglichkeit für eine Ausreise nach Palästina unter Beweis stellen mussten. Schon auf der Zugfahrt von Krefeld, dem Wohnort der Loewys, nach Berlin, setzte eine Korrespondenz zwischen Eltern und Sohn ein, die während der gesamten Zeit der Trennung fortgesetzt wurde (vgl. Loewy, *Jugend in Paläsina*). Dieser fast vollständig im Nachlass Loewys im Deutschen Exilarchiv überlieferte Briefwechsel ermöglicht – trotz zensurbedingter Themenauslässe – einen tiefen Einblick in die Befindlichkeiten und die Erfahrungswelten der Briefpartner. Schon von der Vorbereitungszeit auf Gut Schniebinchen berichtete der Sohn an seine Eltern. Die Jugendlichen wurden konkret auf das Leben in Palästina vorbereitet:

> Wir werden für eine Woche immer mit derselben Arbeit beschäftigt. Holzhacken, Schneekehren, Tischlerei und dergl. mehr, die Mädels in der Küche, daß ich Anstreicher bin, habe ich ja schon geschrieben. Wir haben schon ein Zimmer gestrichen, dann haben wir Möbel gebeizt, nächste Woche kalken wir den Waschraum.
>
> Brief an Erna und Richard Loewy, 20. Dezember 1935

Zur Vorbereitung auf das Leben in Palästina gehörten auch Sprachkurse und Landeskunde: „Iwrith-Kurse sind hier 4, je nach dem Können der einzelnen […] sonst haben wir noch einen Kurs ‚Zion. Geschichte' und ‚Palästinakunde'" (Brief an Erna und Richard Loewy, 27. Dezember 1935).

War bis dahin noch ein Scheitern wegen Untauglichkeit und ein daraus resultierendes Verbleiben bei den Eltern möglich, wurde das Auswanderungsvorhaben mit der sogenannten „Bestätigung" Loewys durch Vertreter der Jüdischen Jugendhilfe aus Berlin konkret. Am 5. Januar 1936 teilte er seinen Eltern das positive Ergebnis dieser Beurteilung mit. Nach der Vorbereitungszeit auf Gut Schniebinchen kehrte Loewy noch einmal zu seinen Eltern nach Krefeld zurück, wo am Tag vor seiner Abreise das beschriebene Erinnerungsfoto aufgenommen wurde. Mit dem am 25. Februar 1936 vom Berliner Palästina-Amt ausgestellten Einwanderungszertifikat und dem zwei Tage später unterzeichneten Vertrag zwischen der Jüdischen Jugendhilfe und seinen Eltern waren alle bürokratischen Hürden für die bevorstehende Ausreise genommen. Beide Dokumente sind Teil der Dauerausstellung *Exil. Erfahrung und Zeugnis* und sind dort den Kapiteln *Fluchtwege* und *Hilfe* zugeordnet.

Ernst Loewys Weg führte von Krefeld zunächst zu Verwandten nach München, von dort mit dem Zug über Salzburg nach Triest und weiter mit dem Schiff nach Haifa. Vom 22. März bis 2. April 1936 war der Jugendliche unterwegs und berichtete den Eltern bereits während der Reise. Mit der Entfernung zu Deutschland nahm Loewy auch eine Erleichterung und das Gefühl einer neuen Zugehörigkeit wahr. „Der ganze Zug voller Juives. Alles Palästinareisende"

ILLUSTRATION 1.3   Einwanderungszertifikat von Ernst Loewy für Palästina

(Brief an Erna und Richard Loewy, 26. März 1936), berichtete er bereits aus dem Zug nach Triest. Seit 1933 hatte der Jugendliche antisemitische Anfeindungen erlebt, die 1935 den frühzeitigen Schulabgang Loewys zur Folge gehabt hatten (vgl. Loewy, *Jugend in Paläsina* 8). In diesem Kontext ist auch sein Bericht von einem Landgang in Spalato in Jugoslawien zu lesen:

> Draußen vor dem Schiff sind wir angetreten und dann, und zwar in voller Kluft, mit Gesang durch die Stadt marschiert. Du mußt Dir das einmal vorstellen, geschlossen durch eine Stadt marschieren und dazu noch jüdische Lieder zu singen. Die Leute haben uns alle bestaunt wie das siebente Weltwunder. Es hat uns keiner etwas gesagt, die Polizei hat uns sogar den Weg gezeigt.
>
> Brief an Lore Traub sowie Erna und Richard Loewy, 29. März 1936

Die Passage ist hier nicht nur eine individuell erlebte Phase des Übergangs zwischen Herkunfts- und Aufnahmeland, sondern auch eine Zeit der kollektiven

Erfahrung, in der die negative Konnotation des in NS-Deutschland definierten Andersseins abgeschwächt wurde. Gerade in der Phase der Adoleszenz kommt dieser gemeinschaftsbildenden Funktion eine besondere Bedeutung zu.

Nach der Ankunft in Haifa fuhren die Jugendlichen nach Kirjat Anavim, einer Kwuzah (einer landwirtschaftlichen Gemeinschaftssiedlung) in der Nähe von Jerusalem, wo sie eine zweijährige Ausbildung erhalten sollten. Etwa 430 Briefe und Karten wurden während der Zeit der Trennung von Eltern und Sohn zwischen Palästina und Deutschland gewechselt, oft mit nur einem oder wenigen Tagen Abstand zwischen den Schreiben. Loewy berichtete den Eltern ausführlich von seiner neuen Lebensumgebung, er schilderte detailliert das Leben in der Kwuzah, die Gemeinschaft, die Arbeitsbedingungen, er informierte über gesellschaftliche und politische Ereignisse und seine eigenen Zukunftspläne. Die Eltern nahmen über die Briefe Anteil am neuen Leben ihres Sohnes, sie kommentierten seine Entscheidungen aus der Ferne, berieten ihren Sohn und unterstützten ihn auch finanziell. In ihren Gegenbriefen schilderten sie ihren Alltag in Deutschland, ihre berufliche Situation und informierten über Verwandte und Freunde. Dadurch blieb Loewy auch nach seiner Exilierung in Verbindung zu seiner „Familienheimat" (Vogel 36) und Teil der früheren Lebens- und Familienkonstellation.

Dem Briefwechsel kommt aber zudem eine zusätzliche Funktion zu, die im Folgenden näher betrachtet werden soll. Die Berichte Exilierter ermöglichten den in Deutschland Zurückgebliebenen über die Distanz hinweg die Annäherung an ihr zukünftiges Aufnahmeland. Richard und Erna Loewy lasen die Beschreibungen ihres Sohnes auch im Hinblick auf ihre eigene Zukunftsperspektive in Palästina, denn sie befanden sich während der mehr als zweijährigen Trennung zunehmend selbst in einer Vorbereitungsphase auf die eigene Exilierung. Bereits während seines Aufenthalts auf Gut Schniebinchen eruierte Loewy, welche Perspektiven seine Auswanderung den Eltern eröffnen könnten:

> Dann habe ich noch mal […] gefragt, wie die Möglichkeiten sind, die Eltern nachkommen zu lassen. […] In den ersten 2 Jahren ginge es natürlich nicht. Wenn ich später nachweisen kann, daß ich meine Eltern ernähren kann (es kann frühestens nach 2 weiteren Jahren möglich sein), so kann ich sie auf Anforderungszertifikate anfordern, und sie können dann in die Kwuzah kommen […]. Also im besten Falle könnt Ihr in 4 Jahren ungefähr nachkommen.
> Brief an Erna und Richard Loewy, 6. Januar 1936

Zunächst blieb Erna und Richard Loewy also nur, „in Gedanken" (Brief an Ernst Loewy, 28. März 1936) mit ihrem Sohn zu reisen, das Land durch seine

Schilderungen kennenzulernen und auf seine Eignung für die eigene Lebens-
perspektive zu prüfen: „als wenn ich das selbst alles erlebt hätte" (Brief an
Ernst Loewy, 15. November 1936), kommentiert die Mutter Loewys Bericht einer Besichtigung Tel Avivs. Bereits einige Monate nach seiner Ankunft in Palästina finden sich in der Korrespondenz erste Hinweise auf einen geplanten Pa-
lästinabesuch der Eltern. Dieser Besuch sollte einerseits dem Wiedersehen mit
dem Sohn dienen, war andererseits zudem als Erkundungsreise für eine spätere Auswanderung der Eltern angelegt, auch wenn der Sohn vehement davon
abriet:

> Dann zum Punkte Elternanfordern. Ich weiß, dass dies am ‚schnellsten'
> durch die Kwuzah geht, aber auf eine Weise, die für Euch *völlig ausge-*
> *schlossen* ist, es ist *unmöglich* [Hervorhebung im Original] (falls es nicht
> durch äußeren Zwang wäre), daß Ihr Eure schöne 4-Zimmerwohnung
> mit einer verwanzten Bude in einer Holzhütte vertauscht, außerdem hät-
> tet Ihr ja ein völlig abgeschlossenes Leben ohne irgend einen Menschen.
> [...] es wird Jahre dauern, bis ich genug verdiene, und wenn Ihr hier wärt,
> müßtet Ihr Euch schon mit 50 Jahren auf die faule Haut legen, denn ei-
> nen neuen Beruf beginnen, könnt ihr nicht.
>
> Brief an Erna und Richard Loewy, 4. Juni 1937

Auch wenn Loewy, der die Situation in NS-Deutschland aus der Distanz nicht
richtig einschätzen konnte, in Palästina keine Perspektive für seine Eltern sah,
waren es dennoch gerade seine Briefe mit ihren detaillierten Schilderungen,
die ihnen das Land näherbrachten.

Im Juli und August 1937 besuchte Richard Loewy seinen Sohn in Palästina.
Gemeinsam unternahmen sie Reisen durch das Land, so dass der Vater die
durch die brieflichen Beschreibungen des Sohnes gewonnenen Eindrücke
durch eigene Anschauung ergänzen konnte. Nach seiner Rückkehr nahmen
die Auswanderungspläne der Eltern in den Briefen immer mehr Raum ein, ihre
Formulierungen wurden drängender. Wie Erna Loewy dem Sohn mitteilte, bereiteten sie sich mit Sprachkursen und dem Erlernen zusätzlicher Fertigkeiten
konkreter auf ein Leben in Palästina vor:

> Ich selbst machte mir nichts draus in einer Kwuzah zu leben, auch wenn
> es nur ein Zimmer für uns wäre. Das Glück hängt nicht alleine von einer
> schönen Wohnung ab, ich kann mich sehr gut umstellen, finde mich
> überall zurecht. Kochen für eine grosse Gesellschaft oder sonst eine Ar-
> beit würde ich jederzeit übernehmen, es würde mir mehr Freude machen
> als hier in den Tag hinein leben. Ausserdem bin ich ja auch noch keine

alte Frau, die nichts mehr leisten kann. Ich habe mir sogar vorgenommen, anfang des Jahres einen Nähkursus mitzumachen, damit ich auch das kann, und mal zugreifen kann. [...] Vater und ich lernen augenblicklich fleißig [Englisch] und ich hätte nicht gedacht, dass ich so leicht dahinter komme.

Brief an Ernst Loewy, 10. Dezember 1937

Sie berichten auch von der Emigration befreundeter Familien, um ihrem Sohn den Ernst der Lage zu verdeutlichen: „Gestern war Helmut Frank hier, um sich zu verabschieden. In letzter Minute hat es noch mit Amerika geklappt" (Brief an Ernst Loewy, 10. Dezember 1937). Mit zunehmender Verschlechterung ihrer Lage – dem als Handelsvertreter tätigen Vater wurde aufgrund seiner jüdischen Herkunft im Februar 1938 eine wichtige Vertretung gekündigt – formulierten sie ihren Ausreisewunsch drängender: „Du gehst immer noch von dem Standpunkt aus, dass man es nicht gut in der Kwuzah hat, aber es geht nicht darum, um gut oder nicht gut, sondern nur darum, dort zu sein" (Brief an Ernst Loewy, 19. Februar 1938), kommentiert Richard Loewy die Einwände seines Sohnes gegen ein Leben in einer landwirtschaftlichen Gemeinschaftssiedlung, das sie durch die brieflichen Schilderungen des Sohnes schon detailliert kennengelernt hatten. Mit zusätzlichen Ausbildungen bereiteten sie sich weiter auf ein Leben in Palästina vor:

> In Europa ist ja auch bald eine Konferenz in Evian, die wir mit vielen Hoffnungen erwarten. Vielleicht ist auch damit mal Leuten geholfen, die nicht als Kapitalisten weggehen können, sondern leider auf die Hilfe der Gemeinschaft angewiesen sind. Vielleicht wird dann auch die Einwanderung erleichtert, dass wir auch daran denken hinüberzukommen. Ende des Monats werden wir beide [...] zu meinem Hemdfabrikanten fahren um dort etwas zu lernen, wenigstens das Notdürftigste, wie man ein Oberhemd und Sporthemd zuschneidet und näht, man muss ja an alles Mögliche denken, damit man dort vielleicht doch mal ein bisschen kann und was beginnen kann, wenn auch nur im allerkleinsten Rahmen. [...] Man versucht ja vieles [...].
>
> Brief an Ernst Loewy, 3. Juli 1938

Letztlich endete die mehr als zweijährige Vorstufe des Exils für Erna und Richard Loewy im November 1938. Mit einem Touristenvisum gelang ihnen die Ausreise nach Palästina. In der Dauerausstellung *Exil. Erfahrung und Zeugnis* wird ein Brief dieser dichten Korrespondenz zwischen Ernst Loewy und seinen Eltern im Kapitel *Familien im Exil* präsentiert. Für Familien bedeutete das

Exil häufig eine Trennung von Ehepaaren, von Geschwistern sowie von Eltern und Kindern. Der Briefwechsel Loewys mit seinen Eltern legt davon eindrücklich Zeugnis ab.

Zurückgelassen werden mussten aber auch Erinnerungsplätze an Verstorbene. In Nachbarschaft des Briefes Ernst Loewys wird in der Ausstellung ein Notizbuch des Schriftstellers Hermann Borchardt präsentiert, dessen Berliner Einträge ebenfalls als gedankliche Vorbereitungen auf das Exil interpretiert werden können. Hermann Borchardt, Autor des erst 2005 auf Deutsch erschienenen Romans *Die Verschwörung der Zimmerleute* (vgl. Borchardt, *Verschwörung*), war von einem Aufenthalt in der Sowjetunion im Januar 1936 nach Deutschland zurückgekehrt. Nach seiner Haft in mehreren Konzentrationslagern und dort erlittenen Misshandlungen konnte er sich 1937 in die USA retten. Zurücklassen musste er die Gräber seiner Eltern auf dem Jüdischen Friedhof in Berlin Weissensee. In einem im Nachlass überlieferten Notizbuch hielt er unter dem Buchstaben „W" die Lage der Gräber seiner Eltern fest (vgl. Borchardt, Nachlass). Das Notizbuch begleitete ihn ins Exil.

Ganz ähnlich ist ein weiteres Exponat zu deuten. Es handelt sich um ein Säckchen mit Graberde, das die Familie von Stefanie Zweig, der späteren Schriftstellerin und Autorin von *Nirgendwo in Afrika,* mit ins kenianische Exil nahm. Mit „Erde vom Grab der lieben Mutter" ist es beschriftet.

> Meine liebe, gute Liesel! Ich hatte ganz fest vor, Dich vor Euerm Breslauer Besuch um ein Säckchen Erde vom Grab unserer Mutter zu bitten, dann habe ich es doch nicht getan. Ich fand, dass wir alle schon mitgenommen genug waren, und wollte nicht auch noch von Gräbern reden. Doch hier in Genua, wo ich mir bereits vorkomme, als wäre ich in ein tiefes Loch gestoßen worden, sehe ich die Dinge in einem anderen Licht. Ein Stück Heimat, und sei es auch nur ein Häufchen Graberde, würde mir sehr viel bedeuten. Ich hoffe, die Reise nach Gleiwitz und dann der Weg zum Friedhof machen Dir nicht den Kummer, den ich Dir ursprünglich nicht zumuten wollte. Es wäre gut, wenn Du Jettel die Erde nicht in einem verschlossenen oder gar versiegelten Behälter schickst. Ich könnte mir nach allem, was ich in Breslau hörte, vorstellen, dass das Ärger beim Zoll gibt, wenn Jettel so weit ist, mir zu folgen. Wenn Gott ausnahmsweise ein Mal mit uns ist, wird das hoffentlich schneller der Fall sein, als wir alle derzeit zu hoffen wagen.
>
> ZWEIG, *Nirgendwo war Heimat* 78

In diesem von ihr erinnerten Brief Walter Zweigs schildert Stefanie Zweig den Hintergrund des Objekts. Das Notizbuch und das Säckchen mit Erde können als Versuche gedeutet werden, für Zurückgelassenes portable Erinnerungsformate zu finden. Mit dieser Transformation geht zugleich ein Bedeutungswechsel einher, denn die Tatsache, dass die Erinnerungsorte selbst nicht mehr besucht werden konnten, lässt diese Formate zu Symbolen für den Verlust der Heimat werden. Die Graberde erfährt in dem Augenblick einen Bedeutungswechsel, in dem Walter Zweig im Begriff ist, Europa zu verlassen.

Der Schriftsteller Heinz Liepman, der 1933 in die Niederlande emigrierte, von dort nach Belgien ausgewiesen worden und über Frankreich in die USA gegangen war, befand sich gleich mehrfach in einer Vorstufe des Exils. 1959, zwölf Jahre, nachdem er aus seinem Exil in den USA nach Deutschland zurückgekehrt war, stellte er in der Zeitung *Die Welt* die Frage „Müssen wir wieder emigrieren?“ Sein Artikel ist in der Ausstellung *Exil. Erfahrung und Zeugnis* Teil des Kapitels *Nach dem Exil* und steht doch zugleich für eine erneute Vorstufe der Exilierung.

> Mit einiger Verwunderung stellten wir kürzlich fest, daß jetzt gerade 25 Jahre verstrichen sind seit der Zeit, da einige zehntausend Deutsche emigrieren mußten, um ihr Leben zu retten – oder ihre Selbstachtung. Fünfundzwanzig Jahre, der gleiche Zeitraum wie der zwischen dem ersten und dem zweiten Weltkrieg. Und heute, 25 Jahre nach der damaligen Emigration beschäftigen sich schon wieder eine ganze Anzahl von Menschen mit demselben Problem: ob sie ihre zweite Emigration vorbereiten sollen – bisher nicht wegen akuter Lebensgefahr, sondern wegen akuter

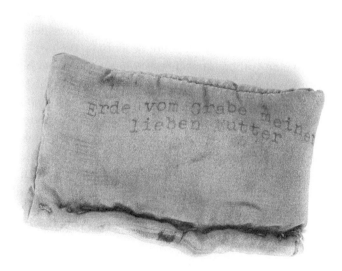

ILLUSTRATION 1.4   Säckchen mit Erde vom Grab der Mutter Walter Zweigs

Gefährdung ihrer Integrität oder besser noch: aus Gründen der Selbst-
achtung. [...] Uns alle stört der Antisemitismus, über den die Zeitungen
jetzt wieder so häufig berichten, hauptsächlich als ein Symptom. [...]
Nein, es ist nicht der mickrige Antisemitismus in diesem Land, der uns beunruhigt. Was uns beunruhigt, ist, daß so viele Übermenschen von Anno
dazumal jetzt – wie auf ein Zeichen – plötzlich Morgenluft wittern –,
daß sie überall in diesem Land plötzlich wieder auftauchen. [...] Was uns
aber am meisten beunruhigt, ist ein altes deutsches Gesellschaftsspiel,
das heute wieder in Mode gekommen ist. Es ist das Spiel mit dem Titel: Wer eine andere Meinung hat als ich ist ein Schuft. [...] Wir, die wir
an persönliche Integrität glauben anstatt an die Dogmen der Parteien,
Religionsgemeinschaften und Verbraucher-Organisationen, wir sind ver-
dammt einsam geworden. (39)

Antisemitismus, unheilvolle Kontinuitäten und das Gefühl einer erzwungenen
Konformität brachten Liepman erneut dazu, über eine Auswanderung nachzudenken. 1961 verlegte er seinen Wohnsitz dauerhaft in die Schweiz.

Es sind ganz unterschiedliche Exponate, die in der Dauerausstellung des
Deutschen Exilarchivs 1933–1945 *Exil. Erfahrung und Zeugnis* für Vorstufen des
Exils stehen. Zu ihnen zählen Objekte, die im Exil eine emotionale, reale oder
imaginäre Verbindung zum Herkunftsland herstellen sollten. Das Exil er-
scheint in der Phase vor Verlassen des Herkunftslands als Chance und Rettung,
ist aber gleichzeitig ein unbekannter Zustand, der auch als beängstigend empfunden wird und in dem die Verbindung zur Herkunftsgesellschaft zu zerbre-
chen droht. Fotografien und Erinnerungsstücke wie das Säckchen mit Graberde fungierten als Verbindungselemente zwischen beiden Welten und erhielten
durch die erzwungene räumliche Distanz besondere Bedeutung. Die Zeit vor
der Exilierung war oft auch eine Vorbereitung auf das Kommende, in der beispielsweise Sprachkenntnisse und Voraussetzungen für andere berufliche Tä-
tigkeiten erworben wurden und Vorstellungen vom Aufnahmeland entstanden. Diese Bilder und Erwartungen wurden einerseits gezielt vermittelt,
beispielsweise durch für Auswanderer verfasste Literatur oder durch mehr-
schichtige Vorbereitungskurse, wie ihn Ernst Loewy auf Gut Schniebinchen
absolvierte. Bilder vom Zufluchtsland erzeugten aber auch die Beschreibungen, die Exilierte an die Zurückgebliebenen übermittelten. Erna und Richard
Loewy lernten Palästina auch durch die Beschreibungen ihres Sohnes kennen.
Dabei kollidierten die aus ihren unterschiedlichen Perspektiven gezogenen
Schlussfolgerungen an einigen Stellen. Was der Sohn aus seiner Erfahrung
vor Ort in Palästina und seiner durch die räumliche Distanz entstandenen

Unkenntnis der zugespitzten Verhältnisse in NS-Deutschland als Lösung für die Eltern verwarf, wurde für diese in der Phase vor ihrer Exilierung dennoch zur Zukunftsperspektive.

Die Erinnerungen an die Vorstufen des Exils sind in vielfältigen materiellen Formen konserviert. In Fotos und ganzen, kontextgebenden Fotoalben, die besonders in vordigitalen Zeiten einen fast unikalen Charakter haben, in überlieferten Souvenirs, wie Mützenbändern und Prospekten von Schiffspassagen, Billetts oder Fahrplänen, in amtlichen Dokumenten oder Briefen. Allen materiellen Zeugen ist gemeinsam, dass sie Bedeutungswechseln unterliegen. Ein Dokument behördlicher Vorgänge kann so zum Erinnerungsstück werden, ein Säckchen mit Erde zum Symbol für Heimat, ein Reisesouvenir zum Exilobjekt. Dass diese oft fragilen Erinnerungsobjekte über die Jahrzehnte aufbewahrt und wie im Falle von Stefanie Zweig sichtbar in ihre spätere Lebenswirklichkeit integriert wurden, indem sie beispielsweise die Mützenbänder in Rahmen gefasst in ihrer Frankfurter Wohnung präsentierte, macht die Bedeutung dieser Objekte für die Familienbiografien zusätzlich deutlich. Auch Ernst Loewy bewahrte das Abschiedsfoto sowie die Briefe der Eltern und seine eigenen Schreiben aus Palästina über die Jahrzehnte auf. Mit der Übergabe der Objekte an ein Archiv wurden diese Zeugen der Vorstufen des Exils in neue Kontexte überführt und auf Dauer gesichert. In der Dauerausstellung des Deutschen Exilarchiv 1933–1945 *Exil. Erfahrung und Zeugnis* werden einige dieser Exponate erfahrbar gemacht.

ILLUSTRATION 1.5 Mützenband, das die Familie Zweig als Andenken
                 an ihre Schiffsreisen nach Kenia 1938 aufbewahrte

Zitierte Literatur

Bermann, Richard A. *Tagebuch von der Saharafahrt.* Nachlass Richard A. Bermann, Deutsches Exilarchiv 1933–1945 der Deutschen Nationalbibliothek, Frankfurt am Main, EB 75/015.

Borchardt, Hermann. Nachlass. Deutsches Exilarchiv 1933–1945 der Deutschen Nationalbibliothek, Frankfurt am Main, EB 96/266.

Borchardt, Hermann. *Die Verschwörung der Zimmerleute.* Weidle, 2005. (Englische Erstausgabe unter dem Titel *The Conspiracy of the Carpenters. Historical Accounting of a Ruling Class.* Simon and Schuster, 1943).

Loewy, Erna. Brief an Ernst Loewy. Krefeld, 28. März 1936. Nachlass Ernst Loewy, Deutsches Exilarchiv 1933–1945 der Deutschen Nationalbibliothek, Frankfurt am Main, EB 95/75.

Loewy, Erna. Brief an Ernst Loewy. Krefeld, 15. November 1936. Nachlass Ernst Loewy, Deutsches Exilarchiv 1933–1945 der Deutschen Nationalbibliothek, Frankfurt am Main, EB 95/75.

Loewy, Erna. Brief an Ernst Loewy. [Krefeld], 10. Dezember 1937. Nachlass Ernst Loewy, Deutsches Exilarchiv 1933–1945 der Deutschen Nationalbibliothek, Frankfurt am Main, EB 95/75.

Loewy, Erna. Brief an Ernst Loewy. [Krefeld], 3. Juni 1938. Nachlass Ernst Loewy, Deutsches Exilarchiv 1933–1945, Deutsche Nationalbibliothek, Frankfurt am Main, EB 95/75.

Loewy, Ernst. Brief an Erna und Richard Loewy. Schniebinchen, 20. Dezember 1935. Nachlass Ernst Loewy, Deutsches Exilarchiv 1933–1945 der Deutschen Nationalbibliothek, Frankfurt am Main, EB 95/75.

Loewy, Ernst. Brief an Erna und Richard Loewy. Schniebinchen, 27. Dezember 1935. Nachlass Ernst Loewy, Deutsches Exilarchiv 1933–1945 der Deutschen Nationalbibliothek, Frankfurt am Main, EB 95/75.

Loewy, Ernst. Brief an Erna und Richard Loewy. Schniebinchen, 6. Januar 1936. Nachlass Ernst Loewy, Deutsches Exilarchiv 1933–1945 der Deutschen Nationalbibliothek, Frankfurt am Main, EB 95/75.

Loewy, Ernst. Brief an Erna und Richard Loewy. Schniebinchen, 26. März 1936. Nachlass Ernst Loewy, Deutsches Exilarchiv 1933–1945 der Deutschen Nationalbibliothek, Frankfurt am Main, EB 95/75.

Loewy, Ernst. Brief an Lore Traub sowie Erna und Richard Loewy. SS Tel Aviv, 29. März 1936. Nachlass Ernst Loewy, Deutsches Exilarchiv 1933–1945 der Deutschen Nationalbibliothek, Frankfurt am Main, EB 95/75.

Loewy, Ernst. Brief an Erna und Richard Loewy. Kirjat Anavim, 4. Juni 1937. Nachlass Ernst Loewy, Deutsches Exilarchiv 1933–1945 der Deutschen Nationalbibliothek, Frankfurt am Main, EB 95/75.

Loewy, Ernst. Brief an Erna und Richard Loewy. Schniebinchen, 20. Dezember 1935. Nachlass Ernst Loewy, Deutsches Exilarchiv 1933–1945 der Deutschen Nationalbibliothek, Frankfurt am Main, EB 95/75.

Loewy, Ernst. *Jugend in Palästina. Briefe an die Eltern 1935–1938*, hrsg. von Brita Eckert, Metropol, 1997.

Loewy, Richard. Brief an Ernst Loewy. Krefeld, 19. Februar 1938. Nachlass Ernst Loewy, Deutsches Exilarchiv 1933–1945 der Deutschen Nationalbibliothek, Frankfurt am Main, EB 95/75.

Liepman, Heinz. „Müssen wir wieder emigrieren?" *Die Welt*, Nr. 44, 21. Februar 1959, S. 39.

Vogel, Jakob. „Die Passage. Annäherungen des Historikers an ein analytisches Konzept *Passagen des Exils*, hrsg. von Burcu Dogramaci und Elizabeth Otto, edition text + kritik, 2017.

Zweig, Stefanie. *Nirgendwo in Afrika*. Langen Müller, 1995.

Zweig, Stefanie. *Nirgendwo war Heimat. Mein Leben auf zwei Kontinenten*. Langen Müller, 2012.

Dank an die Emigration

Egon Schwarz

This essay is contained in the papers of Egon Schwarz in the Olin Library of Washington University as a typoscript corrected by hand. On the basis of a time designation in the text, it can be assumed that Schwarz wrote it in the early 60's as a kind preliminary exercise in the process of writing his later autobiography, *Unfreiwillige Wanderjahre*. However, it also stands by itself as giving witness to many early stages of exile. In spite of the many trials and tribulations of those early stages and exile itself, Schwarz comes a positive conclusion about emigration.[1]

Emigration ist schrecklich wie des Himmels Plagen, doch ist sie auch gut, ein Geschenk der Götter wie sie.

Die Emigration ist eine strenge Lehrmeisterin. Jeder Lebende erfährt den Schmerz, das Gefühl absoluter Sinnlosigkeit beim Verlust eines einzigen vertrauten Menschen. Der Emigrant verliert mit einem Schlag alles, was ihm vertraut im Leben ist, was das Ausharren auf dieser unwirtlichen Erde möglich zu machen scheint.

Ich war sechzehn Jahre alt, als ich emigrieren musste.

Ich glaube, dass ich ein sesshafter Mensch bin, obwohl ich es nicht beweisen kann. Denn ich habe mich seither – und das geschah vor fünfundzwanzig Jahren – pausenlos in der Welt umgetrieben. Es gibt keinen Ort auf der Erdoberfläche, wo ich drei Jahre, keine Wohnung, in der ich zwei Jahre verbracht hätte. Aber die bescheidene Etagenwohnung in meiner Heimatstadt zu verlieren, in der ich von Kindheit an gewohnt hatte, deren jeder Winkel, jedes Möbel, jede rauhe Tapetenstelle mir so vertraut war, dass ich das alles fast wie

---

1 Der Nachlass in der Olin Library ist eine Teilkopie des erweiterten Nachlasses, der sich im Deutschen Literaturarchiv in Marbach befindet. Zu Schwarz' Autobiographie und die Vorstufen des Exils darin vgl. den Beitrag von Helga Schreckenberger in diesem Band. Der Text erschein zum ersten Mal wie folgt: Reinhard Andress, „Leb wohl Südamerika' und ‚Dank an die Emigration' – Texte aus dem Nachlass von Egon Schwarz". *Glossen. German Literature and Culture after 1945*, 44 (2019): http://blogs.dickinson.edu/glossen/glossen-44-2019-current -issue/texte-aus-dem-nachlass-von-egon-schwarz-lebe-wohl-sudamerika-und-dank-an-die -emigration/. Der Essay gelangt hier mit der freundlichen Genehmigung von Schwarz' Witwe, Dr. Irène Lindgren-Schwarz, zum Druck. Zwecks der Publikation wurde eine Reinschrift hergestellt, die die handschriftlichen Korrekturen des Typoskripts berücksichtigt.

einen Teil meines Körpers empfand, war mir lange Zeit kaum erträglich. Ganz ähnlich verhielt es sich mit der Stadt: die Läden, wo ich manchmal einkaufen musste (ein halbes Pfund Butter, das man schnell brauchte, oder die Zeitung, die man vergessen hatte), die Parkanlagen, in denen man mich als Kind spazieren führte und in deren Sandhaufen ich graben durfte, die Brücken, unter denen ich Steine in das Wasser schmiss, die Straßenzüge, durch die mein Schulweg führte – das alles war wie eine leibliche Fortsetzung meiner eigenen Existenz, nicht schön und nicht hässlich, sondern fraglos mein. Schon die Rückkehr von den großen Ferien, so gern ich diese auch hatte, war selige Wiedervereinigung mit all dem entbehrten Trauten, das ein Teil von mir war. Und nun gar die Schule selbst: die Treppen, die geölten Böden, die bekritzelten und zerschnittenen Pulte, die kahlen Wände, die bestaubten Zeusköpfe aus Gips, sogar die scharf nach Desinfektionsmittel und anderem riechenden Aborte! Ich liebte sie nicht, diese Schule. Welcher sensiblere Gymnasiast hätte schon die grauenhafte, von verkrampften Marionetten autoritär regierte Stätte seiner Demütigungen geliebt? Aber sie war unentbehrlich, und sein seither nie mehr erlebtes Glücksgefühl durchströmte mich, wenn im September nach endloser, dreimonatiger Entfernung die Wellen ihres unausrottbaren Geruches wieder über mir zusammenschlugen und ich mit wohligem Schauder in den Stundenplan das neue, mir gänzlich rätselhafte Wort „Physik" eintragen musste, mit dem ich fürderhin leben sollte.

Das alles ging eines Tages plötzlich und unwiederbringlich verloren, als sei es weggewischt, und ich glaubte, nicht weiterleben zu können.

Dem Verlust ging eine Zeit des Aufruhrs und des Hasses voran. Fahnen wurden in allen Fenstern gehisst, neue, rote mit dem bedrohlichen schwarzen Zeichen im weißen Kreis, nicht die harmlosen, gestreiften, die wir bis dahin anzubeten hatten. Aus dem Radio plärrten scharfe, ironische und pathetisch salbungsvolle Stimmen. Alles war voll von Uniformen, Freunde meines Vaters verschwanden und man erzählte Furchterregendes von den KZs, wohin sie, wie es hieß, gebracht worden waren. Fratzen starrten einem aus den Hasszeitungen entgegen und waren Verzerrungen des eigenen Gesichts. Auf den Straßen wurden meinesgleichen in Häuflein fortgetrieben. Es wurde viel marschiert. Die Lehrer zeigten sich noch gehässiger als zuvor, die gestern noch lausbübisch-egozentrischen, aber schülerhaft umgänglichen Kameraden wurden eisig und ablehnend. Und ich wusste, dieser feindselige Aufwand galt mir. Die ganze vertraute Umgebung hatte sich gegen mich gekehrt. Das war nicht schön, es war sogar gräßlich, aber es war und blieb die vertraute Umgebung, und war nicht die Emigration.

Eines Tages war dann alles weg. Die Schule, die Wohnung, die Parks und Plätze, die ganze Stadt. Ich hatte alles verloren: das Gesicht der Hausmeisterin und die roten Hände der Kolonialwarenhändlerin, den Papagei, dem ich immer Plätzchen brachte, wenn ich sonntags ins Weltpanorama ging. Ich hatte plötzlich keine Schulkameraden, ich kannte keinen Menschen mehr und hatte sogar meine Eltern, kurz, meine gesamte Vergangenheit und Zukunft verloren. Das war die Emigration: Ich war gerettet. Aber für eine vertraute Heimat hatte ich trotz der Verfratzung die Leere und Sinnlosigkeit der ganzen Welt eingetauscht.

Das mit dem Verlust meiner Eltern muss ich erklären, denn sie leben heute noch nach fünfundzwanzig Jahren, etwas betagt und gebrechlich, aber im Grunde ganz gesund, worüber ich natürlich sehr froh bin. Aber es sind nicht die Eltern meiner Kindheit. Diese waren nämlich für mein Gefühl unzertrennlich mit der Umwelt meiner Heimatstadt verbunden und büßten für mich zugleich mit dieser ihre ursprüngliche Funktion ein. Mein Vater war der Mensch gewesen, der zu ganz bestimmten Stunden aufstand und fortging, und zu ebenso genau festgesetzten Zeiten heimkehrte, aß, das Radio andrehte und eine Zeitung mit einem unveränderlichen Titel las. Und auch meine Mutter war eine ganz festgelegte Person, etwas erregbar und weinerlich, aber – und darauf kam es an – mit bekannten Ansprüchen und Gewohnheiten, die allesamt auf diese meine Geburtsstadt bezogen waren. Diese beiden Menschen hatten kaum etwas mit den vergrämten, versorgten, ratlos getriebenen Personen zu tun, mit denen ich von nun an eine Zeitlang durch die Welt zog und von denen ich mich bald trennen musste, weil die Emigration eine eifersüchtige Göttin ist, die auf den ungeteilten Dienst ihrer Hörigen besteht. So war ich an dem Tage der Einbuße unter anderem auch plötzlich und mit einem rohen Schlage Erwachsener geworden.

Und jetzt kamen die Jahre der Ruhelosigkeit und der Obdachlosigkeit für einen, der sich für sesshaft hält, ohne es freilich beweisen zu können. Es gab wieder Wohnungen, es gab neue Obst- und Milchhändler, Parkanlagen und Brücken und sogar einen Schulweg, und eine Schule gab es noch einmal auf kurze Zeit, aber das war vollkommen sinn- und bedeutungslos und hätte genauso gut auch nicht zu sein brauchen. Das Furchtbare an der Emigration war nicht das immer wieder eintretende Ablaufen der Aufenthaltserlaubnis, das Einpacken und Verreisen ohne Ziel, das Deportiertwerden und die nächtlichen Grenzüberschreitungen, das Schlangestehen bei den Hilfsvereinen für Flüchtlinge und Konsulaten, das Leben aus Koffern, die Wochen im Lager, die Flucht und das monatelange Verstecktsein, nicht das schlechte oder mangelnde Essen, nicht der Husten, mangelhafte Zimmer, nicht das Verlieren und Suchen des Vaters, die Erkrankung und das Zurücklassenmüssen der Mutter, nicht einmal das Misstrauen der Menschen oder die Hoffnungslosigkeit und

Aussichtslosigkeit der ganzen Existenz. Denn sonderbarerweise war das für mich nicht das Wesen des Exils, nicht die Emigration an sich, sondern lediglich die logische Entsprechung jenes verlorenen Schatzes, die natürliche Folge der Einbuße des Vertrauten und Ererbten, ohne das leben zu wollen mir damals unvorstellbar und leben zu können ehrlos vorkam. Wirkliche Glückempfindungen habe ich jahrelang nur in manchen Nächten, anfangs häufig, dann immer seltener erlebt, stürmische, törichte, selige Räusche von Glück, aus denen ich in Schweiß gebadet, mit klopfenden Pulsen und wahnsinniger Enttäuschung erwachte. Es war fast immer ein und derselbe Traum, in dem ich weiter nichts Schönes sah und in dem nichts passierte, als dass ich mich in eine Straße jener Stadt zurückversetzt sah, deren Bewohner mich grausam bespien und verjagt hatten und die für mich nur den einen, allerdings unwiderruflichen Vorzug besaß, dass ich da geboren war. Das hat nichts mit Sentimentalität zu tun.

Und dann kam wieder ein Tag. An diesem Tag brachte mein Vater die grünen Pässe mit der grauenhaften Rune auf dem Deckel und dem obszönen roten Jot auf der ersten Seite, die er so lange auf den hochmütigen Konsulaten vergebens zu Markte getragen hatte, heim, und es war in jeden ein Visum eingestempelt, ausgestellt auf ein fernes primitives Land, von dem ich in der Schule nichts gelernt und dessen Namen ich kaum jemals gehört hatte. Weiß der Himmel, welchem Zufall oder welcher Ausdauer oder welcher ausgeklügelten Erniedrigung diese Einreisegenehmigung zu verdanken war. Die Stadt, in der wir letzthin mit den Nachtkellnern eines Sektpavillons in einem gemeinsamen Schlafsaal gehaust hatten, war längst auf allen Seiten von Hitlerterritorium umgeben. Aber das Visum war ein Zauberstab, und es öffnete sich für uns die Himmel. Ein Hilfsverein zahlte unsere Passagen, und mein erster Flug hob mich hinaus aus dem Kessel der Treibjagd. Ein paar Tage in einer begehrten Weltstadt, allerdings ohne ein Pfennig in der Tasche – immer wiederkehrende Tantalussituation des Exils – dann saßen wir zwischendecks auf einem Dampfer und überquerten das Meer. Die Reise zu unserem neuen Bestimmungsort dauerte einen ganzen Monat. Und in der Mitte des Ozeans stand eines Tages auf einem schreibmaschinengeschriebenen Anschlag zwischen Nachrichten von einem Tennisturnier und der Verhaftung eines bekannten Gangsters zu lesen, dass die Stadt, der wir entronnen waren, mitsamt den Volksküchen, in denen wir gegessen, und den Pfandleihanstalten, wo wir die Reste unserer Garderobe gelassen, mitsamt den Polizeistationen, Konsulaten und Flüchtlingsstellen, in denen wir Schlange gestanden, und dem grölenden Sektpavillion, über dem wir geschlafen hatten, eine Beute Hitlers geworden war. Dieser Tag war das Ende meiner Emigration und der Beginn meiner Immigration.

Emigration und Immigration sind, obgleich offenbar miteinander verwandt, doch gleichzeitig so grundverschieden, wie Verlobung und Ehe verwandt und verschieden sind. Mit einer grauenhaften Weibsperson ist es entsetzlich verlobt oder verheiratet zu sein, aber es ist auf andere Weise entsetzlich.

Die Verlobungszeit mit der Emigration war voll von stürmischem Auf und Ab, Hin und Her gewesen, voll hektischer Erregungen und tiefer Depressionen. Auf die Dauer konnte man so nicht leben, das war klar. Wir waren bei Schulschluss im Frühjahr ausgewandert, und ich erinnere mich der irren Hoffnung, in der ich den ersten Sommer verlebte, im Herbst nach den großen Ferien bei veränderten Verhältnissen, so als wäre nicht geschehen, wie schon so oft in meine Schule zurückkehren zu können.

Solche Hoffnungen waren nun für immer erloschen. Die Immigration war von vornherein auf Dauer angelegt. Man hatte eine Einreiseerlaubnis, eine unbeschränkte Aufenthaltserlaubnis, ja sogar eine Erwerbserlaubnis. Bald musste man nicht mehr von misstrauisch dargereichten Mildtätigkeiten leben, sondern durfte sich eine Arbeit suchen, eine Wohnung mieten, Mahlzeiten kochen. Man wurde nicht mehr abgeschoben, abends gab es wieder die Pantoffeln und morgens den Wecker. Es hatte Sinn, die neue Sprache zu lernen, denn es würde wohl noch morgen und übermorgen dieselbe sein. Die Misere war jetzt Alltag geworden.

Aber was sollte ein siebzehnjähriger Gymnasiast machen, der in der Erwartung eines geistigen Berufes erzogen wurde und gelebt hatte? Was nützte jetzt das bisschen Algebra und Latein? Die Schule war zu Ende, jetzt musste Geld verdient werden. Während der nächsten zehn Jahre trieb ich – das war schon zum Lebensgesetz geworden – von einem Land zum anderen, von einer Beschäftigung zur nächsten. Ich war Maurer und Elektriker, Bibliotheksgehilfe und Textilarbeiter, Hausierer und Nachtwächter, Sprachlehrer und chemischer Techniker, Bergarbeiter und Kürschner, Buchhalter und Übersetzer, und immer ein Fremder. Einmal Emigrant, immer Emigrant. Diese Wahrheit erfuhr ich am eigenen Leibe. Und obschon ich das neue Land nicht eroberte, entschwand das alte immer mehr. Weit weg war Europa und die Aufgaben der Gegenwart dringend. Zuerst freilich beschäftigte die Vergangenheit noch sehr. Man verkehrte fast ausschließlich mit anderen Emigranten, die Gespräche drehten sich um das politische Geschehen, demzufolge man hier zusammensaß, um das „Früher", das einem jeden in einem verklärten Licht erschien, um die Flucht, deren jede einzelne einem fesselnden Roman glich. Man las die Emigrantenzeitungen, gründete Emigrantenvereine, spielte Emigrantentheater. Und endlich – so empfanden wohl die meisten – brach der gerechte Krieg aus, und jeder Sieg der alten Heimat wurde mit Erbitterung, Niedergeschlagenheit und Angst, jede ihrer Niederlagen mit gieriger Genugtuung und irrsinnigem Jubel aufgenommen. Aber die Gegenwart wurde immer stärker und die Vergangenheit immer schattenhafter. Und als es dann klar wurde, dass der entsetzliche Krieg im Grund entschieden war und die Niederzwingung des Untiers nur mehr eine Frage der Zeit, begann sogar das Interesse an den europäischen Entwicklungen nachzulassen. Man war der grauen Gegenwart nun gänzlich ausgeliefert, weil einen sogar der Hass im Stich gelassen hat, der noch eine Verbindung mit dem Ursprungsort darstellte. Noch einmal wurde man aufgewühlt von den unglaublichen und doch wahren Nachrichten, die aus Europa kamen: die vergasten Millionen von Menschen. Nur durch einen Zufall, ein Missverständnis war man selber nicht dabei.

Und dann kam wieder ein Tag. Der Krieg war zu Ende. Die deutschen Städte und die jüdischen Krematorien rauchten zum Himmel, es war ein und derselbe Rauch. War jemand von den Menschen, die damals, vor undenklichen Zeiten, zur Familie gehört haben, noch am Leben? Was war mit dem Großvater, der Großmutter, den Onkeln und Tanten, den zahllosen Vettern und Kusinen geschehen, die nicht emigrieren konnten, sondern daheim geblieben waren, und von denen jahrelang kein Sterbenswörtchen herübergedrungen war. Und dazu war das Telegramm da, durchs Rote Kreuz weitergeleitet, in französischer Sprache. Es stammte von einem Onkel, der immer als eine Art schwarzes Schaf gegolten hatte, weil er – der Himmel weiß warum – katholisch geworden war. Das Telegramm enthielt nur zwei Worte: *Resté seul*. Die Taufe hatte ihm, wie ich später erfuhr, das Leben gerettet. Wir stammen ja aus einem christlichen Land. Alle anderen tot. Die Großmutter auf der Landstraße mit dem Gewehrkolben erschlagen, der achtzigjährige Großvater im Vernichtungslager verschollen. Ich habe später einen Landsmann getroffen, der mit ihm zusammen in Auschwitz war und es überlebt hat. Er habe in der Küche gearbeitet, erzählte der Mann, und meinem Großvater eine gekochte Kartoffel gebracht, und da habe ihm der sterbende Großvater die Hand geküsst. Und am nächsten Tag sei er verschwunden gewesen. Und verschwunden waren auch alle anderen, Frauen und Männer, Alte und Junge, ebenso wie die kleinen Kinder, vergast, verschleppt, erschlagen, ermordet. *Resté seul*. Auch dieser Tag war ein Tag der Konfrontierung mit der Emigration.

Fünfundzwanzig Jahre sind vergangen, seit ich ausgewandert bin, achtzehn seit der Krieg zu Ende ist. Längst bin ich in einem Land, wo ich eine vierte Sprache gelernt habe. Ich bin sogar Staatsbürger geworden und habe einen neuen Pass. Er ist wieder grün, aber ohne Rune und Jot. Ich habe geheiratet. Ein deutsches, christliches Mädchen. Zufall oder geheime Bewandtnis? Wir haben drei Kinder, die zwei Sprachen sprechen. In dem Maße, wie die weltgeschichtlichen Konvulsionen nachließen, milderte sich auch mein seelischer Aufruhr. Ich habe doch wieder meine Studien aufnehmen und den nie vergessenen, nie aufgegebenen geistigen Beruf ergreifen können. Und was mehr ist: eine unabweisbare Gewissheit sagt mir, dass ich darin mehr und Größeres leiste, ja, dass ich ein bedeutenderer Mann geworden bin, als es ohne die Emigration möglich gewesen wäre.

Und einmal bin ich auch wieder „drüben" gewesen. Nicht bloß in Europa im Allgemeinen, sondern „dort", an der Stelle meines Ausgangs. Es begann harmlos genug mit Frankreich und Italien. Aber dann durchquerten wir die Alpen und näherten uns meinen Ursprüngen, dem Lande meiner Väter, wie es schön heißt. Unsere zwei Kinder reisten mit uns, alle waren ermüdet, ich hatte meiner Frau versprochen, in einer kleinen Stadt zu übernachten. Aber als wir am Nachmittag da anlangten, hatte mich ein sonderbares Fieber ergriffen, von innen her, das Schichten erfasste, die ich für verschüttet gehalten hatte. Ohne auch nur zu halten, durcheilte ich den Ort, immer weiter und weiter. Meine Frau fragte nicht. Spät nachts fuhr ich in meiner Geburtsstadt ein.

Die nächsten Tage verlebte ich in einem Trancezustand. Wie ein Traumwandler zog ich durch die Gassen, meine Familie hinter mir her. Alles schien unverändert. Mit einer fast schmerzenden Hellsichtigkeit wusste ich nach zwanzig Jahren jedes Fenstersims, jeden Torbogen voraus, wusste, dass der übernächste Laden eine Konditorei, dass hinter der nächsten Ecke drei Ahorne und eine Bank sein mussten. Und bei jeder Bestätigung wurde etwas heil. Hier, an diesem Platz hatte mein Vater eine Taxe angehalten und mich hineingesetzt, weil ich verschlafen hatte und zu Fuß zu spät zur Schule gekommen wäre. Hier war zu meinem Entsetzen mein Reifen über das Brückengeländer gesprungen und den Fluss hinuntergetrieben. Wo war er jetzt? Hier unter dem Denkmal des geigenden Künstlers, im Schatten der Fliederbüsche, hatte ich das erste Mädchen geküsst. Und hinter diesem Vorgärtchen hatte ich gewohnt. Fremde Kinder spielten darin. Alle Zeit zwischen jetzt und damals war ausgelöscht. Es hätte gestern, aber auch vor zweihundert Jahren sein können. Willenlos drückte ich die schwere schmiedeeiserne Tür auf. Im Foyer war es stockdunkel. Ich tastete mich bis zur Tür vor, die zum Lichthof führte, wo unsere Wäsche im Sommer zum Trocknen oft gehangen hat. Ich öffnete, und statt des Hinterhauses, in dem wir gewohnt hatten, lagen Ruinen, Berge von Schutt. Und auch die Schule besuchte ich wieder. Wie viele Menschen haben dieses Erlebnis nicht schon beschrieben! Aber man muss es selber haben. Alles, alles haargenau wie vor zwanzig Jahren, ja sogar der Geruch ist bis auf die feinste Nuance derselbe. Wie klein, wie winzig klein sind die Bänke, ist es möglich, dass ich hier gesessen habe? Ja, denn das hier habe ich selbst mit meinem Taschenmesser ins Pult geschnitzelt: „Hier saß ich einst in süßer Ruh und sah dem Katz beim Zaubern zu." Und darunter meine Initialen. Katz war unser Chemielehrer gewesen und Zaubern nannte ich seine stets misslingenden

Experimente. Und dann kam der Schuldiener und fragte, was ich wollte. Es war derselbe Mann mit dem slawischen Namen und Akzent. Nur waren seine Haare brennrot gewesen, als ich ihn zum letzten Mal gesehen hatte, jetzt waren sie weiß. Es war der einzige Mensch, den ich aus meiner Kinderzeit wiederfand. Die Stadt hatte ich, von einigen Bombenschäden abgesehen, bis zur schmerzenden Identität unverstellt gefunden. Die Menschen waren fremd geworden. Fremd und sonderbar beschränkt, wie mir schien. Ganz wehmütig machte mich die Melodie ihrer unendlich vertrauten mundartlichen Rede, aber was sie sagten, blieb mir unverständlich. Sie sprachen von der Politik, aber nur von der des Tages, von den Preisen, aber es waren ganz andere Preise, vom Theater, aber die Schauspieler hießen ganz anders. Und manchmal hieß es, der Krieg, die Amerikaner, die Russen. Ich hatte nichts mit ihnen gemein. Ich merkte, dass ich für ein paar Traumtage in eine verschollene Zeit zurückgekehrt war und nicht in einen Ort. Und als ich das merkte, konnte ich wieder abreisen. Für diese Menschen lief kein Bruch zwischen Vergangenheit und Gegenwart, sie waren ihnen eins. Meine Vergangenheit war hier, aber meine Gegenwart war anderswo, weit weg.

Und als ich diese geheimnisvoll gleiche und doch so fremde Stadt verließ, dankte ich der Emigration, dass sie mich hinausgeführt hatte in die Welt, die mir nun nicht mehr fremd erschien, sondern wieder bekannt und sinnerfüllt. Unendlich war der Preis gewesen. Den Verlust der Heimat verwindet man nicht leicht, und Ersatz für sie gibt es nicht. Sie ist wie ein Teil von einem selbst, und viele sind an dieser Abtrennung zugrunde gegangen. Ich habe überlebt. Und darum weiß ich, wer ich selbst bin, unabhängig von dem Ort, an dem ich mich befinde. Ich habe wieder einen Pass, und ich bin sehr zufrieden damit. Aber er ist mir nur ein Reisepapier. Ein Land hat mich aufgenommen, in dem meine Fähigkeiten anerkannt werden, in dem meine Kinder aufwachsen. Ich bin dankbar dafür, aber ich finde das nur richtig und natürlich. Ich verlange und erwarte das von allen Ländern. Ich lebe gerne in dem Land, dessen Staatsbürger ich bin, aber nichts hindert mich, seine Fehler zu erkennen und öffentlich aufzuzeigen, zu seinem Nutzen, wie ich meine. Und wenn es mir eines Tages nicht mehr gefiele, so würde ich in ein anderes Land ziehen, und das würde mich kein Opfer kosten. Denn seit geraumer Zeit weiß ich, dass ich nicht so sehr in diesem besonderen Land, sondern dass ich in der Welt lebe. Langwierig war das Erlernen dieser Kunst, groß ist der Gewinn, unsanft die Lehrmeisterin. Die dritte Stufe der Emigration heißt Weltbürgertum.

CHAPTER 3

From Estranged Homeland to Strange Asylum

Guy Stern

Abstract

In his contribution to this chapter, Guy Stern also gives witness to the early stages of his exile. They start with school in his native Hildesheim, to learning English, planning for emigration, procuring the necessary affidavits and passport stamps, and saying good-bye. They extend to traveling to the US and St. Louis, and the slow process of Americanization there, which effectively ended his early stages of exile.

"Learn English" were my parents' frequent early morning admonitions when I mounted my bike to get to my high school, the *Oberrealschule* at the outskirts of my native town of Hildesheim in Northern Germany. We were three Jewish boys in the same class of *Untersekunda*, in short in our sixth year. When we were admitted in 1932, we thoroughly enjoyed it. We made new friends from among our largely Protestant fellow students, liked our teachers, studied hard, and—for the most part—stayed out of trouble. One year later, after the Nazis came to power, the pleasant atmosphere slowly changed—and thus began my preliminary steps into exile. Our school became a torture chamber.

In addition, a rather benign English teacher had been superseded by someone whom we had justly named "The Boxer." He went through the classroom, his arms entwined, and stopped to throw a question at a randomly-selected victim. "*Unser Unterricht beginnt um acht.* Translate into a negative question." If you didn't follow orders by shouting, "Don't our classes begin at eight?," his arms would unfold and the back of his right or left hand—you never knew which—would land on your cheek. Rightly or wrongly, we Jewish students felt that his slaps became more forceful when directed at his Jewish victims.

Before another school year could descend upon us, my father, having heard my accounts of our painful school days, took me out of school. Exit the Boxer, enter an eccentric gentleman, gaunt and emaciated, as my private English tutor. Mr. Tittel had taken leave of Hildesheim for five years to become a teacher at an orphanage in Brooklyn. He returned when his contract ran out, filled with memories of American hit songs and of visits to Ebbets Field, then the home ground of the erstwhile Brooklyn Dodgers. He would interrupt his English lessons, fortunately in standard Americanese and not Brooklynese, by humming "On Top of Old Smokey" or exulting in great detail over the impossible catch by a Brooklyn outfielder. His vocabulary stood me in far better stead than the stilted phrases of the Boxer. And he filled me with visions of new horizons: "High schools in America are co-educational!"

In the meanwhile my parents made plans for emigration. My mother intensified her correspondence with one of her brothers, Benno, who resided with his family in St. Louis. Unlike her other brothers, living in Westphalia plus one of them having fought and died in World War I for the German fatherland, Benno had unceremoniously been shipped to America after he sassed his patriarchal father once too often. Could he, my mother asked, furnish affidavits for his sister and her family? The answer came quickly: No, he couldn't. He had lost his job as a baker and pastry maker during the end of the Depression. He was able to support only himself and his family because his union liked him and sent him on every available substitute job. But, my aunt and uncle added, they could manage to take care of one of the children.

At the same time my father appealed to German-Jewish agencies as a further step.[1] He did not know that those bodies passed requests on to American agencies. In fact, one of them furnished an additional affidavit intended to support Uncle Benno's bank statement, which was, however, all but insignificant. He took recourse to a subterfuge. Asked to submit a bank statement, he petitioned every friend, acquaintance, and union buddy to deposit money into his bank account, repayable one month later. The unemployed baker looked like a very affluent personage.

What happened next to complete the paperwork, including the *Zusatzaffidavit* from the German-Jewish Rescue Committee, was not revealed to us, nor the ultimate decision in my favor. Right after my 90th birthday, I had a chance to read the correspondence from back then.[2] Even though my rescue had taken place more than 75 years ago, I read those pages as though that life-or-death

---

1 My father's letter dated 12/6/36 was addressed to a district subsidiary of the *Reichsvertretung der Juden in Deutschland* in Hannover. The letter begins: "Ich bitte Sie höflichst, meinem Sohn Günther zur Ausreise nach Nordamerika verhelfen zu wollen." It is signed: "Mit vorzüglicher Hochachtung, Julius Stern."

2 All the extant letters concerning my immigration found their way into the files of the German Jewish Children's Aid (also called informally, the Committee for the 1,000 Children). After the war this collection and the papers of other refugee children was bequeathed to YIVO, Institute for Jewish Research located in the Center for Jewish History in New York. I own a copy of my file thanks to Gunnar Berg, the archivist of YIVO, and to Feiga Weiss, Chief Librarian of the Holocaust Memorial Center Zekelman Family Campus, Farmington Hills, MI.

decision still hung in the balance. What argued for me was my school record and the excellent recommendations given to me not only by my Jewish teachers, but also my classroom teacher at my high school. But my age, approaching the limit of sixteen years, and the fact that preference was to be given to youngsters who had no relatives in the US—and the overdrawn budget of the St. Louis subsidiary of the committee—argued against me. But then, an unexpected ally turned up: a Mrs. Margaret Esrock, the social worker charged with investigating the suitability of my aunt's and uncle's living quarters and their role as substitute parents. She was overwhelmed by their decency and altruism, and became my advocate. That turned the tide.[3]

Those papers also cleared up a puzzle: Why were those helping hands of the committee members stretched out so surreptitiously? Those fine ladies were utterly aware of the anti-Semitism of the US State Department, which was anxious to keep those rather undesirable aliens far away.[4]

During the summer of 1935, four of us adolescents, two girls, two boys, all belonging to the same Jewish youth group, took a chance. We went on a 1,000 km bicycle trip from Hildesheim to the Rhine. If we should succeed to flee Germany, we would never see the most beautiful regions of our homeland. We were willing to take a chance on encountering Nazi hooligans on the road, being recognized as Jews and being attacked—all that for retaining the memory of a countryside far more peaceful than the militant majority of our fellow citizens. It was another step on the road into exile.

We returned home unscathed. I had scarcely unpacked when my parents, with an unusual touch of formality, urged me into our dining room. Even that was out of the ordinary. That room was normally reserved for the high holidays

---

3 Mrs. Esrock had sent her social worker's report of Feb. 11, 1937 to her director at the Sommers Children's Bureau, Mrs. Viola Oschrin. Her report was summarized during a meeting of July 6, 1937, which finalized the decision of the Sommers Children's Bureau, taking responsibility for me. Mrs. Esrock had provided a most favorable account of my aunt and uncle: "The Silberbergs are kindly, wholesome people with fairly sound ideas in regard to child rearing. Mr. Silberberg, who came to America as an immigrant boy of 14 years himself, was reared by his aunt and uncle, the Markus'. Because of this experience he is eager to be of service to his nephew, and his wife of course, is in accord with the plan. They would be glad to welcome the child as soon as necessary."

4 In this regard David Wyman writes: "On June 29 [1941] the State Department instructed its diplomatic and consular officers to examine applications for permanent visa extremely carefully and to withhold visa from aliens about whom they had 'any doubt whatsoever.' The policy of keeping a very low profile in bringing children to the US is reaffirmed in a letter by Chairman Solomon Lowenstein to Paul Beerwald. He writes in a letter of Sept. 17, 1934: "In repeating our warning with regard to press publicity, we urge you again to see that no items are published in your local press. There is no objection, however, to your writing letters to your members of holding meetings with regard to this important matter."

and for meals with honored elder family members. The dining room table overflowed with documents in German and English, waiting for my inspection and signature. With that task completed, my father had one more piece of news: "You have a date next month with the American Consul in Hamburg."

The speed with which the possibility of my emigration was approaching overwhelmed me. The impressions of my recently-completed trip, the summerly beauty of a river landscape, the repellent black and brown-clad Nazi troopers visible everywhere returned to my mind, now mixed with the prospect of leaving my family and beloved country.

A month later I stood before Malcolm C. Burke, the Vice Consul of the United States for Germany's northern provinces. I had spent long hours preparing for that meeting. Even obscure events in America's history were at my fingertips. An impressive, broad-shouldered man, probably in his mid-fifties, flipped through my papers, looked me over and then shot out the first and feared question: "How much is 48 and 52?" I couldn't believe it. I dutifully answered; he pulled out a rubber stamp, marked my identification card, signed it, and said goodbye.

It is only in retrospect that I can explain these ten minutes with Mr. Burke. Among the many consular officials, he was one of the rare ones, described by historians as sympathetic to the plight of Germany's Jews.[5] I held in my hand the documents so deeply desired by thousands of my fellow Jews.

As luck would have it, the committee in New York decided that my English was good enough to travel alone to St. Louis. And so, some months later, I found myself on a train westward, marveling at the expanse of America. During a layover in Chicago, I was treated to a city tour and observed the unrestrained comings and goings of predominantly Jewish sellers and buyers. I realized that in my new country I had no need to hide for safety.[6]

Upon my arrival in St. Louis, a bevy of relatives descended upon me and welcomed me. My Uncle Benno, a small, squat person who was floored but not counted out by the Depression, was working a night shift and was not among them. My new home with Uncle Benno was a cramped flat very different from

---

5   In spite of Vice Consul Burke's candor and the continuing complaints of social agencies interested in assisting applicants, the State Department did not alter its consular procedures until 1937 (cf. Morse 143).

6   My demeanor during my short sojourn in Chicago is also mirrored in a letter of Nov. 11, 1937 by Mrs. Eleanor Schwartz, a volunteer of the Jewish Children's Bureau of Chicago and my personal tour guide, to Mrs. Lotte Marcuse, the Chair of the German-Jewish Children's Aid in New York: "I found Günther a most [...] responsive boy, who should make an excellent adjustment in this country [...]."

my grandparents' spacious house in Westphalia, and I also had to share space with another refugee boy.

Undeterred by Uncle Benno's modest home, I dreamed of adventure in America. Though my days of cross-country train travel would not resume until five years later, courtesy of the US Army, I discovered hitchhiking and explored St. Louis and its environs, from the sheltering main library with the nearby White Castle to the Jefferson Memorial and art museum. Occasionally, my aunt and I would walk to the Plymouth Movie Theatre, where on Tuesday nights, ladies received reduced admissions. I absorbed Americana from faded matinee idols to rookie players of the St. Louis Browns and Cardinals. I also became knowledgeable about the Wild West (fictitious of course) and learned folk tunes.

Within five days of my arrival, I was enrolled at Soldan High School.[7] An avid student, I was soon immersed in the strict but welcoming environment. On my first day, the principal, Mr. Stellwagen, received me personally and, undeterred by my German-tinged speech, patiently explained the menu of extra-curricular activities. Soon, I found myself scheduled for swimming and the school news-paper, *Scrippage*, where I later earned the moniker "Scoop" for my ability to get interviews of a caliber rarely seen in high school newspapers. Within a couple of weeks I corralled both the jazz idol, Benny Goodman, and the renowned author, Thomas Mann. I counted it, however, as my personal triumph that on my first day at Soldan I got a "G" for "good" on Mrs. Carmody's geometry test after understanding her explanation of the meaning of the isosceles triangle. Some of the teachers even took me under their wing. Rose Kaufman, the Latin teacher, got me my first job as a dishwasher at the Branscom Hotel and as a busboy at the Chase. Even at that time, the Depression had not fully lifted and jobs were scarce. Mrs. Kaufman interceded personally and through her kind-ness and my hard work, I launched a "career" of sorts—eventually I became a room service waiter, then a dining-room waiter with full union standing. These jobs sustained me even through undergraduate college and beyond.

On Jewish holidays, I walked with my family to a small prayer house, a make-shift synagogue presided over by a volunteer cantor, a few blocks away. Uncle Benno did not have the means to afford the hefty membership dues for larger congregations. Despite my growing familiarity with the congregants, the cele-brations were not the same for me. I missed my hometown synagogue, the fa-miliar pronunciation of the Hebrew vowels, the rituals of my youth. This

---

7   Soldan, now a "magnet school," has been renamed Soldan International Studies High School
     (cf. also Stern 3–14).

religious adjustment problem faded into utter insignificance after the trauma-tizing news of November 9, 1938. A newsboy, hawking the *St. Louis Star-Times*, shouted "Synagogues burning in Germany! Read all about it!" To this day, I can hear his voice and feel my sense of loss.

I never stopped searching for a way to bring my family to safety, but all of my efforts were in vain. I had hoped to find Jewish people in St. Louis who were wealthy enough to provide affidavits. One afternoon, on my way to work at the Jefferson Hotel, a man picked me up in a car that spelled affluence. I steered our conversation first to myself, then to the plight of my family. "What's in-volved in getting them over here?" he asked. I told him that someone with means had to guarantee that they won't become a public charge. "Well, I could do that," he said. He added: "I'm not sure the government will accept my pledge. You see, I am a gambler." I asked whether he'd be willing to try it and he replied, "Sure, absolutely! After all, life's a gamble!"

The next week, in the fall of 1938, he and I met with the lawyer designated by the Jewish community to do *pro bono* work for us refugees. The lawyer, Mr. R., turned out to be oblivious to the plight of Germany's Jews and was a stickler for the niceties of the law. Fussing with papers and forms, he asked my new ac-quaintance some routine questions but came to an abrupt halt when my fam-ily's potential savior stated his occupation. "Gambler?" said Mr. R. "We needn't bother. The signer of an affidavit must be a stable citizen with an assured in-come." This terse verdict was delivered with supercilious authority. I have nev-er forgotten nor forgiven Mr. R., who proved singularly unwavering. That after-noon, my new-found friend walked out of the lawyer's office and out of my life, and with him the last concrete chance of rescuing my family.

One incident marks a milestone in my progressive Americanization. I couldn't go to my high school prom because I was busing dishes that night at the Chase Hotel. Had I attended, I would have been in the company of a classmate by the name of Idamae Schwartzberg, who had become my friend through our mutual involvement at the YMHA/YWHA. Idamae had little pa-tience with my German name, Günther, which she proclaimed a tongue-twister. She dubbed me "Guy," and it stuck throughout high school, through my Army service, and I retained it when I became a US Citizen.

Idamae and I enjoyed afternoon outings with a picnic and the outdoor op-era in Forest Park. Neither she nor I had money to speak of, but if we arrived at 3:30 right after classes, we could occupy one of the back row free seats that the city provided. There, we saw Gershwin's *Of Thee I Sing*, Jerome Kern's *Show-boat*, and many other American musicals. We often lingered till the last curtain call, then, humming just-heard melodies, strolled home through the park. Oth-er afternoons I spent with Kurt Salomon, a fellow recent arrival from Germany, learning the intricacies of baseball with the help of a so-called Knothole Pass to games, generously given out to passing high school students by the two major league teams then in St. Louis.

My awareness of America—both its good and bad points—developed rapidly during those intensely-lived years of transition from an emigrant to an immigrant. One person in particular influenced my understanding of my adopted land. Aunt Rae, who was the sister of my aunt-by-marriage Ethel, was an energetic person with a magnetic personality. From pictures of far-away San Francisco to the lectures that she took me to, her influence broadened my horizons. During one of her Ethical Culture Society's meetings, I heard Martha Gellhorn's stories of her experiences during the Spanish Civil War and her impassioned plea for America's involvement in the face of Hitler's quest for global dominance.

Aunt Rae also helped me navigate my newfound knowledge of the darker side of American culture, including the beholdenness of America's press to its advertisers. After Joe Louis' victory over Max Schmeling, she pointed out America's discriminatory practices and ridiculed the myths of racial superiority and ethnic stereotypes. Once, in examining my American history textbook,

ILLUSTRATION 3.1
Guy Stern just before the graduation ceremonies at Soldan High School in St. Louis

she took great offense to its reference to slaves as "Samboes." Many years later, she took an active role in the integration of St. Louis's public swimming pools.

Through these years, I saw America more clearly without loving it less. Yes, I was on the road to Americanization, the early stages of exile were over, but Günther never became a completely American guy. I am, as we all are, a compound of our experiences. But I am grateful to all those who helped me find a home in my new country. As those rapid years of acculturation drew to a close, "I heard America singing" (in the words of Walt Whitman). Today, close to eighty years later, I hope that our love song to "one nation indivisible" will not grow fainter.

Works Cited

Morse, Arthur D., *While Six Million Died; A Chronicle of American Apathy.* Random House, 1969.

Stern, Guy, "The Americanisation of Günther." Deborah Vietor-Engländer, ed., *The Legacy of Exile; Lives, Letters, Literature.* Blackwell Publishers, 1998, pp. 3–14.

Wyman, David S., *Paper Walls. America and the Refugee Crisis 1938–1941.* Pantheon Books, 1968.

PART 2

Politische, kulturelle und intellektuelle Entfremdung / Political, Cultural and Intellectual Alienation

∴

CHAPTER 4

Letting Go of Europe: On Stefan Zweig's Political and Cultural Disillusionment

Gregor Thuswaldner

Abstract

Stefan Zweig's notion of humanism is deeply connected with his idea of a transnational Europe. Even though Zweig escaped continental Europe four years before Hitler's "Anschluss" with Austria, he was unable to metaphorically leave Europe, especially the German-speaking world, behind. It is a well-documented fact that Zweig found his life in exile unbearable. But as this paper demonstrates, Zweig's "impossible exile" (George Prochnik) began well before 1934. As early as 1909, Zweig senses an uneasiness that seemed hard to pin down. What Zweig was sorely missing at the beginning of the 20th century and throughout his life was a sense of belonging and a distinctive European cultural identity. Tracing his early stages of exile starting already in 1909 until his death in 1942, this paper shows Zweig's growing sense of alienation, which intensified significantly during his "last life," his actual time as an émigré.

Stefan Zweig (1881–1942) is known for his humanistic and pacifistic attitude that is recognizable in all his writings, especially after 1917. Zweig's notion of humanism is deeply connected with his idea of a transnational Europe. Even though Zweig escaped continental Europe in 1934, four years before Hitler's "Anschluss" or annexation of Austria, he was unable to metaphorically leave Europe, especially the German-speaking world, behind. It is a well-documented fact that Zweig found his life in exile unbearable and unacceptable. "[L]ittle by little, the world refuses itself to the exiled," he wrote to his newly-exiled friend, the author André Maurois, in 1940 (qtd. in Prochnik 10).

Zweig's "impossible exile"[1] began well before 1934 when he abruptly left his home in Salzburg. As early as 1909, Zweig sensed an uneasiness that seemed hard to pin down when he writes, "Mißbehagen wäre zu viel und Bedauern zu wenig" (Discontent would be too strong of a word, while regret would be too

---

[1] *The Impossible Exile: Stefan Zweig at the End of the World* is the title of George Prochnik's Stefan Zweig biography.

weak) ("Das Land ohne Patriotismus" 7).[2] In any case, the feeling somewhere between discontent and regret can be seen as an early stage of exile. What Zweig was sorely missing at the beginning of the 20th century and throughout his life was a sense of belonging and a distinctive European cultural identity.

Zweig, the cosmopolitan writer, found the political and cultural conditions even before the outbreak of World War I in his native Austria wanting. In his essay of 1909, "Das Land ohne Patriotismus" (The Country without Patriotism), Zweig laments the fact that Austria lacks unity and a comprehensive vision for its future. Unlike citizens of France and Italy, Austrians do not have any sense of patriotism. Being Austrian does not evoke a sense of pride or joy in Austrians while the French get excited whenever they hear their national anthem. According to Zweig, the reason for the absence of patriotism is the complicated conglomerate of Austria-Hungary whose only unifying factor is the long-serving Emperor Francis Joseph. As early as 1909, Zweig suggests that the future of the Austrian monarchy seems questionable, as there is no sense of unity among the empire's diverse ethnic groups and no shared ideological conviction (cf. 7–10). But Zweig was not just critical of the Hapsburg Empire. He also saw very positive aspects of the monarchy that enabled him and fellow writers to find their own voice as he writes in *The World of Yesterday*:

> We were able to devote ourselves to our art and to our intellectual inclinations, and we were able to mold our private existence with more individual personality. We could live a more cosmopolitan life and the whole world stood open to us. We would travel without a passport and without a permit wherever we pleased. No one questioned us as to our beliefs, as to our origin, race, or religion. I do not deny that we had immeasurable more individual freedom and we not only cherished it but made use of it. (89)

Soon after the outbreak of World War I, Zweig became a pacifist. His play *Jeremiah*, which premiered in Zurich in 1917, became his anti-war manifesto. Based on the life of the biblical prophet, Zweig's Jeremiah condemns war and calls on his fellow Israelites to remain peaceful. In order to reach his predominantly Christian audience with his pacifistic message, Zweig's Jeremiah becomes a Christ-like figure whose monologues are anachronistically and quite synchretistically interspersed with quotes from the New Testament (cf. Plank). The play was highly praised in neutral Switzerland and Zweig became renowned for both his humanistic and pacifistic attitudes.

---

2   All translations into English are mine unless otherwise indicated.

In 1919, Zweig settled in Salzburg where he stayed until 1934. During this time period, Zweig emerged as the most successful German author of his time. In 1926, the renowned Burgtheater in Vienna staged his adaptation of Ben Johnson's *Volpone,* which was celebrated as Zweig's best play. A year later, his *Decisive Moments in History: Twelve Historical Miniatures* and his novella *Confusion* appeared which turned out to be instant bestsellers. Zweig became known for his psychological portrayal and analysis of complicated relationships, important thinkers, politicians, and world events. And while writing one successful book after another for a wide readership, he also kept his dream of a unified Europe alive in shorter essays and speeches.

For example, in the early 1930's he wrote a speech on the "Einigung Europas" (Unification of Europe). It is not clear why he never held the speech, which was recently published for the first time. In it, Zweig wants his fellow Europeans to go beyond feelings of patriotism and nationalism. Instead, they need to recognize that they are part of a greater whole, namely Europe, which is not just a continent, but an intellectual and cultural home to millions of people. For Zweig, it will take an intellectual rather than emotional awakening for Europeans to embrace what he calls "the European idea" ("der europäische Gedanke") (Zweig, *Einigung Europas* 11), the ideology of a supranational European identity. Following Enlightenment thought, Zweig seems to imply that strong feelings for a united Europe would follow, once Europeans were persuaded by the importance of "the European idea."

However, as Zweig's Europe lacked a clear political and cultural center, creating a sense of unity was a very difficult task. According to Zweig, Geneva has the potential to become Europe's Washington, but European leaders have lacked political will power to make Geneva the center of European unity (cf. 11). But without a visible center, a concrete manifestation and representation, the European idea remains ephemeral. At the same time, Zweig acknowledges the fact that numerous international events, including writers conferences as well as sporting events, could contribute to both intellectual and emotional ties between European countries. Zweig's intentionally peculiar list of international events also include meetings of European chicken farmers, theologians, wine producers, and medical doctors (cf. 13). As random as this list is, Zweig tries to make the point that international meetings of various guilds that are held at the same time in the same place have the potential to create closer ties between individual countries. Organizing these conventions in the same city would maximize intercultural and international understanding on numerous levels. Zweig's text lacks a clear and realistic outline of how such a concerted effort could be realized. He seems to naively assume that bringing people together to share ideas or trade chickens or wine would somehow automatically lead to an increase of humanism, pacifism, and a growing sense of European unity.

In his essay, "Der europäische Gedanke in seiner historischen Entwicklung" (The European Idea in Its Historical Development) of 1932, Zweig, in a clearly Hegelian vein (cf. Mitterer 153), traces the "europäische[n] Geist" (European spirit) from the Roman Empire to his present day (185–210). Since the times of the Roman Empire, Zweig argues, there have been two opposite forces at work that have shaped and continue to shape Europe. The two forces can be traced back to the Tower of Babel story in Genesis. Because people were united in their endeavor to build a tower that would reach into God's Heaven, God caused the separation by confusing the languages of the people. God, according to Zweig, who had created humans in his image, feared that his creation would be able to topple him. As a result, God put an end to the revolt by making it impossible for humans to communicate in one common language, which had been the unifying element and the source of strength of the people. Despite the fact that the people did not succeed in their unified effort, Zweig maintains, "die Idee unserer menschlichen Einheit ist unzerstörbar" (the notion of our human unity is indestructible) (191).

Zweig describes this dialectic between unity and separation, and compares it to the natural process of ebb and flow as *the* marker of European history. For Zweig, the Roman Empire was the first unifying force in Europe, which was rooted not in military but intellectual power. Zweig speculates that had the Roman Empire survived for another two to three hundred years, Europe would still be a unified continent today and other continents would be subjected to this central idea of a unified Europe. The notion of other continents being subjected or subjugated ("untertan," 190) to the idea of a unified Europe would suggest a highly imperialistic Eurocentric view. But Zweig goes well beyond Eurocentrism here, as he is interested in creating a sense of *human* unity in general. If, according to Zweig, the Roman Empire had lasted longer so that its peoples had truly become united, this model would have inspired the unknown continents of the time to follow suit and to form similar unified political and cultural structures. But since the Roman Empire vanished, Europe became a chaotic place as Europeans did not hold on to unifying cultural and intellectual achievements. In this phase of intellectual amnesia, Europe was dependent on medical knowledge from Arabia, as well as artistic and economic expertise from the Byzantine Empire. Instead of celebrating influences from non-European cultures, Zweig criticizes Europe's incapacity to be self-sufficient and to be the world's leading intellectual and cultural engine.

The rise of the Roman Catholic Church, however, halted and reversed Europe's decline. Following Hegel's train of thought, Zweig claims that once again the European spirit proved to be stronger than matter. For Zweig, the European spirit manifested itself in the Latin language, which was revived and revered by the Catholic Church. And thanks to writers including Plutarch, Latin did not only become the language of the Church and the sciences, but was also used for poetic expression. As a result, Latin was spoken and written all over Europe. It seems important to note that Zweig does not mention the fact that Latin was the *lingua franca* of the European elite only.

The intellectual unity, which Zweig locates in the age of humanism, came to an abrupt end when the Protestant Reformation swept over Europe. The status of Latin as the common denominator began to fade, as Protestants translated the Bible into the respective vernaculars. Europeans did not belong to the one Holy Roman Catholic Church anymore. Rather, depending on the religious and political persuasions of their rulers, they had to become Lutheran or Reformed, while others remained Catholic. It is important to note that in order for Zweig to present his ideas as succinct, he completely ignores the Jewish diaspora in Europe and the influence of Jewish merchants and intellectuals. In his version of the retelling of the manifestations of the European spirit, Jews are not mentioned. As we know from his other writings, however, Zweig *was* very much concerned about European Jews. So why did he utterly overlook Jewish achievements in his condensed historical overview? The answer may have to do with the fact that he saw the future of the European Jewry, and the future of all Europeans, in a cosmopolitan and unified Europe where, by definition, issues of heritage, religion, and ideological convictions would be rather unimportant.

After the Reformation had caused disunity and major wars in Europe, it was not until the 16th and 17th centuries when Europe found a new unifying *lingua franca* in music. Composers such as Händel, Haydn, and Mozart presented operas for librettos written in various European languages. Zweig also highlights Goethe's cosmopolitan notion of "Weltliteratur" ("world literature") that would surpass the parochial idea of national literatures. Goethe famously argued "[...] die Epoche der Weltliteratur ist an der Zeit, und jeder muß jetzt dazu wirken, diese Epoche zu beschleunigen" ("it is time for the era of world literature and everybody must endeavour to accelerate this epoch") (Eckermann 229). In addition, Zweig points out three very different writers who tried to keep the dream of a unified Europe alive: Friedrich Nietzsche, Emile Verhaeren, and Romain Rolland. He quotes Nietzsche's provocative phrase in which he compares the Europe of his time as "the small Asian peninsula" ("die kleine Halbinsel Asiens," 201), but Zweig also refers to a passage in Nietzsche's works where the philosopher talks about his vision of a new and unified Europe. According to Zweig, Nietzsche was the first modern thinker who contended "daß man innerhalb Europas die 'Väterländerei' beende und ein neues, ein übernationales Nationalbewußtsein schaffe, das Vaterlandsgefühl des 'neuen Europa'" (that one needs to end the attachment to fatherlands within Europe, so that one can create a transnational form of national consciousness, the patriotism of the "new Europe") (201).

It is not surprising that Zweig also refers to both Verhaeren and Rolland as the other prime examples of authors promoting a new Europe. Zweig was a close friend of both authors and promoted their works in the German-speaking world. It is rather unexpected, however, when he claims Verhaeren's poetry would evoke "das gemeinsame europäische Rassegefühl" (the shared European race feeling) (202). "Rassegefühl" is a highly problematic term that was part of national socialist discourse (cf. Schmitz-Berning 499). In his book on Verhaeren, Zweig also uses the term "Rasse" (race) when he describes the Belgian poet as a representative of "the Belgian race," which for Zweig is "one of the most diligent ones in Europe" ("Und diese neue belgische Rasse ist eine starke Rasse, eine der tüchtigsten Europas") (qtd. in Le Rider 750). Le Rider points out that Zweig sometimes used the word "Rasse" in order to avoid terms such as "Volk" ("people") and "Nation" ("nation") that were even more closely associated with National Socialism (cf. 750).

Towards the end of his essay, it becomes apparent that for Zweig the two similar sounding words "geistig" ("intellectual") and "geistlich" ("spiritual") are to be seen as related. The European spirit has quasi-religious qualities he indirectly suggests. According to Zweig, creating a sense of unity among people is always accompanied by a feeling of religious emotion. Consequently, Zweig compares the belief in a united Europe to the Christian's belief in the Gospels, which of course suggests that the intended audience of this essay had a Christian background. Finally, Zweig sees a new unifying force, albeit a very impersonal one, in technology which allows people to travel much faster than in the past. And even though he applauds the opportunities that the new technologies provide, he criticizes the fact that technology remains lifeless and without an intellectual or cultural home. As a consequence, technology is incapable of providing a basis for European unity.

Undoubtedly, Zweig's essay is utopian in nature. His description of the continuous ebb and flow of the European spirit which manifests itself in the cultural and intellectual unity and disunity of its people is based on a radically simplified and hence highly flawed historical analysis. Nonetheless, one would think that this conclusion would strengthen Zweig's belief that European unity was within reach in the 1930s. In other words, Zweig was hoping for a resurgence of the European spirit, as he believed that the trying times of European disunity would be followed by a new era of European unity.

Just months before he left Austria for Britain, Zweig published a biography of Erasmus of Rotterdam in 1934, which in 1974 was translated into English as *Erasmus and the Right to Heresy*. In it, he juxtaposes Erasmus with Luther, the "titanic adversary" and personification of the "dark demonic forces of the Germanic peoples" (89), who in his anti-humanistic zeal caused the segmentation of Europe. In the biography, Zweig writes:

> At the outset, both Erasmus and Luther desired the same thing; but their natures were so fundamentally different that they endeavored to achieve the aim by utterly dissimilar methods. Enmity radiated round Luther. Of all men of genius who have lived upon this earth, Luther was, perhaps, the most fanatical, the most unteachable, the most intractable, and the most quarrelsome. He could only tolerate those who were completely acquiescent with his views, so that he could make what use he would of them; those who said him nay served him as targets for his wrath, and provided him with material to grind to powder with his scorn. (93)

As this quote and may similar ones demonstrate, Zweig's depiction of Luther appears quite distorted. Writing during the time of Hitler's political rise in Germany, Zweig saw close parallels between the dangers of National Socialism and the rise of Protestantism in the 16th century in general and between Hitler and Luther in particular. For Zweig, Luther was the precursor of Hitler. Just like the Reich's Chancellor, Zweig's Luther was a proud, dangerous, and violent demagogue. Zweig writes:

> [I]n the home [Luther] was a cheerful and friendly father and housemaster; as an artist in words he gave expression to the magnitude of his cultural attainments; but so soon as the battle was joined, Luther was transformed, becoming a werewolf raging with uncouth and unjustifiable scorn and fury. Out of the necessity of his nature, he was again and again forced into combat; for, not only did he enjoy this, considering it to be the jolliest thing in life, but he looked upon fight as, morally, the fairest and justest form of activity. "A man, and especially a Christian, must be a warrior," he said proudly as he gazed at himself in a mirror; and in a letter written in 1541 he raised this concept into the heavens with the strange remark: "Certain is it that God is a sturdy fighter." (96–97)

Just like Luther, Hitler would divide Europe. Zweig's Erasmus, on the other hand, is depicted as a pacifistic humanist, an alter-ego of Zweig himself. In other words, Zweig's Erasmus book is a thinly-veiled critique of Europe in the first half of the 1930s. Even though Zweig sees himself in Erasmus who appears as a peace-seeking and bridge-building cosmopolitan European, he describes the great humanist's incapacity to save the unity of Europe:

> It was Erasmus's tragical destiny to live through such a time of storm and stress. He, the most unfanatical, the most anti-fanatical of men, living at a moment when the supranational ideal was taking a solid hold upon European thinkers, had to witness one of the wildest out-breaks of national and religious mass-passion that history has ever had to relate. (8)

While praising Erasmus's humanistic zeal, Zweig bemoans his lack of courage to outright reject Luther's separatism. The conflict was expressed in the original German title of his biography, *Triumph und Tragik des Erasmus von Rotterdam* (Triumph and Tragedy of Erasmus of Rotterdam).

On February 18, 1934, Zweig was awoken by members of the *Heimwehr*, the para-militaristic fascist troops. Zweig was alleged to have hoarded weapons for the organization's nemesis, the *Republikanische Schutzbund*, the para-militaristic organization of the socialist party. When the they searched Zweig's house, they did indeed find a rifle accusing Zweig of conspiracy. Knowing that he was framed, Zweig immediately traveled to London and not only escaped the civil war that immediately followed in Austria but also his country's absorption into the Third Reich in 1938 (cf. Matuschek 267 f.). Although he was treated much better than most Jewish emigres, Zweig, the cosmopolitan European, was unable to accept the way the British viewed him during World War II. Even though Zweig insisted on his Austrian identity, he was seen as a German, and hence, an "enemy alien":

> For was a more absurd situation imaginable than for a man in a strange land to be compulsory aligned—solely on the ground of a faded birth certificate—with a Germany that had long ago expelled him as anti-German and to which, as an Austrian, he had never belonged. By a stroke of a pen the meaning of a whole life had been transformed into a paradox; I wrote, I still thought in the German language, but my every thought and wish belonged to the countries, which stood in arms for the freedom of the world. Every other loyalty, all that was past and gone, was torn and destroyed and I knew that after this war everything would have to take a fresh start. For my most cherished aim to which I had devoted all the power of my conviction for forty years, the peaceful union of Europe, had been defiled.
>
> *The World of Yesterday* 435

In 1940, Zweig left his house in the English city of Bath, for Ossining, a town outside of New York City. But since he could not see himself settling down in the United States, he moved to Brazil where he published *Brazil: Land of the Future* in 1941. The book stands out from Zweig's oeuvre because of its naively positive portrayal of Brazil. To this day, scholars debate Zweig's earnestness in writing it (cf. Dewulf). Was it the price Zweig paid so that he and his wife could become permanent citizens? Was he really that optimistic that he could find a permanent home in Brazil? Did Zweig really believe that Brazil would emerge as the "Land of Future," while countries in Europe would remain in ruins after the war?

According to George Prochnik, "Zweig understood that exile wasn't a static condition but a process" (10). For Zweig this process began decades before he left Austria in 1934. As this essay has demonstrated, early stages of his exile can be traced back to 1909, a time when the Austro-Hungarian Monarchy, or at least the emperor's life, was noticeable coming to an end. In his posthumously published autobiography, *The World of Yesterday*, Zweig writes that he "was aware that the past was done for, work achieved was in ruins, Europe, our home, to which we had dedicated ourselves had suffered destruction that would extend far beyond our life. Something new, a new world began, but how many hells, how many purgatories had to be crossed before it could be reached!" (436). In a letter to Abrahão Koogan, Zweig's Brazilian publisher, he writes on February 18, 1944: "Sie wissen, wie sehr ich des Lebens müde war, seitdem ich meine Heimat, Österrich, verloren hatte" ([Y]ou know how I have been tired of my life having lost my homeland, Austria) (qtd. in Renoldner 9). Only four days later, both Lotte and Stefan Zweig committed suicide, which suggests that his vision of Brazil did not give him enough hope to continue living, especially at a time when his utopia of a united and peaceful Europe, "the European idea" he had passionately argued for, seemed completely out of reach.

Works Cited

Dewulf, Jeroen. "Brasilien." Larcati, Arturo, Klemens Renoldner and Martina Wörgötter. *Stefan-Zweig-Handbuch*. De Gruyter, 2018, pp. 330–339.

Eckermann, Johann Peter. *Gespräche mit Goethe in den letzten Jahren seines Lebens*. Ed. Regine Otto and Otto Wersig. Aufbau, 1987.

Le Rider, Jacques. "Europe-Konzeptionen." Larcati, Arturo, Klemens Renoldner and Martina Wörgötter. *Stefan-Zweig-Handbuch*. De Gruyter, 2018, pp. 748–754.

Matuschek, Oliver. *Stefan Zweig: Drei Leben*. S. Fischer, 2006.

Mitterer, Cornelius. "Biography between Poetry and History: Stefan Zweig's 'History as a Poetess.'" Hemecker, Wilhelm and Edward Saunders. *Biography in Theory: Key Texts with Commentaries*. De Gruyter, 2017, pp. 136–147.

Plank, Eva. "Jeremias." Larcati, Arturo, Klemens Renoldner and Martina Wörgötter. *Stefan-Zweig-Handbuch*. De Gruyter, 2018, pp. 128–133.

Prochnik, George. *The Impossible Exile: Stefan Zweig at the End of the World*. Other Press, 2014.

Renoldner, Klemens. "Abschied von Salzburg." Renoldner, Klemens and Peter Karlhuber. *"Ich gehöre nirgends mehr hin": Stefan Zweigs Schachnovelle – Eine Geschichte aus dem Exil*. Verlag des Salzburg Museum, 2017, pp. 9–18.

Schmitz-Berning, Cornelia. *Vokabular des Nationalsozialismus*. De Gruyter, 2007.

Zweig, Stefan. "Das Land ohne Patriotismus." Zweig, Stefan. *Die schlaflose Welt: Essays 1909–1941*. S. Fischer, 2012, pp. 7–16.

Zweig, Stefan. "Der europäische Gedanke in seiner historischen Entwicklung." Zweig, Stefan. *Die schlaflose Nacht: Essays 1909–1941*. S. Fischer, 2012, pp. 185–210.

Zweig, Stefan. *Einigung Europas: Eine Rede*. Tartin, 2013.

Zweig, Stefan. *Erasmus and the Right to Heresy*. Trans. Eden Paul and Cedar Paul. Souvenir Press, 1979.

Zweig, Stefan. *The World of Yesterday*. Trans. Harry Zohn. University of Nebraska Press, 1964.

Thomas Manns Essay „Pariser Rechenschaft" (1926) als Vorstufe seines Exils

Thomas Pekar

Abstract

In 1926 Thomas Mann travelled to Paris as an unofficial cultural ambassador in order to advocate for improved German-French relations, writing about the trip in the same year in his essay "Parisian Account." Mann himself understood this trip and his essay as a caesura in his life that meant turning away from his hitherto hawkish and German nationalistic attitude to a new beginning. This new beginning took place in three respects: (a) his internationalization and assumption of the role as representative of German and democratic culture; (b) his encounter with the problem of exile as he experienced in Paris in the form of Russian émigrés; and (c) his confrontation with a certain German mythological tradition which—especially via Alfred Baeumler—was to flow into totalitarian and National Socialist concepts of mythology. The Paris experience led Mann directly to the conception of his great novel of exile, *Joseph and His Brothers*, which his essay hints at repeatedly.

1   Einleitung

1926, genauer gesagt vom 20. bis zum 29. Januar, reiste Thomas Mann zusammen mit seiner Frau Katia nach Paris. In seinem Essay *Pariser Rechenschaft* (vgl. GKFA 15.1, 1115–1214), der noch in demselben Jahr publiziert wurde, berichtet er über diese Reise, die vor dem Hintergrund einer erheblichen Verbesserung der deutsch-französischen Beziehungen in dieser Zeit stattfand.[1] Das Ehepaar Mann reiste auf Einladung der amerikanischen-philanthropischen Carnegiestiftung nach Paris, um die Völkerversöhnung zu fördern. Mann war „eine Art inoffizieller Kulturbotschafter der Weimarer Republik" (Kurzke 783) und wurde in Paris von der deutschen Botschaft betreut. Er lernte bei

---

1 Diese Verbesserung geschah vor allem durch den Abschluss der Locarno Verträge 1925 (zum politischen Hintergrund der Reise vgl. Beuter und Bock 61–96).

verschiedenen Lesungen und Ansprachen, die er dort hielt, wichtige Persönlichkeiten des geistigen Frankreich kennen. Reise und Essay sind von großer Bedeutung für die schriftstellerische Entwicklung Manns, vor allem, wenn man dies im Kontrast zu seinen früheren Positionen sieht: 1914 hatte er sich mit seinem Aufsatz *Gedanken im Kriege*, wie viele andere bekannte deutschsprachige Autoren auch, in die Reihen der patriotischen Kriegsbefürworter gestellt. Mit seinem Großessay *Betrachtungen eines Unpolitischen* (1918) – die Frucht der Kriegsjahre – versuchte er dem Krieg eine geistige Grundlage zu geben, indem er sich besonders gegen Frankreich wandte, und zwar mit dem von ihm vielfach variierten Grundgegensatz von Kultur vs. Zivilisation[2], also deutsche Kultur vs. französisch-westliche Zivilisation, und mit dem Verständnis des Krieges als „Ausbruch [...] des uralten deutschen Kampfes gegen den Geist des Westens [...]" (GKFA 13.1, 52).

Wie sehr hat er sich nun, acht Jahre später, verändert! Seine Paris-Reise und seine Vorträge dort[3] lassen sich folgendermaßen zusammenfassen: „Die Reise ist von paradigmatischer Bedeutung, weil Thomas Mann hier die Identitätskonstrukte der Weltkriegszeit intellektuell zu durchschauen beginnt und sich endgültig von ihnen verabschiedet" (Kurzke 783). Insbesondere verabschiedet er sich von seiner Antinomie von ‚Kultur' und ‚Zivilisation'. Mann selbst wertet diesen Pariser Aufenthalt wenige Jahre später, nämlich 1929 in einem Brief an den französischen Schriftsteller Charles Du Bos, so: „Ich habe damals [in Paris] einen Anfang gemacht, ein Signal gegeben" (GKFA 23.1, 400).

Für Mann selbst bedeutet diese Pariser Reise und der Essay also weniger einen Abschied von antiquiert gewordenen Positionen als vielmehr einen Anfang, einen wirklichen Neuanfang, eine Zäsur. Dieser Neuanfang Thomas Manns soll hier unter drei Aspekten thematisiert werden, die alle als Vorstufen des Exils, d.h. Vorstufen seines amerikanischen Exils, zu verstehen sind. Diese drei Aspekte lauten: Repräsentation deutscher demokratischer Kultur im Ausland, Exilproblematik selbst und Faschismuskritik.

---

2   So schreibt er gleich am Anfang von *Gedanken im Kriege*: „Zivilisation und Kultur sind nicht nur nicht ein und dasselbe, sondern sie sind Gegensätze, sie bilden eine der vielfältigen Erscheinungsformen des ewigen Weltgegensatzes [...]" (GKFA 15.1, 27).

3   Vgl. seine Ansprache vom 20.1.1926 *Die geistigen Tendenzen des heutigen Deutschlands*, die *Einführende[n] Bemerkungen zur Lesung „Liberté et Noblesse" und „Grace Aristocratique" in Paris* vom 26.1. und die Ansprache *Über den Pen-Club* ebenfalls von diesem Tag (vgl. GKFA 15.1, 1076–1095).

2   Repräsentation deutscher-demokratischer Kultur im Ausland

„Where I am, there is Germany. I carry my German culture in me."[4] Mit diesen Worten betrat Thomas Mann bekanntlich 1938 in New York amerikanischen Boden – und formulierte damit den Anspruch, dass die bessere, demokratische Kultur oder überhaupt die deutsche Kultur mit ihm aus dem faschistischen Deutschland in die USA emigriert sei.

Diese Haltung, Repräsentant des „anderen Deutschlands" zu sein,[5] war Mann nicht unvertraut, ja man kann sagen, dass er sich mit dieser Haltung eigentlich in Paris angefreundet hat. Man erlebt im Paris-Essay in seinen eigenen Worten sozusagen mit, wie er sich diese Haltung aneignet: Im Essay versichert Mann in einer Ansprache den Franzosen zunächst etwas vollmundig (und dann später leider auch von der Geschichte widerlegt), dass „in Deutschland jeden Tag die Idee der Demokratie an Boden gewönne" (GKFA 15.1, 1129), um dann in der anschließenden Diskussion grundsätzlich zu Deutschland und seiner repräsentativen Haltung befragt zu werden. Zunächst wehrt er sich ein wenig kokett: „Im übrigen erklärte ich, die Anmaßung liege mir fern, für die ganze geistige Welt Deutschlands zu sprechen. Wir seien ein sehr dezentralisiertes Land [...]" (GKFA 15.1, 1130). Nach einigem Hin und Her ringt er sich aber schließlich zu diesem Satz durch: „So möge man sich mit einer gewissen Zuversicht der Vorstellung überlassen, Deutschland durch mich sprechen zu hören" (GKFA 15.1, 1130). Und er versäumt es nicht, die Reaktion seiner französischen Zuhörerschaft auf diesen Satz zu überliefern, die nämlich aus einem „Très bien" besteht. Vielleicht ist diese Szene, die Thomas Mann hier so lebendig überliefert, eine Art Urszene seiner Übernahme dieser Repräsentationshaltung, die er seitdem bis zu seinem Tod nicht mehr ablegen wird.

3   Exilproblematik

In Paris trifft sich Thomas Mann mit vier russischen Emigranten, die Anfang der 1920er Jahre dorthin vor der Oktoberrevolution und der Etablierung der kommunistischen Herrschaft in Russland geflohen waren. Es handelt sich

---

4   Die lange verbreitete deutsche Version dieses Satzes: „Wo ich bin, ist die deutsche Kultur", stammte von Heinrich Mann (vgl. Vaget 63 u. 241).

5   Die Problematik dieses antiquierten Begriffs ist mir durchaus bewusst (vgl. dazu u.a. Bischoff/Komfort-Hein).

zunächst um den Philosophen Leo Schestow (1866–1938)[6], dessen 1924 auf
Deutsch erschienenes Buch *Dostojewski und Nietzsche* Mann im Essay hervorhebt.[7] In Schestows Pariser Wohnung, die Mann besucht, trifft er weiter den
Schriftsteller Iwan Bunin (1870–1953). Einige Tage später besucht er den Schriftsteller Iwan Schmeljow (1873–1950), mit dessen 1925 auf Deutsch erschiene-
nem Buch *Die Sonne der Toten* sich Mann intensiv beschäftigt hatte.[8] In diesem
Buch wird die grausame und mit einer großen Hungersnot verbundene Herr-
schaftsübernahme der Bolschewiki auf der Krim-Halbinsel thematisiert. Im
Paris-Essay beschreibt Mann das Buch als „grauenvolle[s] und dennoch in den
Glanz der Dichtung getauchte[s] Dokument aus der Zeit, da die roten Glücks-
bringer die Krim mit ‚eisernem Besen kehrten'" (GKFA 15.1, 1201). Und wenig
später trifft er schließlich noch den russischen Schriftsteller Dmitri S. Mereschkowski (1865–1941), der für Mann insgesamt von großer Bedeutung ist. Hier
erwähnt er Mereschkowskis Buch über Tolstoi und Dostojewski und sagt, dass
es einst auf seine „zwanzig Jahre einen so unauslöschlichen Eindruck gemacht"
(GKFA 15.1, 1210) habe.[9]

Welche Haltung hat nun Mann gegenüber diesen Emigranten, die alle der
Sowjetunion gegenüber oppositionell eingestellt waren und z.T. auch, wie beispielsweise Mereschkowski, mit politisch reaktionären Kräften kooperier-
ten?[10] Er solidarisiert sich mit ihnen weitgehend, wobei diese Solidarisierung
nicht die politische Position der russischen Emigranten betrifft – hier findet
Mann stellenweise vorsichtige Worte der Distanzierung[11] –, sondern auf einer
menschlich, genauer gesagt menschlich-künstlerischen Ebene stattfindet. So

---

6   Schestow gilt als jüdisch-russischer existenzialistischer Philosoph, der an der Sorbonne
     unterrichtete und Einfluss u.a. auf Albert Camus, Gilles Deleuze, Georges Bataille und
     E.M. Cioran ausübte.

7   Auch war Mann der Aufsatz Schestows „Die Nacht des Gethsemane. Pascals Philosophie"
     bekannt, den dieser in dem 1925 u.a. von Thomas Mann und Ernst Bertram herausgegebe-
     nen (einzigen) Band von *Ariadne. Jahrbuch der Nietzsche-Gesellschaft* publizierte (vgl.
     Bertram u. GKFA 15.1, 1171, wo Mann diese Publikation erwähnt).

8   Vgl. Baskakow. Mann hatte dieses Buch 1925 bei einer Umfrage als eines der besten Bü-
     cher des Jahres genannt (vgl. GKFA 15.1, 1054).

9   Zu Mereschkowski und Mann vgl. u.a. Heftrich.

10 So war er beispielsweise Mentor von Arthur Moeller van den Bruck (1876–1925), der als
     herausragender Vertreter der sogenannten ‚konservativen Revolution' gilt. Der Titel sei-
     nes 1923 erschienenen Buches, *Das dritte Reich*, wurde von den Nationalsozialisten als
     Parole benutzt (vgl. dazu Weiß, auch im Zusammenhang mit Thomas Mann).

11 So spricht z.B. Schmeljow zu Mann über die Gräueltaten, die die Rote Armee auf der Krim
     begingen. Dieser wendet sich mit einer rhetorischen Frage wohl nicht direkt an ihn, son-
     dern an die Leser: „Soll man sich von den Gesichten der Entmenschheit, die sich in Ihre
     abgezehrte Miene eingezeichnet haben, Iwan Schmeljow, in die andere Alternative, ins
     strikt Bürgerliche, Reaktionäre drängen lassen?" (GKFA 15.1, 1205).

ist er beispielsweise von der schlechten „Armeleutwohnung" (GKFA 15.1, 1201), in der Schmeljow in Paris wohnen muss, berührt, ja erschüttert.[12] Ebenfalls ist er erschüttert über die Sprachnot der Emigranten, die sich einer anderen Sprache als ihrer ihnen ja auch literarisch ans Herz gewachsenen russischen Muttersprache bedienen müssen.[13] In seiner Sensibilität für diese Sprachnot der Emigration mag man einen Vorgriff auf seine eigene Sprachproblematik sehen, mit der Thomas Mann dann später in Amerika zu kämpfen hatte.

Es gibt allerdings noch eine fast unheimliche Dimension bei Manns Solidarisierung mit den Emigranten, nämlich die, dass er in ihrer Lebensform schon andeutungsweise seine eigene spätere erblickt, sich also mit den Emigranten nicht nur solidarisiert, sondern sogar identifiziert. Man könnte fast sagen: Er erkennt in diesen russischen Emigrantenexistenzen sein eigenes Menetekel. Der Begriff im Paris-Essay dafür ist ‚Eventualkameradschaft', ein von Thomas Mann an dieser Stelle geprägter Neologismus:

> Hier empfinde ich Sympathie, Solidarität, – eine Art von Eventualkameradschaft; denn wir sind in Deutschland ja noch nicht so weit, daß ein Schriftsteller vom ungefähren Charakter Bunins den Staub des Vaterlandes von den Füßen schütteln und das Brot des Westens essen muß. Aber ich habe gar nicht zu zweifeln, daß unter Umständen mein Schicksal das seine wäre.
>
> GKFA 15.1, 1173

Es ist ein äußerst bemerkenswertes Zitat, das eine ganz andere Sprache als Manns eben erwähntes Statement zum Ausdruck bringt, dass in Deutschland die Demokratie „an Boden gewönne" (GKFA 15.1, 1129). Verräterisch ist nun dieses „noch", dass man in Deutschland „ja *noch* [Betonung T.P.] nicht so weit" sei. Solche Literaten wie Iwan Bunin, sind eigentlich ganz unpolitisch und tragen, wie Thomas Mann über ihn sagt, „die unvergleichliche epische Überlieferung

---

12   „Ich bin erschüttert, wie ich dann bei ihm sitze, an dem improvisierten Notbehelf von Schreibtisch, und in dies zerfurchte, abgezehrte Gesicht im weißen Barte blicke [...]" (GKFA 15.1, 1202).

13   Über Schmeljow heißt es: „Er spricht weder Deutsch noch eigentlich Französisch und sucht, was ihm an Möglichkeit des Ausdrucks fehlt, durch verstärkte Tongebung und heftige Bewegung seiner blassen Krankenhände zu ersetzen [...]" (GKFA 15.1, 1202). Auch von Mereschkowski wird gesagt, das ihn „die fremde Sprache" beenge: „Sie drücke das Ausdrucksniveau in einer Weise, daß man sich beständig wie ein Idiot vorkomme" (GKFA 15.1, 1212).

und Kultur seines Landes" (GKFA 15.1, 1172) in sich.[14] Doch nun werden sie von ihren – im Falle Bunins kommunistischen – Feinden ‚politisiert', indem sie als, wie Mann schreibt, „ein Konterrevolutionär, bourgeois, widerproletarisch, politisch verbrecherisch" (GKFA 15.1, 1172) stigmatisiert werden. Dies scheint also Thomas Mann auch in Deutschland für möglich zu halten, was ihn dann eben in die Emigration treiben würde.

Der entscheidende Unterschied zu Bunin ist, dass Mann keineswegs eine kommunistische Revolution für Deutschland erwartet, sondern in seinem Essay schon vor dem Faschismus warnt – und dieses Wort „Faschismus" auch in Bezug auf Deutschland benutzt (vgl. GKFA 15.1, 1162).[15] Mann erkennt also in Deutschland faschistische Tendenzen am Werk, die dazu führen, dass er bereits in diesem Jahr 1926 die Möglichkeit einer Emigration in Erwägung zieht.

4   Faschismuskritik

Thomas Manns Faschismuskritik ist in erster Linie literarischer Art, und zwar findet sie vor allem in Form seiner Roman-Tetralogie *Joseph und seine Brüder* statt, die vielleicht als das bedeutendste literarische Dokument des deutschsprachigen Exils überhaupt anzusehen ist. Wie hängt nun der Paris-Essay mit dem *Josephsroman* zusammen?

Man kann ihn als dessen Ankündigung und Exposition verstehen. Zunächst zum Aspekt der Ankündigung: Eine erste, allerdings rein private Erwähnung des *Josephsromans* ist in einem Brief Manns an Ernst Bertram am 4. 2. 1925 zu finden (vgl. GKFA 15.2, 825 u. Jens 136). Hans Wysling datiert den konkreten Schreibbeginn am Roman auf Dezember 1926.[16] Zwischen Februar 1925 bis Dezember 1926 liegt also die ‚heiße' Formierungsphase der gedanklichen Konzeption dieses Romans. Im Essay selbst sind eine ganze Reihe von Anspielungen

---

14   Darin erkennt Mann natürlich sich selbst, der sich eben genau als ein solcher „Schriftsteller vom ungefähren Charakter Bunins" versteht. Das Nobelpreiskomitee sah dies auch so, insoweit es Mann 1929 und Bunin 1933 den Nobelpreis für Literatur verlieh (Bunin war der erste Russe, der diesen Preis erhielt).

15   Zum Verhältnis Manns zum Faschismus vgl. grundsätzlich Pikulik.

16   Vgl. Wysling/Eich-Fischer 7. Die Arbeit am Roman wurde dann von Thomas Mann ab 1933 im Schweizer bzw. dann ab 1939 im amerikanischen Exil fortgesetzt. Mann lebte erst ab 1938 in Princeton, dann ab 1941 in Kalifornien, in Pacific Palisades, wo er 1943 den Roman auch abschloss. Der erste Band erschien im Oktober 1933 noch im nationalsozialistischen Deutschland. Zwischen August 1936 und August 1940 hatte Mann allerdings in Hinsicht auf den *Josephsroman* eine Schreibpause eingelegt, um in der Zeit hauptsächlich *Lotte in Weimar* (1939) zu schreiben. 1943 erschien bei Bermann-Fischer in Stockholm der letzte Band der Tetralogie, betitelt *Joseph, der Ernährer*.

Manns auf seinen im gedanklichen Entstehungsprozess befindlichen Roman zu finden, die natürlich *a posteriori* leicht entschlüsselbar sind, für die damaligen Leser allerdings unverständlich bleiben müssen. Mit ihnen treibt Mann eine Art Verhüllungsspiel. Es sind hauptsächlich Anspielungen auf Ägypten (der *Josephsroman* spielt fast zu zwei Drittel dort)[17], die im Essay zu finden sind. Dafür ein Beispiel: In Andeutung auf seine Mittelmeerreise 1925, die ihn von Venedig nach Ägypten geführt hatte[18], schreibt er im Essay, dass „das Ägyptische" in seiner Literatur „noch nie zum Vorschein gekommen" sei – und fügt dann kryptisch hinzu: „Es wird schon" (GKFA 15.1, 1166). Auch das erwähnte Treffen mit Mereschkowski hat einen ‚ägyptischen' Bezug, da dieser Mann sein Ägypten-Buch *Die Geheimnisse des Ostens* schenkt[19], welches für den *Josephsroman* zu einem wichtigen Quellenwerk wird (vgl. Lehnert). Zum anderen erfährt er von Mereschkowski, dass dieser einen „Tut-ench-Amon-Roman" plane, was er „nicht ohne Schrecken" hört, da er „einigermaßen verwandte Träume zu gestehen" (GKFA 15.1, 1212) habe.[20]

Diese zwischen Verrätselung und Offenbarung pendelnde öffentliche Ankündigung des *Josephromans* geht im Paris-Essay in eins mit seiner Exposition – und diese betrifft dann den Kern der Mann'schen Faschismuskritik, die seine Auseinandersetzung mit dem totalitären, faschistischen Mythos betrifft. Manns Gegenspieler im Paris-Essay ist der spätere Nazi-Philosoph Alfred Baeumler (1887–1968) mit seiner langen Einleitung *Bachofen der Mythologe der Romantik* in einem Auswahlband der Werke des Baseler Gelehrten Johann Jakob Bachofen (1815–1887), betitelt *Der Mythus von Orient und Occident* (vgl. Schroeter).

Diese Mythos-Problematik und die Auseinandersetzung mit Baeumler können hier nur angedeutet werden und sind ohnehin ein viel diskutiertes Thema

---

17   Zu Mann und Ägypten vgl. Assmann.

18   Vgl. GKFA 15.2, 825 und zu dieser Reise seinen Reisebericht *Unterwegs* (GKFA 15.1, 952–962).

19   Thomas Mann gibt dem Buch allerdings versehentlich einen falschen Titel (vgl. GKFA 15.1, 1211 u. GKFA 15.2, 850).

20   Viele weitere Anspielungen auf Ägypten und seinen Roman durchziehen den Essay weiter. So gleitet die Beschreibung von Paris am Ende des Essays sogar ins Orientalische ab: Angesichts des Eiffelturms denkt er „natürlich" gleich an den „Turm zu Babel", der „stärker gewirkt haben" muss. Allerdings ist der Eiffelturm „elektrisch illuminiert", was Mann zu der Bemerkung veranlasst: „Selbst Abraham hätte es prächtig gefunden und wäre vielleicht nicht ausgewandert, hätte der Turm von Esagil dergleichen zu bieten gehabt" (GKFA 15.1, 1170 f.). Damit ist er am Anfang seines *Josephsromans*, wo er vom „Mardug-Tempel Esagila zu Babel" bzw. vom „Sonnen-Tempelturm von Babel, genannt Esagila", spricht (GKFA 7.1, XII u. XXXV).

der Thomas-Mann-Forschung.[21] Mit dem Paris-Essay eröffnet Mann den Kampf gegen Baeumler und eine bestimmte deutsche mythologische Traditi-on. Er zeichnet im Paris-Essay den Irrweg einer von Baumler verfolgten roman-tischen Traditionslinie nach[22], die im Irrationalismus mündet und die, wie Mann sich hier ausdrückt, „von dem großen ‚Zurück', von der mütterlich-nächtigen Idee der Vergangenheit" (GKFA 15.1, 1159) bestimmt sei. Davor warnt Mann eindringlich[23] und entwirft dazu seine Gegenposition, die er im Paris-Essay nur mit dem emphatischen Schlagwort der „Humanität von mor-gen" (GKFA 15.1, 1162) umreißen kann, deren Exemplifikation jedoch der ge-samte *Josephsroman* ist.

5   Schluss

Thomas Manns Entwicklung ab 1926 lässt sich als ein Prozess ansehen, an des-sen Ende der wirkliche 1933 vollzogene Schritt ins Exil steht. Sein Pariser Auf-enthalt und sein Essay darüber sind Vorstufen dieses Exils in vielerlei Hinsicht: intellektuell, da Mann sich politisch umorientiert, existentiell, da er in Paris mit der Lebensform des Exils konfrontiert wird und schließlich künstlerisch, da dieser Aufenthalt mit der Konzeption seines großen, dann zu wesentlichen Teil im amerikanischen Exil geschriebenen Romans zusammenfällt. Ein Kreis wird eröffnet, der dieses Exil und seinen *Josephsroman* umfasst, ein Kreis, der sich mit seiner 1942 in der Washingtoner *Library of Congress* auf Englisch ge-haltenen Rede *The Theme of the Joseph Novels* schließen wird. Dort sagt Mann diese berühmten Sätze über seinen Roman: „In this book, the myth has been

---

21   Die Beziehung Manns zu Baeumler ist recht ambivalent (vgl. dazu u.a. Baeumler/Brunträ-ger/Kurzke). Während Mann ältere Arbeiten von Baeumler schätzte (vgl. GKFA 15.2, 821 f.), lehnt er ihn hier ab, obwohl seine Anerkennung auch noch hier zum Ausdruck kommt, wenn er über Baeumlers Einleitung schreibt: „Man kann nichts Interessanteres lesen, die Arbeit ist tief und prächtig, und wer sich auf den Gegenstand versteht, ist bis in den Grund gefesselt" (GKFA 15.1, 1159). Dann folgt allerdings ein „Aber" und eine kritische Diskussion.

22   Diese von Baeumler favorisierte Traditionslinie verläuft über den Lyriker der Befreiungs-kriege sowie Franzosen- und Judenhasser Ernst Moritz Arndt (1769–1860), über den ka-tholischen und anti-judaistischen Publizisten Joseph Görres (1776–1848) und die Brüder Grimm, also Jacob (1785–1863) und Wilhelm (1786–1859), bis hin zu Bachofen. Sie klam-mert Novalis (1772–1801) und Friedrich Schlegel (1772–1829), also die Jenaer Romantik, aus. Diese Traditionslinie ist Baeumler die „wirkliche Romantik" (vgl. Baeumler CCL), von der er im Übrigen auch Nietzsche ausschließt, der „das heilige Dunkel der Vorzeit nicht" (CCLI) kenne.

23   Er spricht in Hinsicht auf Baeumler von „Nachtschwärmerei" und „revolutionären Obsku-rantismus" (GKFA 15.1, 1159).

taken out of Fascist hands and humanized down to the last recess of its language, – if posterity finds anything remarkable about it, it will be this“ (Mann, *The Theme* 21).[24] Damit, nach etwa 16 Jahren, ist die Aufgabe erfüllt, die sich Thomas Mann in der *Pariser Rechenschaft* gestellt hat, nämlich, den Faschisten den Mythos, dessen sie sich – einem Wort Walter Benjamins zufolge – zu bemächtigen versuchten, zu entreißen.[25]

Siglenverzeichnis

GKFA = Mann, Thomas. *Große kommentierte Frankfurter Ausgabe.* Hg. Heinrich Detering u.a., Frankfurt a.M.: S. Fischer Verlag, 2002 ff. (Bandangabe arabisch, Seite).
GW = Mann, Thomas. *Gesammelte Werke in dreizehn Bänden.* Frankfurt a.M.: S. Fischer Verlag, 1960 ff. (Bandangabe römisch, Seite).

Zitierte Literatur

Assmann, Jan. *Thomas Mann und Ägypten: Mythos und Monotheismus in den Josephs-romanen.* Beck, 2006.
Baeumler, Alfred. „Einleitung. Bachofen der Mythologe der Romantik“. *Der Mythus von Orient und Occident. Eine Metaphysik der Alten Welt. Aus den Werken von Bachofen,* herausgegeben von Manfred Schroeter. C.H. Beck'sche Verlagshaus, 1926, S. XXIII–CCXCIV.
Baeumler, Marianne/Hubert Brunträger/Hermann Kurzke (Hg.). *Thomas Mann und Alfred Baeumler. Eine Dokumentation.* Königshausen u. Neumann, 1989.
Baskakow, Alexej. „Thomas Mann und Iwan Schmeljow“. *Thomas-Mann-Jahrbuch,* Bd. 13. Vittorio Klostermann Verlag, 2000, S. 133–146.
Benjamin, Walter. *Gesammelte Schriften II.2.* Hg. Rolf Tiedemann/Hermann Schweppenhäuser. 2. Auflage, Suhrkamp, 1977.
Bertram, Ernst u.a. (Hg.). *Ariadne. Jahrbuch der Nietzsche-Gesellschaft.* Verlag der Nietzsche-Ges., 1925.

---

24 Die deutsche Übersetzung dieses Essays in Manns *Gesammelten Werken* unterscheidet sich von dem englischen Originaltext in vielerlei Hinsichten. Nur im deutschen Text ist etwa auch der Ausdruck „Umfunktionierung des Mythos“ (GW XI, 658) in Hinsicht auf den *Josephsroman* zu finden.

25 Bei Benjamin heißt es: „[N]ichts Geringeres schwebt den Faschisten vor, als des Mythos sich zu bemächtigen“ (582).

Beuter, Ruth. *Thomas Manns Pariser Rechenschaft und die Metaphorik der deutsch-französischen Beziehungen. Zu Thomas Manns Frankreich-Diskurs als Teil einer sprachlichen Selbstinszenierung.* Freiburg: Univ., Diss., 1995.

Bischoff, Doerte/Susanne Komfort-Hein. „Vom ‚anderen Deutschland' zur Transnationalität. Diskurse des Nationalen in Exilliteratur und Exilforschung". *Exilforschung. Ein internationales Jahrbuch,* Bd. 30. edition text + kritik, 2012, S. 242–273.

Bock, Hans Manfred. *Topographie deutscher Kulturvertretung im Paris des 20. Jahrhunderts.* Narr, 2010.

Heftrich, Urs. „Thomas Manns Weg zur slavischen Dämonie. Überlegungen zur Wirkung Mereschkowskis". *Thomas-Mann-Jahrbuch,* Bd. 8. Vittorio Klostermann Verlag, 1995, S. 71–91.

Jens, Inge (Hg.). *Thomas Mann an Ernst Bertram. Briefe aus den Jahren 1910–1955.* Neske, 1960.

Kurzke, Hermann. „Kommentar [zu *Pariser Rechenschaft*]". GKFA 15.2, S. 781–858.

Lehnert, Herbert. „Thomas Manns Vorstudien zur Josephstetralogie". *Jahrbuch der deutschen Schillergesellschaft,* Bd. 7. De Gruyter Verlag, 1963, S. 458–520.

Mann, Thomas. *The Theme of the Joseph Novels* [1942]. U.S. Government Printing Office, 1943.

Mereschkowski, Dimitri S. *Tolstoi und Dostojewski als Menschen und Künstler.* Schulze, 1903.

Mereschkowski, Dimitri S. *Die Geheimnisse des Ostens.* Welt-Verlag, 1924.

Moeller van den Bruck, Arthur. *Das Dritte Reich.* 3. Auflage, Hanseatische Verlags-Anstalt, 1931.

Pikulik, Lothar. *Thomas Mann und der Faschismus: Wahrnehmung – Erkenntnisinteresse – Widerstand.* Olms, 2013.

Schestow, Leo. *Dostojewski und Nietzsche. Philosophie der Tragödie.* F.J. Marcan, 1924.

Schmeljow, Iwan. *Die Sonne der Toten.* Fischer, 1925.

Schroeter, Manfred (Hg.). *Der Mythus von Orient und Occident. Eine Metaphysik der Alten Welt. Aus den Werken von Bachofen. Einleitung: Alfred Baeumler.* C.H. Beck'sche Verlagshaus, 1926.

Vaget, Hans Rudolf. *Thomas Mann, der Amerikaner. Leben und Werk im amerikanischen Exil.* 2. Auflage, S. Fischer, 2012.

Weiß, Volker. „Dostojewskijs Dämonen. Thomas Mann, Dmitri Mereschkowski und Arthur Moeller van den Bruck im Kampf gegen ‚den Westen'". *Völkische Bande. Dekadenz und Wiedergeburt. Analysen rechter Ideologie,* herausgegeben von Heiko Kauffmann/Helmut Kellershohn/Jobst Paul. Unrast, 2005, S. 90–122.

Wysling, Hans/Marianne Eich-Fischer (Hg.). *Thomas Mann Selbstkommentare „Joseph und seine Brüde".* Fischer Taschenbuchverlag, 1999.

CHAPTER 6

Outcast—the Period from the "Anschluss" to Exile in Egon Schwarz's Autobiography *Unfreiwillige Wanderjahre*

Helga Schreckenberger

Abstract

As Egon Schwarz's autobiography reveals, his most traumatic experiences took place in Vienna, before his emigration. In this preliminary state of exile, Schwarz experienced an erosion of legal, civil, and human rights that diminished his sense of security, identity, and belonging. He witnessed radical anti-Semitism combined with public humiliation and abuse, social isolation, and economic destruction aimed at the demoralization of Austria's Jewish population to the point where emigration seemed the only option for survival. These experiences left their mark on the then sixteen-year-old Egon Schwarz, leaving him with doubt in individual power to influence the direction and course of one's own destiny, and with a rejection of any essentializing nationalistic and ethnocentric identification.

In his autobiography, *Unfreiwillige Wanderjahre. Auf der Flucht vor Hitler durch drei Kontinente* (2005),[1] Schwarz describes the difficulties of adapting to the foreign geographical, social and cultural environment of exile in South America. For Schwarz, the experience of exile constituted

> [...] das Erlebnis der Rechtlosigkeit und des Ausgestoßenseins aus der menschlichen Gemeinschaft, den Verlust an Heimatgefühl und innerer Sicherheit, an Identität und kultureller Zugehörigkeit, das Herausgerissenwerden aus Kindheit und Zukunftserwartungen, aus Freundschaft

---

1 Egon Schwarz published his autobiography first in 1979 under the title *Keine Zeit für Eichendorff. Chronik unfreiwilliger Wanderjahre Unfreiwillige Wanderjahre*. In 2005, a paperback edition of the work was issued with the new title *Auf der Flucht vor Hitler durch drei Kontinente*. With the title change, the publisher aimed to reach a broader audience. The new edition received the renowned Johann-Friedrich-von-Cotta-Literaturpreis of the city of Stuttgart in 2008.

und Studium, und am allerschlimmsten vielleicht die trübe Hoffnungslosigkeit eines ganzen langen Jahrzehnts. (244)

His autobiography however suggests that most of these experiences—loss of
civil rights, banishment from the community, the erosion of inner security, the
fracturing of childhood, the effects of being torn from friends and school and
future expectations—had in fact already occurred in Vienna before the family's actual emigration to Bolivia. The "Anschluss" unleashed an attack on Jewish Austrians that resulted not only in their loss of legal rights but also in their
complete social isolation. The young Egon Schwarz found himself expelled
from a number of communities to which he thought he had belonged. There
can be no doubt that this had a severe impact on the adolescent's sense of security, identity, and cultural belonging. It is thus not geographical banishment
that marks the beginning of exile for Egon Schwarz and Austrian Jews; instead,
early stages of exile can already be seen in the erosion of basic social and civil
rights within the borders of the country that they had considered their home.

Already in antiquity, geographical banishment marked the end and not the
beginning of exile. In her discussion of Ovid's exile in Tomis, Sabine Grebe
points out that according to Roman law, exile meant not only expulsion from
the community but also the confiscation of property and the effective loss of
citizenship, since exiles could no longer exercise their civic rights. Grebe con-
cludes: "Exile was a measure designed to encourage the expelled to renounce
his Roman citizenship and take up the franchise of a new state" (505, n. 54).
The developments following the "Anschluss" suggest a similar goal on the
side of the new administration with regard to Austria's Jewish citizens. The
abrogation of their civil rights occurred almost immediately. Jewish citizens
were abused, intimidated, and unrightfully imprisoned; their businesses and
residences plundered. They were prohibited from participating in the April 10
plebiscite, which supposedly was to decide the question of the "Anschluss."
Moreover, the quick implementation of the Nuremberg Racial Laws accelerated the exclusion of the Jews both from public and professional life. The rapid
"Aryanisation" of Jewish property further destroyed the Jewish community's
economic means to sustain itself. The intention, according to Oskar Karbach,
was "to engender and maintain abroad a state of mind conducive to the utmost
concessions as regards emigration" (264). The new rulers kept the Austrian Jews in a constant state of uncertainty, making emigration appear the
only possible solution. In anticipation of the success of this strategy, the
Völkische Beobachter promised already on April 26, 1938: "By the year 1942 the
Jewish element in Vienna will have to have been wiped out and made to disappear" (2).

The second and third chapters of Egon Schwarz's autobiography relate the effectiveness of these measures. The constant attacks on the Jewish community diminished their ability to adequately respond to the new situation. Deeply shocked, they helplessly endured the harassment and persecution ranging from "amtlichen Schickanen bis zur physischen Vernichtung" (Schwarz 50) that set in immediately after the "Anschluss." Particular devastating were public humiliations from which no Jewish person was safe and which specifically targeted orthodox Jews. Schwarz describes the familiar scenes, which became daily occurrences with little variation:

> [...] ein Mann oder eine Frau, ausgerüstet mit primitiven Hilfsmitteln, etwa einem Eimer und einer Bürste, bemüht sich, die Spuren der vaterländischen Wahlkampagne zu entfernen, Plakate von Litfaßsäulen und Wänden zu kratzen, Parteiensymbole oder politische Parolen, die mit weißer Ölfarbe auf Mauern und Gehsteige gemalt worden waren, wegzuscheuern. (50)

Forcing Jewish citizens of both sexes to perform demeaning labor such as scrubbing the streets to remove the signs of the deposed government, cleaning barracks or defacing Jewish-owned stores with anti-Semitic slogans were symbolic acts aimed at the destruction of any sense of a Jewish Austrian identity.[2] The most disconcerting aspect of these attacks against Austrian Jews was that they were not carried out by the German occupiers but by fellow Austrians. As Gerhard Botz states in his article, "The Jews of Vienna from the 'Anschluß' to the Holocaust,"

> [...] the Anschluss was not just a transfer of power by a kind of occupation, but was at the same time an internal take-over of power by the Austrian Nazis and a popular rising. The political and social discontent that had accumulated over the years among the middle-class following of National Socialism was discharged with elemental force against the Jewish part of the population. (320)

Not only Austrian Nazis vented their long-held resentment against the Jewish population. Fellow-travelers and even people who were not affiliated with National Socialism also joined in (cf. Botz 320). Moreover, public humiliation of Jews was not enough to abate the resentment the Viennese population.

---

2   Despair over these developments resulted in a high number of suicides among Viennese Jews. Herbert Rosenkranz puts the number at 220 for March 1938 alone (39–40).

Weeklong raids on Jewish-owned apartments and businesses soon followed. It did not matter if their owners were affluent or barely above the poverty rate. The targets included big "department stores of the *Mariahilfer-Strasse* as well as the pathetic little shops in the *Leopoldstadt*" (Botz 320). These occurrences shattered any hopes of Austrian Jews that they would be able to continue their lives, albeit in a more restricted framework in the country they regarded as their home.[3]

Schwarz recalls the feelings of insecurity and impotence that engulfed the Jewish community. Particularly unbearable was the "zermürbende Unsicherheit" of the situation:

> Ständig mußte man sich fragen: Wann trifft es mich? und sich sagen: Das darf man mit mir tun, ohne daß ich mich wehren oder protestieren kann. Mir war es, als werde mir der Boden unter den Füßen und, wie ich es noch zu berichten gedenke, das Dach über dem Kopf weggezogen. (51)

Witnessing the constant humiliations of the Jewish community and the realization of his utter powerlessness to defend against such perpetrations of injustice destabilized Schwarz's once so predictable world. He indeed soon became the target of an unfounded accusation. Their next door neighbor claimed to have received obscene notes directed at his young granddaughter, and as the only young Jew living in the house, Egon Schwarz was identified as the perpetrator: "Schließlich galt Laszivität und obszönes Sexualverhalten als eine jüdische Spezialität" (53). This racial stereotype was sufficient proof of guilt, and Schwarz and his father had to move out of their apartment the same day. The young Schwarz was deeply affected by the eviction:

> In dieser Wohnung, in diesem Haus war ich aufgewachsen, hatte da gelebt, soweit ich zurückdenken konnte. Meine Vorstellung von Häuslichkeit und Seßhaftigkeit war an diese Stiegen, diese Treppenabsätze, diese Räume und Wände gebunden. Von der falschen Bezichtigung und schweren Ungerechtigkeit ganz abgesehen, empfand ich den Auszug wie eine Vertreibung. (53)

The apartment in which he had lived all his life represented permanence and security for the sixteen-year-old. The grief over the loss of the apartment is even more poignantly expressed in Schwarz's early biographical text "Dank an die Emigration," which is also contained in this volume:

---

3 Oskar Karbach points out that many Jews had put their hope in the continued protection of minorities assured by the treaty of St. Germain that Austria had signed in 1919 (cf. 264).

> Aber die bescheidene Etagenwohnung in meiner Heimatstadt zu verlie-
> ren, in der ich von Kindheit an gewohnt hatte, deren jeder Winkel, jedes
> Möbel, jede rauhe Tapetenstelle mir so vertraut war, dass ich das alles fast
> wie einen Teil meines Körpers empfand, war mir lange Zeit kaum er-
> träglich. (18–19)

For Schwarz, the apartment stood for familiarity, for belonging, for a sense of
being rooted ("Seßhaftigkeit"). These are emotions generally associated with
the concept of home in the sense of the German word "Heimat." In his essay,
"How Much Home Does a Person Need?," fellow Austrian and exile Jean Améry
defines "Heimat" as follows:

> Home is security, I say. At home we are in full command of the dialectics
> of knowledge and recognition, of trust and confidence. Since we know
> them, we recognize them and we trust in ourselves to speak and to act—
> for we may have justified confidence in our knowledge and recognition.
> The entire field of related words loyal, familiar, confidence, to trust, to
> entrust, trusting belongs to the broader psychological area of feeling se-
> cure. (47)

For Schwarz, the apartment fulfills the same function as "Heimat" for Améry. It
provides emotional security, familiarity and an environment of mutual trust. It
is thus not surprising that he equates the loss of the apartment with being
banished in the sense of exiled. The eviction not only robs him of a safe and
familiar place but also destroys his trust in his environment. The neighbor who
denounced Schwarz had only a few weeks earlier assured the family of his sym-
pathies. After the "Anschluss," the situation had changed completely and the
lines were sharply drawn: "Weil mir Nazis san, und Sie san a Jud" (53) Schwarz
is told when he inquires about the neighbor's motivation for his betrayal.

As Améry's definition of "Heimat" also suggests, the feeling of security it
provides is derived from the bonds to community that establish trust and familiarity. Security is lost when the bonds are severed and one is expelled from
the community. This parallels the experience of the sixteen-year-old Schwarz.
Shortly after being evicted from his home, he is also thrown out of his school as
a consequence of the quick implementation of the Nuremberg Laws in Austria.[4] It was not so much the Nazi administration's desire to purge the schools

---

4   According to Botz, approximately 16,000 secondary school students were affected by the "de-
    schooling" that started in April 1938. At first, the city provided alternative accommodations,
    but by the end of the 1938/39 school year, Jewish children were prohibited from receiving
    public education (322).

of Jews that hurt the young Schwarz, but rather his fellow students' tacit agreement with the measure: "Dieser Umschwung, der über Nacht eine alte Kameradschaft auflöste, gehörte zu den unvergeßlichen Lektionen, die mir jene Tage erteilten" (55). The same sense of betrayal haunted Jean Améry. As he writes in his essay, it was not just the loss of home and possessions that hurt but also, and perhaps even primarily, the abrupt ending of personal relationships: "[...] but we also lost the people: the schoolmate from the same bench, the neighbor, the teacher. They had become informers or bullies, at best, embarrassed opportunists" (42). The ability of the Austrians to casually turn away from or even turn against their fellow citizens causes Améry to question whether Jews could ever have claimed Austria as their home: "We, however, had not lost our country, but had to realize that it had never been ours. For us, whatever was linked with this land and its people was an existential misunderstanding" (50). More than a geographical place, "Heimat" represents for Améry a feeling of well-being and security that results from the knowledge of being a legitimate and accepted member of a community. The "Anschluss" and its aftermath destroyed this feeling of well-being and security, and thus the belief in being at home in Austria.

As his autobiography reveals, Schwarz's relationship to Vienna had been ambiguous even before the "Anschluss." The Jewish lower-middle class to which Schwarz's family belonged clearly felt the impact of the economic and political instability of the interwar period, the anti-Semitism of the Viennese and the growing threat of neighboring Germany's National Socialism. Moreover, there were no satisfying models of identification available for the adolescent Schwarz. His half-hearted attempts at becoming a practicing Jew failed, and he rejected Zionism because of its nationalism. Although a very good student whose talent was promoted by both his parents and his teachers, he felt stifled by his school's empty routine and hierarchical structure. In addition, he had become increasingly alienated by the anti-Semitism that he encountered at school and beyond. Still, he regarded Vienna as his home:

> Trotz allem und allem war Wien "meine Heimat". Sind es die Worte oder Erinnerungen? Vokabeln wie Prater, Schönbrunn, Neuwaldegg bewahren ihren zauberischen Klang. Aus keiner Wasserleitung hat mir das Wasser besser geschmeckt als aus der in unserer Wiener Küche, wenn ich erhitzt vom Fußball nach Hause kam und [...] meinen Mund direkt und unter den Hahn hielt, und wenn ich ein Brötchen esse, dann vergleiche ich sie immer noch zu ihren Ungunsten mit den Wiener Kaisersemmeln. Noch Jahre später in der Emigration [...] habe ich denselben selig-melancholischen Traum geträumt, dem ich jedesmal lange nachhing, nachdem ich zu

einem gänzlich unwienerischen Tag erwacht war: Ich ging die Kärntner-
straße hinunter und war wieder "zu Hause". (46–47)

The fond memories that Schwarz connects with Vienna are also memories of
his childhood, a time that he associates with intense pleasures derived from
sensations:

> Zu den unersetzlichen Dingen, die man mit der Kindheit verliert, zähle
> ich die intensiven Lustempfindungen, die von Licht und Farben ausge-
> hen, aber auch von Geschmackserfahrungen und anderen sinnlichen
> Eindrücken. Keine noch so steile intellektuelle Entwicklung kann volle
> Entschädigung für die Einbuße dieser Wahrnehmungen bieten, die das
> Entzücken der ersten Lebensjahre sind [...]. (15)

Schwarz's positive memories of Vienna are such perception of sense—of the
taste of the water straight from the spigot, of the freshly baked rolls or of the
vibrancy of the Prater or Schönbrunn. Thus, they are memories of childhood
and of the security and innocence it represents. The "Anschluss" and its aftermath put an end to this period even if it did not erase Schwarz's memories and
the longing for what was lost.[5]

For Schwarz, the loss of security and belonging was augmented by his sense
of powerlessness, and the impunity with which the oppressors were allowed to
act. With the formal introduction of the Nuremberg Racial Laws on May 20,
1938, the Austrian Jews officially lost their civil rights and thus any possibility
of recourse to legal action over the injustices suffered.[6] Schwarz states:

---

5   In his "Dank an die Emigration" text that is also published in this collection of essays, Schwarz
    equates emigration with the loss of home: "Die ganze vertraute Umgebung hatte sich gegen
    mich gekehrt. Das war nicht schön, es war sogar gräßlich, aber es war und blieb die vertraute
    Umgebung, und war nicht die Emigration. Eines Tages war dann alles weg. Die Schule, die
    Wohnung, die Parks und Plätze, die ganze Stadt. Ich hatte alles verloren: das Gesicht der
    Hausmeisterin und die roten Hände der Kolonialwarenhändlerin, den Papagei, dem ich im-
    mer Plätzchen brachte, wenn ich sonntags ins Weltpanorama ging. Ich hatte plötzlich keine
    Schulkameraden, ich kannte keinen Menschen mehr und hatte sogar meine Eltern, kurz,
    meine gesamte Vergangenheit und Zukunft verloren. Das war die Emigration: Ich war ger-
    ettet. Aber für eine vertraute Heimat hatte ich trotz der Verfratzung die Leere und Sinnlosig-
    keit der ganzen Welt eingetauscht" (19–20). This quote suggests that the young Egon Schwarz
    would have preferred to remain in Vienna despite the increasing hostility and danger. While
    emigration meant safety, it also meant disorientation.
6   The implementation of the Nuremberg Racial Laws accelerated the complete isolation of the
    Jewish population. They were banished from all public spaces, including parks, playgrounds,
    restaurants, theaters, concert halls, and museums (cf. Karbach 265).

> Es gab keine Behörde, keine Instanz, bei der man sich gegen eine Beleidi-
> gung hätte verwahren, wo man sich über die gröblichsten Rechtsverlet-
> zungen und körperlichen Ausschreitungen hätte beschweren können. Im
> Gegenteil, diese Dinge waren ja von Amts und Gesetzes wegen angeord-
> net oder wurden von den höchsten Stellen augendzwinkernd geduldet.
> Es war ein sonderbares Gefühl, plötzlich vogelfrei zu sein. (52)

Already before he left Austria, Schwarz experienced a kind of exile by being
deprived of the most elementary civil rights to physical safety and due process.
This is indicated by his use of the term "vogelfrei" in its original meaning.[7] According to medieval German law, "vogelfrei" meant to be "without the protection of the law." Just like an outcast in the Middle Ages, Schwarz felt himself at
the mercy of the violence and capriciousness of his former compatriots and
their new rulers. Although the cause of his misery was clearly identifiable and
had very real perpetrators, Schwarz felt "verraten und schutzlos bösen Mächten
ausgeliefert zu sein" (53).

The constant attacks on the Jewish population had the desired effect of ac-
celerating their decision to emigrate. In contrast to the German Jews, who initially did not see the danger that Hitler and his regime posed and therefore had
put off emigration until it was too late, Austrian Jews did not hesitate. Schwarz
notes: "Der Vorteil der österreichischen Juden bestand darin, daß sie auf Grund
dieser Erfahrungen und Beobachtungen völlig illusionslos waren, als die Ka-
lamität nun auch über sie hereinbrach. Ich glaube nicht, daß es viele unter ihnen gegeben hat, die meinten, ohne Auswanderung mit dem Leben davonzu-
kommen." (57). However, by 1938 emigration had become almost impossible as
many countries had closed their borders to refugees and visas were hard to
obtain. Moreover, the Nazi government imposed their own bureaucratic stipu-
lations, including the charge of a *Reichsfluchtsteuer* intended both to relieve
the emigrants of their possessions and, perversely, to make leaving the country
as difficult as possible.[8]

Schwarz and his father were successful in obtaining papers that allowed
them to leave the country and, despite lacking a visa, they were able cross the
border into Czechoslovakia. Looking back, Schwarz wonders at the feelings of
his father who at age forty-five "nun alles zurückließ, was er sich aufgebaut

---

7 "Vogelfrei" can also mean to be free of any restrictions. It is clear that this is not the meaning
   Schwarz intended.
8 Despite these difficulties, 126,445 Austrian Jews managed to emigrate by November 1938; another 24,500 were able to leave during the war (cf. Botz 325).

hatte, und ohne Besitz und Erwerb, ohne Bleibe und Beruf einer ungewissen Zukunft entgegen ging" (59). The loss of economic and social status, which commonly characterizes the fate of those forced to emigrate, occurred for Schwarz's father already in the preliminary stages of exile as a result of Nazi policy that combined "anti-Semitic persecution and the satisfaction of material interests" (Botz 318). In Czechoslovakia, Schwarz and his father joined Mrs. Schwarz who at the time of the "Anschluss" had been visiting her parents in Pressburg, where it had been deemed safer for her to remain. However, Hitler's regime caught up with them again. After the occupation of the Sudetenland and the partition of Czechoslovakia, a fascist government was installed in the new Slovak state. This new government had little sympathy for the refugees from the expanding Third Reich. Schwarz and his parents were arrested and, along with other refugees, deported to the demarcation line between Slovakia and Hungary. The group of refugees, which included small children, pregnant women, and frail old people, was left in a no-man's-land without shelter, adequate clothing, food or medical supplies during the month of November. Several people died during the first night, among them young children. For Schwarz, this experience was "eine der absurdesten, ganz aus dem Rahmen der Herkömmlichkeiten fallende Episode" of his life (69–70). He writes:

> Armut und Arbeitslosigkeit, Streik und Protest, selbst Krieg und Revolution, Inhumanes von Menschen über andere Menschen Verhängtes gehörten vergleichsweise zu den "normalen" Erscheinungen, machten den Vorrat des Erfahrenden oder wenigstens des Vorstellbaren aus. Aber die Existenz von Ausgebürgerten und Geächteten, sozusagen ausgestrichen aus den Listen der standesamtlich Zugelassenen und Lebensberechtigten, war damals vor dem Krieg in Mitteleuropa, deren Machthaber ständig salbungsvolle Worte von Abendland und Gesittung im Munde führten, noch eine Neuheit, etwas Unverständliches, in keiner Rubrik Unterzubringendes. (70)

With the deportation to the no-man's-land between Slovakia and Hungary, Schwarz's experience of being outcast reaches a climax. In Vienna, he found himself excluded from the legal and social community; here, in the no-man's-land, deprived of the most basic rights, he was banned from the human community as such. He and the other refugees were no longer part of the known and knowable world of order and of life. This experience left Schwarz with the conviction "daß jede Zugehörigkeit, jedes Recht, jede Gemeinschaft auf Illusionen beruht, bis auf Widerruf von den jeweils Mächtigen gewährt, nach Willkür wieder entzogen" (73). At age sixteen, Schwarz experienced a permanent loss of ontological security and of trust in human justice.[9]

While his youth and resilience helped him to overcome the obstacles of exile and even to have the distinguished career his parents had wished for him, Schwarz's worldview was irrevocably shaped by the experiences in Vienna and in the no-man's-land between Slovakia and Hungary. They left him with the knowledge of the individual's limited power to influence the direction and course of his own destiny.

> Nur unter glücklichen Umständen, so möchte ich mit aller Vorsicht meinen, bleibt dem Individuum je nach seiner besonderen Situation eine gewisse Bewegungsfreiheit. Es kommt dann zu einer Begegnung zwischen den immer noch übermächtigen Gegebenheiten und dem, was der Mensch selber ist, mit seiner Schlauheit, seiner Vitalität, seinem ethischen Willen. Daraus kann, wenn die Zeiten günstig sind, einiges werden. (234)

Despite this pessimistic view of individual freedom, Schwarz considers upholding freedom and reason in order to safeguard the concept of human dignity to be the most meaningful human task.

The second lesson Schwarz took from his experiences in Vienna and the no-man's-land was to reject any nationalistic and ethnocentric identification. He learned the danger and arbitrariness of such constructs as well during his experiences in the "außermenschlichen Niemandsland" (232) between Hungary and Slovakia. This allowed Schwarz not to judge people as members of nationalities or ethnic groups for atrocities such as the Holocaust or the Vietnam War, but rather as "Individuen, die für sich und darüber hinaus für bestimmte Gruppen und Strömmungen standen" (211). It also shaped his relationship to Judaism which he grants a decisive role in his life. However, he contends this

---

9 In an earlier, unpublished version of the autobiography with the title "Abenteurer wider Willen," Schwarz tells the no-man's-land episode quite differently. Realizing their impending threat of getting arrested by the Slovakian government, the family reports voluntarily to the authorities. They are allowed to keep their possessions and initially seem to stay with relatives in Hungary before being deported to the no-man's-land together with the other refugees. In his article, "Unfreiwillige Wanderjahre von Egon Schwarz. Die Entwicklung einer Autobiographie von der Früh- zur Schlussversion," Reinhard Andress argues that these changes are informed by Schwarz's objective of integrating his story into the larger historical context. In addition, Andress points out that the retelling in the later version of the episode more strongly supports Schwarz's conviction that individuals cannot escape the power of historical forces (64–65).

point not in a religious, cultural, national, and certainly not in a biological sense, but in a historical one: "Jude bin ich nur insofern, als ich mich, da ich ein jüdisches Schicksal durchlebt habe, zur jüdischen Schicksalgemeinschaft bekenne" (232). Conversely, his rejection of essentialism with regard to people, ethnicities, and nationalities allowed him to later reconnect with his former Austrian homeland. As he emphasized in his speech at his former school on the occasion of receiving an honorary diploma, he could never forget the hardships and horrors of the thirties and forties. However, he could still align himself with the progressive elements of Austrian society. In his autobiography, Schwarz quotes from his speech:

> Die Härten und das Grauen der dreißiger und vierziger Jahre können und wollen wir nicht vergessen. Vergessen und Verdrängen verträgt sich nicht mit dem Begriff der Menschenwürde, und man weiß heute, daß unaufgearbeitete Erlebnisse psychische Schäden verursachen können. Aber die Erinnerung verträgt sich nicht mit dem Geist der Versöhnlichkeit und der Freude an den positiven Veränderungen, die sich in unserem Ursprungsland und unserer Heimatstadt während der letzten Jahrzehnte segensreich ausgewirkt haben. (246)

While Schwarz expressed satisfaction about the positive changes he noted during his visits to Austria, he also acknowledges that the experiences in Vienna in 1938 have caused him to fight against and finally lose "das einst stark in mir lebende Gefühl der Anhänglichkeit und Dazugehörigkeit" (245). However, as he states in "Dank an die Emigration," he has not been able to replace what has been lost:

> Den Verlust der Heimat verwindet man nicht leicht, und Ersatz für sie gibt es nicht. Sie ist wie ein Teil von einem selbst, und viele sind an dieser Abtrennung zugrunde gegangen. Ich habe überlebt. Und darum weiß ich, wer ich selbst bin, unabhängig von dem Ort, an dem ich mich befinde. [...] Denn seit geraumer Zeit weiß ich, dass ich nicht so sehr in diesem besonderen Land, sondern dass ich in der Welt lebe. Langwierig war das Erlernen dieser Kunst, groß ist der Gewinn, unsanft die Lehrmeisterin. Die dritte Stufe der Emigration heißt Weltbürgertum. (25)

Both "Dank an die Emigration" and his autobiography suggest that Schwarz has made peace with his involuntary adventures as an emigrant. The initial loss of self resulting from forced emigration has been more than offset by the gain of a confident and independent self. While he confesses a discomfort with the "presumptuousness" of the term "citizen of the world" in his autobiography, he admits to leaning "entschieden in diese Richtung" (232).

In retrospect, it can be said that Egon Schwarz's most traumatic and most formative experiences happened in Vienna and at the demarcation line between Slovakia and Hungary, rather than during his later exile in Bolivia. It was in the preliminary state of exile that he lost his sense of home and belonging, as well as his faith in a just world and his ability to shape his own destiny. The ensuing period in Bolivia, its own specific hardships notwithstanding, served only to reinforce these early lessons. It speaks to Egon Schwarz's intelligence, resilience, vitality, and ethical motivation that he could recover from these lessons and turn them into a positive philosophy of life—an enlightened cosmopolitanism.

Works Cited

Amery, Jean. "How Much Home Does a Person Need?" *At the Minds' Limits: Contemplations by a Survivor on Auschwitz and Its Realities.* Trans. Sidney Rosenfeld and Stella P. Rosenfeld. Indiana UP, 1980, pp. 41–61.

Andress, Reinhard. "Unfreiwillige Wanderjahre von Egon Schwarz. Die Entwicklung einer Autobiographie von der Früh- zur Schlussversion." *Zwischenwelt*, Vol. 35, no. 1/2, 2018, pp. 61–67.

Botz, Gerhard. "The Jews of Vienna from the 'Anschluß' to the Holocaust [1987]." *Historical Social Research Supplement*, Vol. 28, 2016, pp. 316–334. JSTOR, www.jstor.org/stable/43941256.

Grebe, Sabine. "Why Did Ovid Associate His Exile with a Living Death?" The Classical World, Vol. 103, no. 4, 2010, pp. 491–509. JSTOR, www.jstor.org/stable/27856652.

Karbach, Oskar. "The Liquidation of the Jewish Community of Vienna." *Jewish Social Studies*, Vol. 2, no. 3, 1940, pp. 255–278. JSTOR, www.jstor.org/stable/4464348.

Rosenkranz, Herbert. *Verfolgung und Selbstbehauptung: die Juden in Österreich 1938–1945.* Herold, 1978.

Schwarz, Egon. *Unfreiwillige Wanderjahre. Auf der Flucht vor Hitler durch drei Kontinente.* Beck, 2005.

Schwarz, Egon. "Dank an die Emigration." Vorstufen des Exil / Early Stages of Exile. Ed. Reinhard Andress. Brill, 2020, pp. 18–25.

Völkischer Beobachter. April 26, 1938, p. 2.

PART 3

Praktische, politische und pädagogische Arbeit / Practical, Political and Pedagogical Work

∵

Motility and Mobility of Exile: Gross-Breesen's Institutional Preparation for Migrating from Nazi Germany to Kenya

Jutta Vinzent

Abstract

This essay explores the term motility of exile, suggesting that Exile Studies should not only consider those who fled Nazi Germany, but also those who intended to flee but were unable to succeed, if preparation is considered as an early stage of exile. A case in point is Gross-Breesen, a training farm in Nazi Germany providing agricultural classes for 370 young male and female non-Zionist Jews. It was founded in 1936 with the aim of its trainees leaving Nazi Germany as a group and settling on a farm abroad, a purpose overridden by the events of the Kristallnacht. While most Gross-Breeseners were able to flee, the last pupils were transported to and killed in Ausschwitz-Monowitz in 1942. Apart from investigating preparation as an early stage of exile, this essay will also evaluate the usefulness of the training at Gross-Breesen, exploring farming in Kenya in light of the seven Gross-Breeseners able to reach its coast.

What do the early stages of exile encompass? What time period and which place is meant? While the English title of this book—*Early Stages of Exile*—seems to suggest the time at the beginning of being in exile (the settling-in-period, whose ending Guy Stern has marked in his contribution to this volume as the time when everyday-life began), the German equivalent—*Vorstufen des Exils*—seems to mark rather the time before leaving. It is the latter which this essay addresses, arguing that preparation for going into exile can be seen as part of exile itself. An intriguing case in point is Gross-Breesen (originally spelled Gross Breesen), the only non-Zionist Jewish emigration training farm in Nazi Germany, which provided agricultural classes for 370 young male and female Jews between 1936 and 1942. The initial plan was to settle jointly at some overseas destination, to which further trainees should follow, after finishing their education at Gross-Breesen. While this plan could not be realised, most of the Gross-Breeseners did flee Nazi Germany, though not all.

ILLUSTRATION 7.1   Sign at the entrance of Gross Breesen

Much has already been written about the so-called Gross-Breeseners, who went all over the world (see Angress, Pelz, Walk, Cramer). The four major destinations were Australia (covered by Matsdorf), Kenya, the UK, which was also used for transit, and the USA (the latter being the subject of a touring exhibition, travelling throughout the USA since 2008). However, so far no publication has focused on those seven pupils who went to Kenya, despite Kenya having been studied, in light of German-speaking émigrés, by Berman, Bourcet-Salenson, Carlebach, Eppelsheimer, Franz and Halbrainer, Joseph, Marx, Schestokat, and myself.

Thus, apart from the question of the early stages of exile, this essay will bring to the fore new research on Kenya in light of Gross-Breesen based on material in the private archives of Gerd Braun, Norbert Landecker, and the National Archives in London and Nairobi. A focus on Kenya is significant to evaluating preparation as an early stage of exile. While getting ready for exile may designate anything from thinking about it to taking actions, it is the latter that are easier to prove. Signing up for a two-year course seems proof for the intention to go into exile. However, how beneficial was the course? The focus on Kenya allows us to question the usefulness of the training at Gross-Breesen: Kenya arguably being the country, of the four main destinations, most different from Gross-Breesen in terms of climate, and therefore affecting farming, in addition to being initially not intended as a destination. This comparison between Gross-Breesen and Kenya will therefore provide an insight into the imaginings of exile, on which the school's education was based, and its experience—so often thought of as a mismatch (cf. Cramer, "Personal conversation" 40, Pelz 44).

Moreover, an examination of Gross-Breeseners in Kenya provides insight into flight from Nazi Germany: the various stages of preparation, including practicalities. It also queries to what extent preparing to leave in the second half of the 1930s was even possible—a time when emigration became a sudden flight, rather than a planned undertaking.

Finally, a focus on Gross-Breesen is significant because it draws attention to those Jews in the Third Reich who prepared their emigration and attempted to flee but were unable to find haven abroad. Should the latter therefore be excluded in a study on preparation as an early stage of exile? This essay will thus end with a debate on the usefulness of applying the term motility, developed in sociology, to the study of the early stages of exile, a term which emphasises the potential to move rather than the actual move and, therefore, has been seen as an antonym for mobility. Defining émigrés, exiles, and refugees from Nazi Germany in light of motility would have far-reaching consequences for the field of German and Austrian Exile Studies, as it would extend its focus from exile as a success story to an area that encompasses all aspects relevant for migrating, including opportunity, chance, and failure.

1   Beginnings in Gross-Breesen

The training in Gross-Breesen, a small Silesian town situated 18 miles north of Breslau (now Wrocław), began with circa 120 male and female adolescents in the summer of 1936. As described in sources and secondary literature and proven by photographs, the farm consisted of large areas of farmland, meadows, woods and buildings, including a large manor house which was remodelled in order to provide quarters for the majority of the staff and trainees (cf. Angress, "Auswandererlehrgut" 168–187, 172–173).

The foundation of Gross-Breesen, as the training centre came to be known, had not been uncontroversial. Being used to training facilities established all over Germany for the purpose of emigration to Palestine, the Zionist journal *Jüdische Rundschau* published disapprovals on Gross-Breesen, critiquing its focus on agricultural training rather than Jewish education (cf. Communiqué and K.L.). It was only because of the restrictive entry quotas for Palestine, unable to cope with the number of Jewish adolescents needing to leave Nazi

Germany, that they accepted that Curt Bondy, Gross-Breesen's first director, could begin his work with the support of the Reich Representation of German Jews with Leo Baeck as its elected president.

According to Angress, the course at Gross-Breesen lasted two years ("Aus-wandererlehrgut" 182–185). Over three two-year courses, Gross-Breesen educated 370 adolescents, mainly male, until 1942, when the training farm was closed by the Gestapo. 118 of these trainees and six members of the staff had emigrated by summer 1939. The second course was interrupted by an SS raid on 10 November 1938, during which all members of Gross-Breesen were arrested. All those who were over 18 (including the director Bondy and two teachers) were transferred to the concentration camp Buchenwald and released after six weeks upon the provision that they would emigrate immediately. One of those who fled to Kenya was Heinz Lichtenstein. Like most, he was able to leave Buchenwald on 4 December 1938, as detailed by his son David. Despite the devastating fate of the second course, Gross-Breesen continued until 1942 with 114 trainees in the third course, although for Bondy, the 'original' Breesen ended on the day of the raid (183). Angress reports that the number decreased rapidly between the end of 1940, when there were still 110, to 38 by July 1941. Those who were still there in 1942 were unable to flee, all being transported and killed in Ausschwitz-Monowitz ("Auswandererlehrgut" 185).

2   From Gross-Breesen to Kenya

It must have been at the beginning of November 1938, before the November Pogrom, when Braun and Lichtenstein were among those from Gross-Breesen who were interviewed by Colonel Charles Knaggs, the Kenya agent seconded to the UK, and Mr. Stephany, Secretary of the Plough Settlement Association, regarding their acceptance as settlers for Kenya. The Plough Settlement Association was formed by members of long-established Anglo-Jewish families, who sought to organise the migration and placement abroad of trained Jewish agriculturists. Both Braun and Lichtenstein passed successfully, in addition to 27 others mentioned in the records of the White Settlement papers held by the National Archives in London (White Settlement). These interviews took place in Berlin, to where Braun went, but also at Neuendorf and Wieringen, two other training farms for Jews.

Wieringen played a particular role for the Gross-Breeseners's migration route from 1938. In an early *Gross-Breesener Rundbrief*, a newsletter circulated to all alumni from 1938 to 2003, Bondy suggested that Gross-Breeseners should leave via Holland, stopping over at Wieringen, founded on 13 March 1934 and run by Moshe and Lea Katznelson. By 1939 it had 245 graduates, out of whom 111 had gone to Palestine. In his autobiographical notes, however, Braun mentions that he left Cologne by train via Hoeck (Holland) on 6 January 1939, arriving the following day in the UK without stopping over at Wieringen (10 ff.).

Braun also remembers that he met Lichtenstein at the Jews Temporary Shelter in East London on 10 January 1939. Here, the refugees were given food and lodging, while waiting for their departure to Kenya. Before leaving the port of Southampton, the Head Office Plough Settlement Association provided a small amount of money to go shopping in preparation for Africa. Braun remembers that about 30 destined for East Africa bought "sun helmets, moskito nets and boots, spine-pads, blankets, karki shirts and shorts" (Braun, "Autobiographical Notes"). David Lichtenstein recalled in 2018 that his father told him that he had with him on his journey five British pounds and two items from Gross-Breesen: "their farm training book with wonderful photographs of farming implements and animals which we used to pore over as children and a microscope which he gave to me to give to my son, in later years" (Email). Not all Gross-Breeseners who boarded the SS Watussi had stayed at the Jews Temporary Shelter. According to the List of Passengers, nineteen-year-old Gerhard Fraenkel gave his last address in the UK as 65 Greencroft Gardens in South Hampstead, and eighteen-year-old Jochen Feingold as 71 Templars Avenue in Golders Green (cf. List of Passengers).

The four Gross-Breeseners left Southhampton on a six-week journey to Mombasa on 13 January 1939. On board were also eleven alumni from Wieringen, among them three women: nineteen-year-old Marianne Lesser, nineteen-year-old Renate Fraenkel, married to Werner Fraenkel, probably Gerhard's brother, and 35-year-old Selma Heilmann. Except for Selma Heilmann and Renate Fraenkel, all others stated their profession as either farmer, gardener or agriculturist on the List of Passengers (cf. List of Passengers). The four Gross-Breeseners (Braun, Feingold, G. Fraenkel, and Lichtenstein) were not the first alumni to flee to Kenya. According to David Lichtenstein in 2018, Gerd Pfingst and Max Neumann had already left in 1937 and 1938. Together with Traute Fleischer, who arrived in Kenya after the four Gross-Breeseners and married Feingold, a total of seven students from the training farm went to Kenya (cf. Email).

The details of how the Gross-Breeseners made their way from Nazi Germany to Kenya shed light on the training farm's preparation. This preparation consisted of establishing contacts with Wieringen and the Plough Settlement Association and suggesting escape routes. However, the ultimate circumstances are also testament to a sudden flight from Nazi Germany to save their lives, substituting for the carefully planned emigration originally intended by Bondy.

Before the November Pogrom in 1938, he had searched for a 'New Gross-Breesen,' a training farm overseas to which all graduates from Gross-Breesen should emigrate. Explorations began as soon as Gross-Breesen became operative in May 1936, but remained fruitless despite visits and negotiations, and any plan to this extent was thwarted by the events of the Crystal Night, after which, as Angress notes in 1956, "the best that could be expected was to leave in small groups, and to settle wherever an opportunity for immigration opened up" (182). Ernst Cramer, who was instrumental in assisting Bondy in his efforts to help his pupils, formulated it as follows: We "had to speed up emergency arrangements, warning boys and girls: 'Get out—to wherever you can!'" ("Personal conversation" 40).

3   Refugees in Farming in the 1930s and 1940s in Kenya

Surprisingly, as farming played such an important role in immigration to Kenya, Bondy never seemed to have deliberated it in his efforts to emigrate the farm in its entirety, despite contacts (outlined in detail in Eppelsheimer's forthcoming book *Roads Less Traveled*) between the German Jewish Emigration Council and the Nairobi Hebrew Congregation, as early as 1934, which discussed the aptness of Kenya as an immigration country for German Jews and subsequently advertising Kenya as a suitable destination. Having not been considered by Bondy as a possible destination, the preparation that the pupils received at Gross-Breesen may have been less useful for Kenya than for those countries with a similar climate as Gross-Breesen. In order to evaluate the training at Gross-Breesen, the following section is based on the documents about the seven Gross-Breeseners who ended up in Kenya, supplemented by two unpublished reports that provide meticulous insights into population, culture, education, climate, vegetation, and farming in Kenya at the time. These were written by Mark Wischnitzer, Secretary General of the Aid Organisation of German Jews (*Hilfsverein der Juden in Deutschland*), after his visit to Kenya in November 1936, and Asaph Grasovsky, Senior Horticultural Officer of Palestine, who inspected Kenya from January to Februrary 1938. Both were sent by the German Jewish Emigration Council with the intention to explore settlement opportunities for German Jews in Kenya. Grasovsky's professional training and seeming objectivity are particularly useful in the consideration of farming in Kenya in the 1930s and 1940s.

After their arrival in Kenya, the Gross-Breeseners began working on various farms. According to Lichtenstein's son, David, in 2018, Gerd Pfingst, and Max Neumann, whose sister stayed with him, went to a farm owned by the German

Alfred Jacob Minkel, who had already been in the country for five years, in Gilgil (cf. Email). Lichtenstein, together with Gerhard Fraenkel, worked briefly in Kiambu before going up-country to start at Daisy Griffin's farm in nearby Ol Kalou. Jochen Feingold mentioned to Lichtenstein that he worked for a Mrs. Watkins, who had a Tyrol accent, on a coffee farm of 100 acres in Kiambu. This farm might have been the same as that initially offering a place for Lichtenstein and Fraenkel. Braun mentions in his autobiographical notes that he began in Turi, being employed as a farm pupil by G.C. Underwood (cf. "Autobiographical Notes"). Before joining the British Army in January 1943, he worked on three further farms. In October 1939, he became assistant manager to Fred Nye Chart on the Satimma Farm, near the Aberdare mountain range, c. 90 miles north of Nairobi. Two months later, he began work as Farm Manager on H.C. Allison's Farm at Gilgil, transferring to Loltian Farm (also in Gilgil) in May 1940. Loltian Farm belonged to Otto Hahn, who was a refugee himself and a trained lawyer. Taking into account that Gerd Pfingst, Max Neumann, and his sister were also in Gilgil on Minkel's farm starting in 1939, Gilgil seems to have been central for German emigration, already in 1938, when Grasovsky, without mentioning the farms' names, reports that he visited "farms of young German refugees in Upper Gilgil" (4). The last place where Braun worked as farm manager was called Murimani in Molo, a farm belonging to P.W. Lewin, who, according to Cilli Kasper-Holtkotte's research on German Jews in Kenya, was Jewish (Emails). Braun stayed in Molo for nearly a year, from 14 January to 24 December 1942. All these farms were run either by German refugees or by families whose names sound British.

The Gross-Breeseners worked as farm assistants, but mainly as managers. According to David Anderson and David Throup, assistant managers of farms were responsible for overseeing the farming, which was mainly undertaken by Africans (329). Thus, farm assistants and managers seem likely to have been less involved in the farming itself. In fact, even if they wanted, they were not allowed to help unless they owned a farm, according to Kasper-Holtkotte (cf. Emails). Hence, Braun as well as Lichtenstein, who also worked as farm manager, would have needed managerial skills. These, however, were not mentioned by Angress as being part of the training at Gross-Breesen, where pupils undertook all the practical work. In this respect, the training at Gross-Breesen was deficient.

The farms mentioned above were located in various parts of Kenya marked by differences in climate and vegetation. Gilgil, where most of the Gross-Breeseners worked for some time, was situated on the East African Railway from Nairobi to Nakuru. According to Grasovsky, the annual rainfall in the area around Gilgil was irregular and the pink soils were not very fertile. Cattle would not thrive, "as seven to eight acres of grazing are required for each animal" (47). However, the closeness to the railway meant that farm products such as crops could be used for export. The area around Nyeri and the Aberdares (where Braun was) had "little coffee" growing, the climate being "a little too cold" (47). It was a region considered suitable for wheat and cattle (cf. 48), while in Kiambu (not far from Nairobi), Lichtenstein and Gerhard Fraenkel worked on coffee plantations. According to Lichtenstein, they only stayed for a short period, possibly because of their lack of experience in coffee growing (cf. Email). The other farms might have suited them better because of their training at Gross-Breesen which involved crop growing, hay making, cattle farming and dairy production (cf. Angress, "Auswandererlehrgut" 168–187). Carpentry and blacksmith skills, also part of the training in Gross-Breesen, might have been useful too, particularly for Braun, who was asked to build a house when working on Underwood's farm in Turi (cf. "Autobiographical Notes"). Furthermore, a basic understanding of animal husbandry, grain, vegetable, fruit and poultry farming gained at Gross-Breesen may well have helped them understand farming in Kenya better. However, the more specific knowledge of grains, vegetables, and fruits grown in Kenya but not in Gross-Breesen might have been provided by the Africans. The Gross-Breeseners were certainly new to coffee farming and large-scale agriculture for export that involved packing and transportation.

One can therefore conclude that the training at Gross-Breesen, while not intended for farming in Kenya, may have not been entirely useless. It reflects to some extent, the assessment of training at Gross-Breesen by Bondy's assistant Ernst Cramer, who estimates retrospectivly in 1971 that only "in rare cases was it possible to prepare the young people thoroughly for the country into which they intended to immigrate" ("Personal conversation" 40). Regardless of its usefulness, however, the training in farming provided these seven Gross-Breeseners with the possibility to immigrate to Kenya and save their lives.

4   Exile as Motility and Mobility

An exploration into Gross-Breesen in light of Kenya brings to the fore that an early stage of exile from Nazi Germany encompassed a period of preparation for migrating characterised by careful planning, as undertaken by the director Bondy between 1936 and 1938, as well as by the pupils who underwent training to increase their chance for emigration. However, preparation for an emigration as an institution had to be substituted by a rushed flight as individuals after the pogrom of November 1938.

Indeed, preparation as undertaken in Gross-Breesen meant that exile actually began before departing. Gross-Breeseners made a decision to prepare for migration and thus went to a place where they stayed amongst Jews only, as if already in exile, thus living as an island in the sea of Nazi Germany, an island that was invaded in 1938 and destroyed in 1942 by the National Socialists. Therefore, before 1938, exile seems to be a process marked by an increasing alienation from Nazi Germany without physically leaving it yet and without a fixed date of departure. From 1938 onwards, preparation became increasingly impossible. While Gross-Breesen continued to educate German Jewish adolescents, its function changed from being a place for preparation to offering education with a slim hope to escape.

Regarding exile as a period that begins before actual migration conceives of exile not as an interstice or liaison between a point of departure and a destination, but as a phenomenon characterised by what Vincent Kaufmann, Manfred Max Bergman and Dominique Joye have termed motility. Taking this term from its originally biological context and applying it to sociology, motility emphasises the *potentiality* to move rather than an *actual* move (745–756). Motility in view of exile would therefore include all those who prepared but in the end were unable to leave Nazi Germany, demonstrating hencewith their intention to go into exile. Motility foregrounds options and conditions which make exile possible; it leaves room for considering opportunity, chance and what Egon Schwarz has called "a misunderstanding" ("Dank an die Emigration" 23), which can result in failing and/or succeeding in emigrating and shows that going into exile is not marked by being a straight-forward line of occurences.

If exile is understood in terms of motility and mobility, then Exile Studies as a research field is not defined by the success of being able to leave Nazi Germany, but the potentiality of doing so. It would include a study of the preparation, attempts, and impossibilities to leave. While such an understanding of Exile Studies raises issues as to how to prove intentions and define potential to migrate, the application to and subsequent attendance at an institution such as Gross-Breesen, set up with the expressed aim of migration, seems an indication that the intention of those undergoing such an institutional preparation was more than an idea or short-lived thought. However, the study into Gross-Breesen demonstrates that flight from Nazi Germany was anything but a logical consequence of preparation. Firstly, not all who prepared for exile were able to flee and, secondly, migration was increasingly difficult to carefully plan, organise and structure, particularly after the November Pogrom. Nonetheless, it seems that a concept which recognises the potentiality of going into exile in addition to the actual flight, as this edited volume has undertaken, seems more appropriate to capture the entirety of exile from Nazi Germany.

Works Cited

Anderson, David and David Throup. "Africans and Agricultural Production in Colonial Kenya." *The Journal of African History*, vol. 26, no. 4, 1985, pp. 327–345.

Angress, Werner T. "Auswandererlehrgut Gross-Breesen." *Yearbook of the Leo Baeck Institute*, no. 10, London 1956, pp. 168–187.

Angress, Werner T. *Generation zwischen Furcht und Hoffnung*. Christians Verlag, 1985. Translated as Werner T. Angress. *Between Fear and Hope*. Columbia UP, 1988.

Berman, Nina. *Germans on the Kenyan Coast. Land, Charity, and Romance*. University of Indiana Press, 2017.

Bondy, Curt. "Letter to Gertrude van Tijn." Printed in Werner T. Angress, *Between Fear and Hope*. Columbia UP, 1988, pp. 107–108.

Bourcet-Salenson, Lucile. "Das Exil der kleinen Leute in Kenia 1938–1947." *Alltag im Exil*. Ed. Daniel Azuelos, Königshausen & Neumann, 2011, pp. 127–137.

Braun, Gerd. "Autobiographical Notes. Late 1970s, handwritten, 72 pp." Private Archive Lavinia Braun.

Communiqué (without name) to the Editorial, "Eine 'jüdische' Auswanderungsschule," *Jüdische Rundschau*, no. 6 (21 January 1936), p. 4.

Carlebach, Julius. *The Jews of Nairobi 1903–1962*. Nairobi Hebrew Congregation, 1962.

Cramer, Ernst. "Personal conversation with Matsdorf on 24 May 1971." Cited in Wolfgang Simon Matsdorf. *No Time to Grow*. University of Australian Judaica, 1994, p. 40.

Cramer, Ernst. "Opening Comments." *Gross Breesen. In Memomoriam Curt Bondy (1894–1972)*, typescript, 1994. Harvey P. Newton Collection, Leo Baeck Institute Archives, New York.

Eppelsheimer, Natalie. *Homecomings and Homemakings*. University of California, Irvine (PhD dissertation), 2008.

Eppelsheimer, Natalie. *Roads Less Traveled. German Jewish Exile Experiences in Kenya 1933–1947*. Peter Lang, 2019.

Going East – Going South. Österreichisches Exil in Asien und Afrika. Ed. Margit Franz and Heimo Halbrainer. Clio, 2014.

Grasovsky, Asaph. "The White Highlands, Its Settlement Possibilities." KNA (Kenya National Archive, Nairobi): BN/46/61 and TNA (The National Archives, London): CO 533/497/8.

Joseph, Tommy. *Why There Were Jews in Nakuru*. Tommy Joseph, 1998 (printed privately, copy in the private collection of Lavinia Braun).

K.L., 'Unbegreifliches.' *Jüdische Rundschau*, no. 4 (14 January 1936), p. 3.

Kasper-Holtkotte, Cilli. "Emails to the author." April 2018.

Kaufmann, Vincent, Manfred Max Bergman and Dominique Joye. "Motility." *International Journal of Urban and Regional Research*, vol. 28, no. 4, 2004, pp. 745–756.

Lichtenstein, David. "Email to the author." May 2018.

List of Passengers Departing Southampton on 13 Jan. 1939 on S.S. Watussi, Voyage 69. London Metropolitan Archive.

Marx, Leonie. "Konkurrierende Netzwerke im Kenianischen Exil." *Networks of Refugees from Nazi Germany*. Ed. Helga Schreckenberger. Brill, 2016, pp. 11–37.

Matsdorf, Wolfgang Simon. *No Time To Grow*. University of Australian Judaica, 1994.

Pelz, Werner. *Distant Strains of Triumph*. Victor Gollancz, 1964.

Schestokat, Karen. "Memories of Africa: Stefanie Zweig's Autobiographical Works." *AUMLA*, vol. 108, 2007, pp. 51–63.

Schwarz, Egon. "Dank an die Emigration." *Vorstufen des Exils / Early Stages of Exile*. Ed. Reinhard Andress. Brill, 2020, pp. 18–25.

Stern, Guy. "My Early Stages of Exile." *Vorstufen des Exils / Early Stages of Exile*. Ed. Reinhard Andress. Brill, 2020, pp. 26–33.

Vinzent, Jutta. "The British Internment of Refugees from Nazi Germany in Kenya during WWII." *The Yearbook of the Research Centre for German and Austrian Exile Studies*, vol. 19, Amsterdam 2019.

Walk, Joseph. "The Diary of Günther Marcuse." *Yad Vashem Studies*, vol. iii, 1970, pp. 159–181.

White Settlement. "Settlement of German Jewish Refugees." TNA (The National Archives, London): CO 533/497/8.

Wischnitzer, Mark. "Bericht." Digitised manuscript (https://www.lbi.org/digibaeck/, access number MS 695).

CHAPTER 8

Should I Stay or Should I Go? Regional Functionaries, Political Networks, and the German-Czechoslovakian Borderlands in 1933

Swen Steinberg

Abstract

The National Socialist seizure of power in March 1933 was followed by the persecution of political opponents. Members and officials of the trade unions or the Social Democratic, Socialist, Liberal, and Communist parties often escaped this persecution by fleeing to border areas such as Northern Bohemia in Czechoslovakia. The decision to flee was frequently *ad hoc*. However, in many cases within this group of political refugees, the decision to go into exile was a process lasting months, sometimes even years. This process is analyzed in the following essay as a preliminary stage of exile by using the example of the Social Democratic party secretary, August Tröndle, from Dresden.

For most of the political and trade union officials on the regional and local level, the violent seizure of power by the Nazis in March 1933 came surprisingly and hit them largely unprepared: secretaries and employees of the Social Democratic, Socialist, Liberal, and Communist parties, officials from the workers' sports, leisure or consumer associations, journalists and staff of political newspapers, bookstores, printing and publishing houses, as well as members of parliaments on the local and regional level. But how did people from this group or these milieus react to the new political situation in the spring of 1933? When and where was flight discussed as a possibility or even a necessity to save one's own life? When did they ask themselves the question should I stay or should I go? Which preliminary stages can be identified until exile itself? When did these political refugees turn their gaze away from their German homeland and start reflecting on identity? (cf. Koepke, Benz, Kuhlmann).

An important point of reference is provided by perspectives of recent migration history (cf. Arcarazo/Wiesbrock, Lucassen) and their interest in aspects such as knowledge, gender, or age (cf. Donato/Gabaccia, Lässig/Steinberg 2017 and 2019). These perspectives—irrespective of the reason for the movement of the individual or group in question—are mostly based on the idea of direct and indirect forms of migration, the latter also being analyzed as "indirect movement in stages" (Wagner 5): whatever the reason, the migration decision itself does not have to be an *ad hoc* decision. Rather, in the context of flight from the German Reich or later from Nazi-occupied Europe, not only examples of "panic flight" can be found (cf. *The Universal Jewish Encyclopedia* 551–552, Röder/Strauss XXVII). On the one hand, there are also examples in which forms of isolation and social ostracism can sometimes be interpreted and analyzed as preliminary stages of exile over months or even years (for example, through work prohibitions and strategic pauperization, social stigmatization and isolation after the Nuremberg Laws, or violence like in November 1938). On the other hand, going abroad was often by no means the 'final step' into a 'new life.' This was especially true for political officials from the regional and local level because they were mostly middle-aged men who fled over the closest border without their families. This phase of reorientation was for many refugees associated with the slow realization of a new life situation. And in many cases, this phase—often lasting more than two or three years—was also a kind of a preliminary stage of exile since emigration had previously simply not been thought of as a state of life without a return option.

This paper examines these questions and perspectives using the example of the region of Saxony and the area of Dresden, where the nearby green border to Czechoslovakia played a specific role in many ways. On the one side, the 300-kilometer-long Saxon-Czechoslovakian borderlands had always been a fluid space, which was defined more and more in a nationalist way during the course of the 1920s and therefore became increasingly impenetrable (cf. Murdock 2010, 17–180). However, on the other side, tourism and the cross-border cooperation of political parties and organizations (e.g. workers' sports, hiking and climbing, youth organizations) as well as the cooperation of social democratic or communist newspapers in Saxony and in the German-speaking northern part of Czechoslovakia had also made these borderlands a place of encounter and cooperation—and thus the border virtually invisible. As in other border regions of the Reich (such as France, Austria until 1934, or the Saar region until 1935), the contacts and networks that were created in the 1920s helped to save lives from March 1933 on (cf. Steinberg 2016a and 2018a). This was also possible because the Czechoslovak Republic under Tomáš G. Masaryk (1850–1937) implemented—at least initially and until 1935—a liberal asylum policy towards the German refugees (cf. Čapková/Frankl). At the same time, "resistance infrastructures" were developed in the border regions of Silesia, Saxony, and Bavaria which were largely organized and financed by the Socialist, Social Democratic, and Communist parties in the ČSR. Border offices, houses of the workers' hiker and sports movement, party offices and trade union houses or publishing and printing houses were used to organize the resistance in central Germany and to document the injustice occurring there. And not least, this infrastructure was used to provide the German refugees with accommodations, cloth and food (cf. Bachstein, Steinberg 2018a and 2018b).

This development made it possible for many political activists at the local and regional level to remain in the German Reich and Saxony despite all threats, to use the contacts in Czechoslovakia to lead the resistance, and at the same time to pass on information from Saxony via the resistance infrastructure and the permeable border, which were then, for example, printed in exile newspapers and magazines or in camouflaged books and smuggled back to Saxony. In this constellation described here as a preliminary stage of exile, many officials of the local and regional levels in central Germany became active since in the German Reich they moved in an environment that became increasingly alien due to the political changes and gave them a feeling of isolation. This 'state of transition' persisted for local illegal functionaries in Saxony in some cases until 1935 when the infrastructures of exchange of printed material and information were uncovered by the Gestapo, especially in large cities

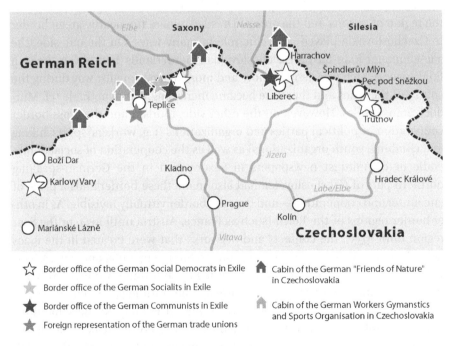

ILLUSTRATION 8.1   Map of the Ore Mountains (Erzgebirge) between Saxony and Northern Bohemia / Czechoslovakia with the infrastructure of the political borderland resistance in 1934

such as Dresden or Leipzig. Those who were not arrested finally fled across the 'green border' to Czechoslovakia. Often they then went into an exile they had already been considering as a possibility, sometimes for years.

With the example of the Social Democrat party secretary from Dresden, August Tröndle (1891–1958), this article elaborates on such a local case. When he finally crossed the border for the last time and went into exile at the end of June 1933, he wrote down his resistance experience in Bodenbach (cf. Decin-Podmokly). This report, which directly describes the transition into exile and its preliminary stages, is at the center of this paper. In addition to Tröndle's career, his reactions and strategies in dealing with the National Socialist takeover are described: when did exile become an option? Which constellations or conflicts resulted from the choice between going and staying? Furthermore, his several months of "transitional life" are presented. Finally, some perspectives are outlined regarding the constellations of the preliminary stages of exile, especially in the ČSR until 1936/37 and the group of political refugees.

1 Into Emigration—and Back

August Tröndle was born in Bachheim near Schaffhausen and learned the profession of a bricklayer. Military service in a Berlin telegraph battalion from 1911 to 1913 was followed by his conscription in August 1914. Tröndle fought first in France and was seriously wounded in Verdun in 1916; later he served at the Serbian-Turkish border. He did not return to Germany until 1919, was unemployed for a longer period of time and finally got a job as a professional fire fighter in Dresden in 1920. Tröndle was mainly active in trade unions and involved in the integration of the professional group of fire fighters into a free trade union organization (*Allgemeiner Deutscher Gewerkschaftsbund*). In 1924/25, his union sent him for studies to the Academy of Labor (*Akademie der Arbeit*) in Frankfurt/M. At that point, he switched to politics. Tröndle, who had belonged to the Social Democratic Party (SPD) since 1912, was elected in 1926 as SPD secretary in Oelsnitz/Vogtland, where he also had been deputy mayor since 1928. He ran a close-party publishing house there as well (cf. RAS, I Justitiedepartementet, M 69, Rapport 27.12.1946). Probably at the end of 1931, Tröndle became the SPD secretary in Dresden; in July and November 1932, he ran for the Reichstag parliament in the constituency of Dresden-East Saxony. Besides Tröndle, the SPD in Dresden had a second secretary, Arthur Kunze (born 1900), appointed also at the end of 1931; Wilhelm Sander (1895–1978) was the secretary for East Saxony, in addition to several employees of the organizations of the party (cf. *Handbuch* 275–276). Tröndle was, therefore, part of a larger regional party administration. But compared to others, he was in a more exposed position, especially in the fight against the political opponents both on the left and right, not only because of his activity for the party or parliamentary candidates. Tröndle appeared publicly and at the end of 1932 and the beginning of 1933 took on an increasingly aggressive tone against the National Socialists. He belonged to the "Kampfleitung" (executive committee) of the "Eiserne Front" (Iron Front) in Dresden. On February 26, 1933, he marched, for example, at the head of a mass demonstration against "the fascist attacks on democracy" with about 60,000 participants (cf. BArch, NY 4090, 280, Bericht 1). In the Reichstag election in March 1933, Tröndle ran again for the SPD and spoke, for example, on March 1, 1933, in Dresden "against the [National Socialist] four-year plan of distress—for freedom, work and bread!" (cf. "Gegen den Vierjahresplan der Not—für Freiheit, Arbeit und Brot!").

The election for the Reichstag on March 5, 1933 was followed by the violent seizure of power by the Nazis because the election did not result in the desired absolute majority in parliament. In addition, this election was no longer free and fair as a result of the measure that followed the Reichstag fire. In Dresden, for example, the Communist or Social Democratic newspapers were banned and initial arrests occurred in the first days of March 1933. For functionaries

ILLUSTRATION 8.2
August Tröndle as a candidate of the
Social Democrats for the Reichstag
election in summer 1932

like Tröndle, however, a radical system change seemed unthinkable. Probably not least because of this, he describes the violent occupation of town halls, administration buildings, and parliaments, but even more the property of the labor movement (e.g. party offices, printing houses, trade union centers, sports facilities) in a depressed way, a dull atmosphere in which the workers waited for a sign of resistance (cf. Steinberg 2016b, 91).

On March 8, 1933, Brownshirts attacked and occupied the party offices of the Dresden SPD at Wettin Square under the protection of the police. The editorial office and printing house of the daily *Dresdner Volkszeitung* (Dresden Peoples Newspaper) and a bookstore were also located in the building. Immediately after the occupation, a pyre of books, documents from the offices as well as flags and pictures was erected and put on fire (cf. Steinberg 2016b 93–94). Tröndle describes this incident in his report as a phase of transition: "We were wandering around the newspaper, trying to arrange a meeting of the executive committee. [...] Everything got mixed up" (BArch, NY 4090, 280, Bericht 8 and 11). Tröndle himself recalled that exile was already being discussed as a possibility in those days: "They all told me to cross the border" (ibid.12). When he was to be arrested on March 13, 1933, the threat became more concrete. He escaped the second attempt to arrest him on March 17, 1933 by crossing the border to Czechoslovakia.

A result of his flight was that he began to become aware of a sort of new isolation because the protagonists of the newly established illegal structures in Dresden refused to cooperate with "runaways" like him (ibid. 14). Hence, Tröndle had the choice between isolation in exile and isolation within German society. Although the SPD was not yet banned, its officials were being persecuted. On April 3, 1933, Tröndle decided to return to Dresden and remained unnoticed until April 26. Then massive house searches took place in his apartment, and parts of his property were confiscated. However, this persecution primarily affected his wife Elsa Tröndle (1897–1940) and son Leo (1929–2000) because Tröndle had not slept at home after April 3 (cf. ibid. 35). This phase of transition continued until June 25, 1933. It can be described as a preliminary stage of exile because Tröndle not only organized the party structures in Dresden. In addition, he published the illegal mimeographed magazine "Der Rufer" (The Voice) in the city, starting on May 1, 1933, which caused him some more problems. Since the SPD was not yet banned, this unregistered magazine isolated Tröndle in his own group of political activists because some of them rejected his strategy of illegality (cf. ibid. 22–23). An essential source of information for this periodical was Czechoslovakia, which Tröndle kept visiting until the end of June 1933. In many ways, he alternated between an exile and non-exile for several weeks from April to June 1933.

ILLUSTRATION 8.3   The burning of books, files, posters, and flags on March 8, 1933, in
                         front of the house of the Social Democratic party at Wettin Square
                         in Dresden

But was the situation of flight and emigration after March 8, 1933 really surprising? Tröndle's suggestion that the "Iron Front" in Dresden had "partially destroyed, partially taken away" the files of the executive committee one week before the Reichstag election on March 5, 1933 points to preparations as well as the fact that Dresden SPD Reichstag deputy Toni Sender (1888–1964)—doubly stigmatized as a Socialist and a Jew—went to Czechoslovakia the night before the Reichstag election (cf. ibid. 7 and Sender 292–294). It seems, however, that the issue of escape as a possibility was apparently not a topic of public discussion within the Social Democratic Party before March 5, 1933. A look into the 1932/33 issues of the SPD daily *Vorwärts* (Forward), published in Berlin, shows that this was indeed the case. The *Vorwärts* reported at this time only about other groups of emigrants, such as the Italian Socialists and Democrats who fled from Fascist Italy (cf. "Nach 10 Jahren Faschismus"), or about emigrants who fled the Russian Revolution in 1917 and thereafter (cf. "Paläste für feudale Clubs").

However, there had been unofficial preparations for a possible emigration. Already at the beginning of 1933, the party executive of the SPD in Berlin had started to transfer money to Switzerland and Czechoslovakia. The negotiations with the German Social Democrats in Czechoslovakia in late autumn 1932 about the publishing house Graphia and their printing plant in Karlsbad (Karlovy Vary) followed similar intentions (cf. Buchholz/Rother XXVII and XXXVII). As Tröndle found out while on a visit from Dresden to Czechoslovakia at the beginning of June 1933, those early preparations for exile can be observed almost simultaneously at the regional level. For example, at the beginning of 1933, the SPD district of Chemnitz-Erzgebirge deposited parts of its party funds in Northern Bohemia. This money was the starting point of the first Social Democratic border office, founded in May 1933 in Karlsbad, and followed by several of these important institutions of Social Democratic resistance work and refugee relief at the border (cf. Schmeitzner 2012a, 169–172). The SPD district Dresden-East Saxony, the *Dresdner Volkszeitung* and the Dresden "Eiserne Front"—whose board Tröndle had actually belonged to—also deposited money in the Czechoslovak border town Bodenbach before the general election on March 5, 1933. At the beginning of June 1933, the refugees from Dresden, therefore, had about 65,000 *Reichsmark* available, and thus wanted to found the weekly journal "Illustrated" (*Illustrierte Zeitung*), which was to be distributed in an edition of 10,000 especially among the German emigrants. This plan was supported by the still operable party executive committee in Dresden-Eastern Saxony, which wanted to smuggle this newspaper over the border to Dresden. In general, it was thought that "some immigrants could work on the newspaper and thereby find a modest existence" (BArch, NY 4090, 280, Bericht 28 and 31–32, cf. Buchholz/Rother XXVII–XXX and XXXIV and *Exil und Asyl* 375).

Threatened by persecution, Tröndle finally fled permanently via train to Czechoslovakia on June 25, 1933. His family followed shortly after. Once out of Nazi Germany, he continued where he had left off before fleeing. Already on August 14 and later on October 18, 1933, Tröndle attended the conferences of the German border offices (cf. Buchholz/Rother 421–422). The family lived first in the close-border town Eulau (Jílove u Děčína), then briefly in Prague, and later in Bodenbach, where Tröndle organized the resistance in Dresden and East Saxony with the escaped party functionaries Oskar Edel (1892–1958) and Arthur Kunze from Dresden (cf. BArch, NY 4090, 280, Bericht 35, NaP, Policejní ředitelství Praha—evidence obyvatelsta, card Tröndle, Augustin, and ibid., Zpravodojaská ústředna Praha, 200-77-1, card Tröndle, August).

This work ended abruptly when Kunze returned to Dresden in January 1934 because he gave the Gestapo comprehensive information on the resistance structures and, more importantly, on the distribution network of illegal, smuggled-in literature (cf. Schmeitzner 2012b and 2009 55–66). This not only led to arrests in Dresden; in March 1934, 58 persons were sentenced to prison and concentration camps for being part of this illegal distribution network (cf. "Zuchthaus für 'Vorwärts'-Verbreitung!"). It also isolated Edel and Tröndle in emigration; they were now also considered traitors. Especially for Tröndle, this event became a very significant problem. He had not only worked with Kunze before the Nazi seizure of power and then in resistance. In addition, he had been in Dresden with Kunze several times after he had gone into exile in the summer of 1933. The suspicion of being a traitor was not substantiated in an internal party investigation (cf. Buchholz/Rother 26, 37–38, 43, and 427), but the rumor was in circulation and evidently did not disappear when the Tröndle family moved to Reichenberg (Liberec) in spring of 1934. Later they lived in Gablonz (Jablonec nad Nisou, cf. NaP, Policejní ředitelství Praha I [1931–1940], T1166/26, Ka. 11577, letter of the German legation in Prague, 22.5.1937).

What activity August Tröndle pursued in the following years is unclear. Presumably, the family was supported by German Social Democratic refugee aid, which was located in Prague under the leadership of Tröndle's former functionary colleague Wilhelm Sander. A way back to Germany was certainly out of the question; however, Czechoslovakia became an emigration impasse for him. In September 1936, Tröndle was still under surveillance of the Gestapo in Saxony (cf. BArch, R 58, 2012, 34, 36); in May 1937, the German legation in Prague asked for information on him (cf. NaP, Policejní ředitelství Praha I [1931–1940], T1166/26, Ka. 11577, letter of the German legation in Prague, 22.5.1937). It was clear that Tröndle had to search for a different path for himself and his family.

In January 1937, Tröndle arrived in Stockholm as a "politisk flyktling" (political refugee) via Prague; his wife and son joined him in July 1937 (cf. RAS, SUK Kanslibyrån F1B, 2546 Tröndle August, entry 28.12.1945, and ibid., questionnaire, 20.4.1940). However, Tröndle did not become politically active again. His 'long road' into exile—due to the affair surrounding Kunze—was the path back into his life before politics. Tröndle, who had first been supported by the Socialist refugee relief in Sweden ("Arbetarrörelsens flyktingshjälp"), started working as an electrician at the Stockholm Fire Department in May 1937 and became politically independent. In December 1946, the expatriate—expelled from Germany eight years earlier—was granted Swedish citizenship (cf. ibid., Rapport 18.10.1939, ibid., entry 28.12.1945). Here his exile finally ended (cf. Benz). A return to the communist-ruled Saxony after 1945 was unthinkable for the Social Democrat in any case (cf. Steinberg 2016b, 145–155 and Scholz).

2   Accept Emigration?—an Outlook

The perspective on the preliminary stages of exile focuses on the temporality and chronology of forced migration. Individuals like August Tröndle did not simply go into exile. On the contrary, behaviors are evident in border regions that point to longer decision-making processes. For Tröndle, for example, the question "should I stay or should I go" was omnipresent to him and his family during this time. He escaped a concrete threat to the safety of Northern Bohemia, but then returned to Dresden for several weeks. Tröndle ended up traveling several times from Dresden to Northern Bohemia until his exile in Czechoslovakia in order to be active in his networks. Precisely in the spaces with permeable and therefore less controlled borders, this oscillation was possible. It was also the case with Arthur Kunze who went back to Dresden in early 1934. In his as in many other instances, a motive was without question the separation from family and the social environment as well as the lack of prospects for emigration to Czechoslovakia, where there was only limited support for German refugees. Only those who worked artistically, for example in the area of literature, were permitted to work (cf. Heumos 414 and Čapková/Frankl 90–94). For this reason, we also find in this period many cases of individuals who did not resign themselves to the exile situation and returned.

The flight to Czechoslovakia can be seen as a preliminary stage of exile for the group of political refugees focused on here. For many Social Democrats, Communists, and trade unionists from Saxony, Northern Bohemia was already a well-known space through cross-border cooperation until 1933. Furthermore, they could continue working in their own language and were generally tolerated in their political work at first. Individuals such as Tröndle thus moved in a space they were familiar with. This changed increasingly in 1935, not only because of the tightening of Czechoslovak asylum policy (cf. Eckert 30–31). Those who had worked 'face to Germany' and organized resistance gradually realized that the National Socialist regime was probably more consolidated and stable than initially assumed. As a result, tendencies can be observed in the political groups, especially in 1935–1936, that show acceptance of emigration and the search for a new home.

How strong this narrative of the search for a 'new home' must have been for the German Social Democrats in Czechoslovakia is obvious in statements made in 1938, when many members of this group left the country to France and Sweden—"Now our emigration begins" (Steinberg 2016b 178). The socialist journalist Edgar Hahnewald wrote in fall 1939 in Stockholm: "Prague has replaced the homeland for us" (ibid.). Evidently, emigration to Czechoslovakia was not similar to the 'feeling' of exile for some members of this group—for them, it was more like a preliminary stage of exile.

Primary Sources

Bundesarchiv Berlin (BArch)

NY 4090, 280, Bericht „Vom 26. Februar bis 26. Juni 1933".
R 58, 2012.

Národni archiv Praha (NaP)

Policejní ředitelství Praha—evidence obyvatelsta, card Tröndle, Augustin.
Policejní ředitelství Praha I [1931–1940], T1166/26, Ka. 11577.
Zpravodojaská ústředna Praha, 200-77-1, card Tröndle, August.

Riksarchivet Stockholm (RAS)

SUK Kanslibyrån F1B, 2546 Tröndle, August.
I Justitiedepartementet, M 69.

Works Cited

Arcarazo, Diego Acosta/Wiesbrock, Anja (eds.). *Global Migration. Old Assumptions, New Dynamics*, 3 Vols. Praeger, 2015.

Bachstein, Martin K. "Die Beziehungen zwischen sudetendeutschen Sozialdemokraten und dem deutschen Exil: Dialektische Freundschaft." *Drehscheibe Prag. Zur deutschen Emigration in der Tschechoslowakei 1933–1939*. Ed. Peter Becher/Peter Heumos, Oldenbourg, 1992, pp. 41–52.

Benz, Wolfgang. "Wann endet das Exil? Migration und Akkulturation. Überlegungen in vergleichender Perspektive." *Literatur und Exil. Neue Perspektiven*. Edited by Doerte Bischoff/Susanne Komfort-Hein. De Gruyter, 2013, pp. 71–82.

Buchholz, Marlies/Rother, Bernd (eds.). *Der Parteivorstand der SPD im Exil. Protokolle der Sopade*. Dietz, 1995.

Čapková, Kateřina/Frankl, Michal. *Unsichere Zuflucht. Die Tschechoslowakei und ihre Flüchtlinge aus NS-Deutschland und Österreich 1933–1938*. Böhlau, 2012.

Donato, Katharine M./Gabaccia, Donna. *Gender and International Migration. From the Slavery Era to the Global Age*. Russell Sage Foundation, 2016.

Eckert, Rainer. *Emigrationspublizistik und Judenverfolgung. Das Beispiel Tschechoslowakei*. P. Lang, 2000.

Exil und Asyl. Antifaschistische Literatur in der Tschechoslowakei 1933–1938. Volk und Wissen, 1981.

"Gegen den Vierjahresplan der Not—für Freiheit, Arbeit und Brot!" *Dresdner Volkszeitung* 50, 28.2.1933.

Glaser, Hans-Georg. *Prag und die Deutsche Emigration. Verfolgte Juden halfen verfolgten Deutschen.* Shaker, 2009.

Heumos, Peter. "Tschechoslowakei." *Handbuch der deutschsprachigen Emigration.* Ed. Claus-Dieter Krohn/Patrik von zur Mühlen/Gerhard Paul/Lutz Winckler. Wissenschaftliche Buchgesellschaft, 1998, pp. 411–426.

Koepke, Wulf. "On Time and Space in Exile—Past, Present, and Future in a No-Man's Land." *Exile Traveling. Exploring Displacement, Crossing Boundaries in German Exile Arts and Writing 1933–1945.* Ed. Johannes F. Evelein, Rodopi, 2009, pp. 35–49.

Kuhlmann, Jenny. "Exil, Diaspora, Transmigration." *Aus Politik und Zeitgeschichte* 42 (2014), pp. 9–14.

Lässig, Simone/Steinberg, Swen. "Knowledge on the Move. New Approaches toward a History of Migrant Knowledge" *Geschichte und Gesellschaft* 43, 3 (2017): Special Issue „Knowledge and Migration", pp. 313–346.

Lässig, Simone/Steinberg, Swen. "Why Young Migrants Matter in the History of Knowledge." *KNOW: A Journal on the Formation of Knowledge* 2 (2019): Special Issue: "Knowledge and Young Migrants," forthcoming.

Lucassen, Jan (ed.). *Migration History in World History. Multidisciplinary Approaches.* Brill, 2010.

Murdock, Caitlin E. *Changing Places. Society, Culture, and Territory in the Saxon-Bohemian Borderlands, 1870–1946.* University of Michigan Press, 2010.

"Nach 10 Jahren Faschismus. Eine Blütenlese." *Vorwärts* 516, 1.11.1932.

"Paläste für feudale Clubs." *Vorwärts* 265, 8.6.1932.

Röder, Werner/Strauss, Herbert A. (eds.). *Handbuch der deutschsprachigen Emigration nach 1933.* K.G. Saur, 1980.

Schmeitzner, Mike. *Doppelt verfolgt. Das widerständige Leben des Arno Wend.* Vorwärts, 2009.

Schmeitzner, Mike. "Erneuerung und Wandel im Exil. Zur Politik der sozialdemokratischen Organisationen 1933–1945." *Deutsche Sozialdemokratie in Bewegung. 1848–1863–2013.* Ed. Anja Kruke/Meik Woyke. Vorwärts, 2012a, pp. 169–175.

Schmeitzner, Mike. "Arthur Kunze. Die (un)freiwillige 'Karriere' eines SPD-Überläufers." *Braune Karrieren. Dresdner Täter und Akteure im Nationalsozialismus.* Ed. Christine Pieper/idem/Gerhard Naser. Sandstein, 2012b, pp. 86–93.

Scholz, Michael F. *Skandinavische Erfahrungen erwünscht? Nachexil und Remigration. Die ehemaligen KPD-Emigranten in Skandinavien und ihr weiteres Schicksal in der SBZ/DDR.* Steiner, 1999.

Sender, Tony. *The Autobiography of a German Rebel.* Routledge, 1940.

Steinberg, Swen. "Grenz-Netzwerke, Grenz-Arbeit, Grenz-Exil: Der deutsch-tschechoslowakische Grenzraum als politischer Ort, 1920–1938." *Grenze als Erfahrung und Diskurs.* Ed. Hermann Gätje/Sikander Singh. Attempo, 2018a, pp. 175–192.

Steinberg, Swen. "How to Become Isolated in Isolation? Networks in the German Political and Trade Union Exile after 1933." *Networks of Refugees from Nazi Germany. Continuities, Reorientations, and Collaborations in Exile.* Ed. Helga Schreckenberger. Brill, 2016a, pp. 89–108.

Steinberg, Swen. "Kochen im Kollektiv. Selbstorganisation und Verpflegung in tschechoslowakischen Flüchtlingsheimen (1933–1938)." *Küche der Erinnerung. Essen und Exil.* Ed. Ursula Seeber/Veronika Zwerger. new academic press, 2018b, pp. 128–147.

Steinberg, Swen. *"Karl Herschowitz kehrt heim." Der Schriftsteller-Journalist Edgar Hahnewald zwischen sächsischer Heimat und der Heimkehr ins Exil.* Metropol, 2016b.

The Universal Jewish Encyclopedia, Vol. 7. Universal Jewish Encyclopedia Inc., 1942.

Wagner, Kathrin. "The Migrant Artist in Early Modern Times." *Artists and Migration 1400–1850. Britain, Europe and Beyond.* Ed. Kathrin Wagner. Cambridge Scholars Publishing, 2017, pp. 2–20.

"Zuchthaus für 'Vorwärts'—Verbreitung! Massenprozesse vor dem Dresdner Sondergericht." *Neuer Vorwärts* 40, 18.3.1934.

KAPITEL 9

Zwischenstationen – zur politischen und pädagogischen Arbeit Ernst Papaneks als Vorstufen des Exils

Inge Hansen-Schaberg

Abstract

Ernst Papanek (1900–1973) was already a well-known politician of the German-Austrian Social Democratic Labor Party (SDAPDÖ) when he had to flee Vienna in February 1934 and leave his family behind. The time before his escape was characterized by intensive political work and dedication to pedagogical concerns, despite being under constant threat. This case study shows how he managed to organize resistance against Austrofacism and National Socialism, and set up help for children in need. Papanek's letters to his family, his personal notes, and the documentation of his pre-exile activities all serve clearly to illustrate how at that time political struggle against fascism began to spread through all of Europe. They also go on to show how strong the relationship between Papanek and his family remained during their time of separation, as well as the lifelong sense of belonging to Austria. Papanek and his family eventually fled to the USA.

Am Beispiel der jahrelangen pädagogischen und politischen Arbeit Ernst Papaneks vor dem eigentlichen Exil in den USA soll untersucht werden, vor welchem Hintergrund der Widerstand gegen den Austrofaschismus und den Nationalsozialismus und Rettungsaktionen insbesondere für Kinder organisiert werden konnten. Darüber hinaus soll gezeigt werden, in welchem Selbstverständnis der aus Österreich geflohene Protagonist handelte.[1]

---

1   Mein Beitrag ist Hanna Papanek, der Schwiegertochter Ernst Papaneks, gewidmet, die am 16. Dezember 2017 im Alter von 90 Jahren verstorben ist. Wir haben über viele Jahre zusammen in der Arbeitsgemeinschaft „Frauen im Exil" in der Gesellschaft für Exilforschung e.V., deren Ehrenmitglied sie ist, gearbeitet.

©   KONINKLIJKE BRILL NV, LEIDEN, 2020 | DOI:10.1163/9789004424715_010

1   Vor dem Exil in Wien

Ernst Papanek, als Sohn einer jüdischen Familie in Wien geboren und in klein-
bürgerlichen Verhältnissen aufgewachsen, engagierte sich bereits 1916 in der
sozialdemokratischen Mittelschülerbewegung und wurde 1919 Funktionär der
Sozialistischen Arbeiter-Jugend (SAJ). In den letzten Jahren vor seiner Flucht
arbeitete er in der Zentralstelle für das Bildungswesen sowie als Berater im
Amt für Wohlfahrtswesen und soziale Verwaltung im Wiener Magistrat, übte
eine Lehrtätigkeit bei den „Kinderfreunden" und in Volkshochschulen aus, war
als Vorsitzender des Reichsbildungsausschusses, als Landesobmann Wien und
als letzter Verbandsvorsitzender der SAJ tätig (vgl. *Biographisches Handbuch*
548). Nachdem der gewählte Kanzler Engelbert Dollfuß eine Geschäftsord-
nungskrise bei der Nationalratssitzung vom 4. März 1933 zu einem Staats-
streich genutzt hatte, regierte er diktatorisch per Notverordnung und begrün-
dete den austrofaschistischen Ständestaat. Ernst Papanek schreibt in seinem
Bericht, dass die Sozialistische Jugend sofort mit der „Vorbereitung für die Ille-
galität" begonnen und „einen Kampf für die Demokratie" gegen die illegitime
Dollfuß-Regierung geführt habe (24 f.), denn: „Wir hielten die Situation für die
Arbeiterbewegung in Europa *nicht* für aussichtslos" (24). Der aus der Sozialdemokratie erwachsende Widerstand gegen das Regime führte am 12. Februar
1934 zu bürgerkriegsähnlichen Verhältnissen: Die Sozialdemokratische Partei
wurde verboten, die Führer des Republikanischen Schutzbundes wurden verhaftet, misshandelt und einige ermordet, bzw. später zu Gefängnisstrafen und
zum Tode verurteilt. Auch gegen Ernst Papanek lag ein Haftbefehl vor, dem er
sich durch Flucht in die Tschechoslowakei entziehen konnte (*Bericht* 28). Viele
in Österreich verbliebene SAJ-Mitglieder tauchten unter und formierten sich
als Revolutionäre Sozialistische Jugend Österreichs (RSJ).[2]

2   Erste Zwischenstation in Brünn und Prag – 15. Februar 1934 bis
         Mai 1938

2.1   *Die politische Tätigkeit*
Der Aufenthalt in der Tschechoslowakei wurde von Ernst Papanek nicht als
Exil wahrgenommen, sondern eher als vorübergehende Verlagerung seines
Arbeitsplatzes ins Ausland angesehen. Weiterhin von einem Optimismus
geprägt, die politische Situation in Österreich und Europa durch Parteiarbeit

---

2   Zur Geschichte der RSJ von 1934 bis 1945 siehe Wolfgang Neugebauer, *Bauvolk der kommen-*
    den Welt 287–326.

verändern zu können, war Ernst Papanek am Aufbau der Zentrale der österreichischen Emigration beteiligt und wurde der offizielle Vertreter der RSJ im
Auslandsbüro österreichischer Sozialdemokraten (ALÖS) in Brünn. Es ging
zum einen darum, den Widerstand gegen den Austrofaschismus von außen zu
unterstützen, indem illegale Arbeiterzeitungen und Zeitschriften produziert
und nach Österreich geschmuggelt wurden (*Bericht* 28). Dazu gehörte auch die
von Ernst Papanek verfasste Broschüre *Die Idee steht mir höher als das Leben.
Ein Bericht über Josef Gerl und seine Freunde* (1935), die in einer Auflage von
20000 verbreitet wurde (Brief Papaneks vom 10.11.1966), und die von ihm organisierten Schulungskonferenzen für die im Untergrund tätigen RSJ-Genossen,
z.B. in Brünn und Mährisch-Trübau (Neugebauer 318), das vor dem Münchner
Abkommen vom 29. September 1938 zur Tschechoslowakei gehörte. Zum anderen nahm Ernst Papanek als Mitglied des Exekutivkomitees in der Sozialistischen Jugendinternationale (SJI) und im Auftrag der Sozialistischen Internationale eine Reisetätigkeit in Europa auf. Sein erster Einsatz wäre jedoch fast
sein letzter gewesen, wie Ernst Papanek im Brief vom 7. Mai 1968 an Wolfgang
Neugebauer berichtet: „Ich ging im Jaenner 1935 nach Danzig, um bei der letzten Wahl, die dort noch stattfand, bei den Vorbereitungen der Wahl und der
Vorbereitung der illegalen Bewegung mitzuarbeiten, [...] wurde waehrend einer Zusammenkunft der Untergrundgruppe [...] unter dramatischen Begleit-
umstaenden gefangen genommen" (Brief Papeneks an Neugebauer). Eine Intervention des Völkerbundkommissars, ihn zu finden, sei ohne Erfolg geblieben,
denn er habe sich in der Gewalt der SS gefunden, einen Hungerstreik begonnen und habe Glück gehabt: „Ein Genosse der Untergrundbewegung, der mir
vorher nicht bekannt war und der im Gefangenenhaus Dienst machte, ermoeg-
lichte mir zu entkommen" (Brief Papeneks an Neugebauer).

Es folgten politische Arbeitstreffen und Konferenzen in Paris, Amsterdam,
London, Oslo, Stockholm, Kopenhagen, Zürich und Madrid etc., wie aus seinen
Briefen an Gustav, Georg und Helene Papanek aus den Jahren 1934 bis 1937 und
seinen Taschenkalendern 1937 bis 1940 erschlossen werden kann. Insbesondere übernahm Ernst Papanek 1936 (bis 1939) unter dem Decknamen Ernst Pek
die Vertretung der SJI in Spanien und beteiligte sich an der Organisation politischer und materieller Unterstützungsmaßnahmen für die Volksfront im Spanischen Bürgerkrieg (*Bericht* 23 f.). In seinem Brief vom 10. November 1966
schreibt er: „Viele Hunderte von Tonnen von Lebensmitteln und Kleidern wurden auf diese Weise nach Spanien gebracht; in der anderen Richtung noch
während der Kaempfe wurden Hunderte von Kindern, deren Eltern im Kriege
umgekommen waren, nach Frankreich und zum Teil auch nach England gebracht" (4). Mit Unterstützung des Hilfswerks von Pablo Casals und den Quäkern habe er zur Rettung von über 800 Kindern nach Frankreich und über 1000

Kinder nach England beitragen können (*Bericht* 31). Später, nach dem Sieg der
Putschisten, sei er daran beteiligt gewesen, Tausende von katalanischen und
baskischen Kämpfern „den Rueckzug ueber die Pyreneen und den Eintritt
nach Frankreich zu ermoeglichen" (Brief vom 10.11.1966, S. 5).

2.2   *Die pädagogische Arbeit*

Neben seiner Funktionärstätigkeit ging Ernst Papanek auch seinen pädagogischen Ambitionen nach: „Ich versuchte so, wie ich es in der legalen Zeit in
Österreich gemacht hatte, nicht Partei-Angestellter zu sein und hatte wiederum mit der pädagogischen Arbeit begonnen" (*Bericht* 30). Er schreibt in seinem *Bericht* an Wolfgang Neugebauer 1968, dass er eine Berufung an die Universität von Teheran abgelehnt und eine Einladung als Gastvortragender der
Clark University in Worcester/USA nicht angenommen habe, weil ihn das zu
weit weg von Österreich geführt hätte, und dass seine Unterrichtstätigkeit an
der Internationalen Schule in Genf 1936 durch seine Ausweisung aus der
Schweiz beendet worden sei (vgl. 30). Allerdings gelang es Ernst Papanek in
Zusammenarbeit mit der Bibliothek des Völkerbunds Genf, die *Internationale
Pädagogische Information* (*I.P.I.*) auf Deutsch, Englisch und Französisch von
1936 bis 1938 herauszugeben, mit der Intention, „alle Veränderungen und Neu-
erungen auf pädagogischem Gebiete" aufzuzeichnen (Papanek, „Die *I.P.I.*" 19),
„sozialistische Kritik an Erziehungsfragen" zu üben und „über die Gegenreform
im österreichischen Schulwesen" zu informieren (*Bericht* 30). Auch nutzte er
seine politisch bedingten Aufenthalte im Ausland für Besuche von Schulen,
zum Beispiel Olafslid Lund in Stockholm und „Den frie Skole" in Kopenhagen
(vgl. *Notizen*).

3   In Verbindung mit Wien – Unterwegs in Europa 1934 bis 1937

Die Auswertung der insgesamt erhalten gebliebenen 48 Briefe vor allem an seine Söhne Gustav, Georg und nur wenige an Helene Papanek ergeben, dass Ernst
Papanek 1934 aus Genf und Zürich schreibt; 1935 schickt er aus Danzig, Stockholm, Kopenhagen, Brüssel und Paris jeweils einige Briefe; 1936/37 hält er sich
für längere Zeit in Paris auf, korrespondiert aber auch aus London und Rotterdam mit seiner Familie. Oftmals in Versform, geschmückt mit Skizzen, schickt
er vor allem Reisebeschreibungen über die Bahnfahrten, Schiffspassagen und
Flüge, über die Landschaften und besuchten Städte mit ihren Sehenswürdigkeiten und Museen, schreibt über Opern- und Theaterbesuche in Paris und
die Weltausstellung in Brüssel 1936, berichtet über die jeweilige industrielle
Entwicklung und soziale Lage der Bevölkerung und über die Kinder und
ihre Vergnügungen. In seinem Brief vom 11. Januar 1935 schildert er seinen

Söhnen beispielsweise Bemerkenswertes der Zugreise von Prag nach Danzig: in Mährisch-Ostrau die Fördertürme für den Kohlenbergbau; nach dem Grenz-übertritt in Polen die Bergwerke, Fabrikschornsteine, Kirchtürme mit Zwiebel-dächern und strohgedeckte Hütten ohne Rauchfang; in Warschau die Koffer-träger am Bahnhof, Autos, Einspänner, Pferdeschlitten, Kutscher mit dicken Pelzmänteln und Pelzmützen, große Kälte, offene Feuer an den Straßenecken, Schlitten fahrende Kinder; in Danzig am Hafen die alten großen Speicher, eine Fahrrinne im aufgebrochenen Eis, Schlittschuhlaufen, vereiste Schiffe, aber Heizer in Hemdsärmeln.

Ein den Briefen vermutlich durch Hanna Papanek bei der Verwaltung des Nachlass zugeordneter Notizzettel Ernst Papaneks enthält eine Auflistung von Themen, die er bearbeiten möchte und die mir eine Entdeckung ermöglichte: Offenbar hatte er den Plan, „Reisebeschreibungen f. Kinder", „Städteschilde-rung", einen „Baedeker f. Kinder" zu verfassen, und auf einem weiteren Blatt finden sich mit der Schreibmaschine geschriebene Stichpunkte, in denen auf Stockholm bezogene Sehenswürdigkeiten und Besonderheiten, die Kinder in-teressieren könnten, zusammengestellt sind (vgl. *Notizen*).

Aber nicht nur durch die Korrespondenz besteht der Kontakt zu seiner Familie – es hat regelmäßige Treffen gegeben, wie sein Sohn Gustav Papanek mir in einer E-Mail vom 3. Oktober 2017 mitgeteilt hat:

> We always met him during our summer vacations in different places. We met him wherever he had vouchers for hotels. He got these vouchers from newspapers for which he had written articles on various issues. The newspapers in turn had gotten the vouchers from advertisers who had advertised in the newspapers. It was in fact a barter economy. This was the period of the Great Depression and nobody had much money. Hotels and especially resort hotels advertised in newspapers but did not pay with money but with vouchers. These entitled the holder of the voucher to spend a certain number of days at the hotel and have two meals there usually breakfast and dinner. The newspaper then paid its contributors with hotel vouchers if they were willing to accept them which Ernst was. So we did not have to pay for the hotel. Ernst had very little income as far as I know. We lived primarily on the income of my mother as a physician so we were always trying to save money.

Demzufolge haben sie sich wahrscheinlich 1934 in Prag, 1935 in Belgien, 1936 in Dalmatien in der Nähe von Dubrovnik und 1937 an der Riviera getroffen, „somewhere near Monaco because we went to the Monaco motor car races. Ernst went into the casino. I was very worried that he would gamble away all of our money. But he had set aside a fixed amount, which he was prepared to lose after which he would stop. He in fact came back with winnings, much to my relief" (E-Mail vom 3.10.2017). Außerdem gab es ein weiteres Treffen, vermutlich Weihnachten 1936: „[...] we met Ernst at least once during Christmas vacation in Prague (or Prag) [...]. I cannot remember whether we met him during other Christmas vacations but if we did it would have been in Czechoslovakia, either in Prag or in Brno (or Bruenn)" (E-Mail vom 3.10.2017).

Zur Frage der Rückkehr nach Österreich schreibt Ernst Papanek in seinem *Bericht* für Wolfgang Neugebauer, dass „des öfteren darüber gesprochen, dies jedoch nicht für wünschenswert gehalten" wurde (5), er sich dennoch nach Beratung „mit den Genossen meines Wahlbezirkes Meidling, mit Vertretern verschiedener Jugendgruppen" ausgerechnet Anfang März 1938 dazu entschlossen habe: „Trotz Abratens von Otto Bauer, machte ich mich auf den Weg" (31). Er sei jedoch noch rechtzeitig gewarnt worden: „Am 12. März 1938 wurde ich am Wege nach Wien von Genossen Taub und Karl Kern zurückgerufen, da die Nachricht vom Einmarsch Hitlers in Österreich vorlag" (5). Er habe einsehen müssen, dass „eine Rückkehr Selbstmord bedeuten würde" (31).

4   Zweite Zwischenstation in Paris – Mai 1938 bis Herbst 1938

Da sich auch in der Tschechoslowakei die politische Lage weiter zuspitzte, wurde der Sitz des Auslandsbüros verlagert: „[I]m Mai 1938 übersiedelte ich

ILLUSTRATION 9.1   Gustav, Ernst, Georg und Helene Papanek in Prag 1936

wie die meisten anderen Genossen des ALÖS und gefährdete Funktionäre der illegalen Bewegung in Österreich nach Paris" (*Bericht* 31). Die anfangs optimistische Haltung war nun in Resignation umgeschlagen:

> Wir waren nicht mehr hoffnungsvoll, dass wir im stande sein würden, in absehbarer Zeit politische Arbeit in Österreich unter dem Hitler-Terror von aussen zu unterstützen oder durchzuführen, und so beschloss ich, [...] wenigstens die Kinder gefährdeter oder toter Politiker und Kinder von Eltern, die wegen ihrer jüdischen Abstammung getötet oder im KZ waren, zu retten.
>
> BERICHT 31

Das wurde mit Hilfe von französischen Philanthropen, des jüdischen Kinderhilfswerks OSE (Organisation de la Santé et de l'Education / Oeuvre de Secours aux Enfants) und des American Jewish Joint Distribution Committee bewerkstelligt: „Wir organisierten Gruppen in Österreich, Deutschland, der Tschechoslowakei für offizielle Transporte nach Frankreich, und mit Hilfe von französischen Bürgern, hauptsächlich Müttern, die einen Pass für Kinder hatten, war es uns möglich, hunderte von Kindern aus diesen Ländern zu ‚kidnappen' und nach Frankreich zu bringen" (*Bericht* 31). Da diese Kinder dann auch untergebracht und versorgt werden mussten, wurde Ernst Papanek im Herbst 1938 von der OSE gebeten, Zufluchtsorte zu organisieren.

Diese Anfrage kam zu einem Moment, in dem die Emigration der Papaneks in die USA bereits entschieden worden war. Vermutlich hatten mehrere Faktoren zu diesem Entschluss geführt: Zu der enttäuschten Hoffnung auf eine demokratische Zukunft Europas war nach dem „Anschluss" Österreichs und der sofort einsetzenden Verfolgung der jüdischen Bevölkerung und Ausschaltung der politischen Opposition eine realistische Einschätzung der Gefahr für ihr Leben hinzugekommen. Helene Papanek war es glücklicherweise zusammen mit ihren Söhnen im Juli 1938 gelungen, einer drohenden Verhaftung durch ihre Flucht aus Wien zu entgehen. So war die Familie nach viereinhalb Jahren in Paris wieder vereint, jedoch fast mittellos und verbrachte den Sommer am Meer, weil dort die Möglichkeit bestand, den Lebensunterhalt durch Kinderbetreuung zu finanzieren, wie Gustav Papanek in seiner E-Mail vom 3. Oktober 2017 schreibt: „The summer of 1938 we had already joined him in France and we spent it at La Baule in France where Ernst and Lene had some other children [...]. Taking care of them helped to pay part of the cost since their parents had considerably more money than we did." Auch finanzielle Erwägungen können eine Rolle gespielt haben, den Auftrag der OSE anzunehmen und damit ein Startkapital für die Ankunft der Familie in New York zu erarbeiten.

Obwohl die Visa für die USA erteilt und Billetts für die Überfahrt nach New York bereits gekauft worden waren, entschied Ernst Papanek sich dafür, dem Aufbau von Kinderheimen ein halbes Jahr zu widmen. Er nahm den Auftrag jedoch erst an, nachdem ihm Freiheit in der pädagogischen Gestaltung zugebilligt worden war, denn eine religiöse Ausrichtung der Erziehung lag ihm fern, kam jedoch dem Wunsch der OSE und den Bedürfnissen jüdisch orthodoxer Eltern und ihren Kindern nach, indem er später ein eigenes Heim mit koscherer Küche und religiösen Riten und Festen einrichtete (vgl. Papanek, *Pädagogische und therapeutische Arbeit* 130–134).

5   Dritte Zwischenstation in Montmorency – Herbst 1938 bis Juni 1940

Der Aufenthalt in Montmorency muss als retardierendes Moment in der Abreisesituation eingeschätzt werden, das vollkommen dem pädagogischen und politischen Selbstverständnis Ernst Papaneks entsprach: „Ihre Leben zu retten, war schon eine wichtige Aufgabe, aber es gab mehr als das zu tun. Es war notwendig, den Kindern und ihren verzweifelten Eltern in den Konzentrationslagern Hoffnung und Aussicht auf eine bessere Zukunft zu geben" (Papanek, *Pädagogische und therapeutische Arbeit* 92). Über die Rettung des Judentums hinausgehend, hatte er das Überleben der individuellen Persönlichkeit im Blick, wenn er schreibt:

> The goal of the OSE was, quite simply, to save as many children as possible. Their client, if they had been forced to put it into words, was the seed and culture of Middle European Jewry. My goal, as executive director, while perhaps less grandiose was also more arrogant. My goal was to see to it that these children who had been brutalized in so many ways not only survived but survived whole.
>
> PAPANEK / LINN, *Out of the Fire* 13 f.

Die Konzeption der Kinderheime entwickelte Ernst Papanek in Anlehnung an die pädagogischen Prinzipien der Wiener Schulreform, und das heißt, dass die individuelle Förderung und Selbsttätigkeit des Kindes und das Leben in der Gemeinschaft im Mittelpunkt stehen, dass eine tatsächliche Mitbestimmung in den Kinderheimen installiert und Verantwortung delegiert wurde,[3] „damit

---

3 Zur Konzeption und Umsetzung der Pädagogik in den Kinderheimen siehe Inge Hansen-Schaberg, „‚Sie waren unentbehrlich' – Ernst Papanek und die Rettung traumatisierter Kinder", und die Texte von Ernst Papanek in dem Sammelband *Pädagogische und therapeutische Arbeit* sowie den Text von Hanna Papanek „Als Jugendliche in den OSE-Heimen: Geschichte und Geschichten zu Ernst Papanek".

sie trotz aller widerwärtigen Umstände – den Tod der Eltern, den Verlust der Heimat, entwurzelt zu sein – trotz der Grausamkeiten des Nazismus und des Krieges doch an die Menschheit glauben und ein ganzer Mensch werden könnten" (*Bericht* 18).

Angesichts der politischen Entwicklung und Dringlichkeit, weitere Zufluchtsstätten für die verfolgten Kinder aufzubauen, wurde die Abreise der Papaneks immer wieder verschoben. Im Juni 1940 war Ernst Papanek schließlich Generaldirektor der elf über ganz Frankreich verteilten OSE-Kinderheime mit 1600 Kindern, und Helene Papanek war als Ärztin in den Kinderheimen und zeitweilig auch Direktorin während der Internierung Ernst Papaneks als „enemy alien" tätig (Hanna Papanek, *Elly und Alexander* 128).

Vor der Besetzung Paris durch die deutschen Truppen am 14. Juni 1940 gelang die Evakuierung der Kinderheime und die Flucht der Kinder in den unbesetzten Teil Frankreichs, jedoch waren politische Flüchtlinge aus Deutschland und Österreich durch Artikel 19 des Waffenstillstandsabkommens mit der Vichy-Regierung gefährdet, in dem die „Auslieferung auf Verlangen" (Hanna Papanek, *Elly und Alexander* 170–189) vereinbart worden war. Ernst Papanek konnte mit Hilfe eines der Visa für in größter Gefahr befindliche sozialistische Führungspersönlichkeiten, die der American Federation of Labor (AFL) von Präsident Roosevelt zur Verfügung gestellt wurden, und der „underground railroad between Marseille and Lisboa" im Sommer 1940 mit seiner Familie aus Frankreich fliehen (Papanek / Linn, *Outline* 21–26).

6   Exil in New York – 1940 bis 1973

Das größte Anliegen Ernst Papaneks in den ersten Jahren in New York war, sein vor der Flucht gegebenes Versprechen einzulösen, die 1600 Kinder aus den OSE-Heimen in die USA zu holen (vgl. Hanna Papanek, *Elly und Alexander* 239 f.). Er fand jedoch nur Gehör bei dem Investmentbanker und Verleger Marshall Field, der als Vorsitzender des U.S. Committee for the Care of European Children (vgl. Papanek / Linn. *Outline* 30–31) zusammen mit dem American OSE Committee, dem American Jewish Joint Distribution Committee und den Quäkern zwei Kindertransporte organisierte (vgl. Papanek, „Die Kinderfürsorge der ‚OSE'" 8). Insgesamt konnten so 197 jüdische Kinder im Sommer 1941 über Marseille in die USA gebracht werden (vgl. Hanna Papanek, *Elly und Alexander* 240).

Die fatale Fehleinschätzung, dass die Kinder im „unbesetzten" Frankreich nicht in Gefahr waren, wurde mit dem Einsetzen der Deportationen am 26. August 1942 offensichtlich, so dass 5000 Notstandsvisen bei Präsident Roosevelt erwirkt werden konnten (vgl. Papanek, *Die Kinder von Montmorency* 178). Wiederum war es Marshall Field, der ein Schiff umrüsten ließ und nach Marseille schickte, um die von den OSE-Rettungsteams versammelten Kinder aufzunehmen (vgl. Papanek / Linn, *Outline* 31). Der Plan scheiterte allerdings daran, dass die deutschen Truppen im November 1942 alle Mittelmeerhäfen schlossen. Trotzdem konnten Tausende jüdische Kinder durch umfangreiche Rettungsaktionen überleben (vgl. Samuel, *Die Kinder retten*).

Nach dem Master of Science 1943 an der School of Social Work an der Columbia University New York war Ernst Papanek als Sozialarbeiter und pädagogischer Berater der Children's Aid Society New York in Displaced Persons Camps tätig (Papanek / Linn, *Outline* 4). Auch hier folgte er seinem Ansatz, „to help the individual child master his past experience and establish normal relations with present and future", wie er 1946 in seinem Artikel „They Are Not Expendable: The Homeless and Refugee Children in Germany" schreibt (316).

Es finden sich keine Unterlagen über die Frage einer möglichen Rückkehr nach Österreich. So bleibt nur zu vermuten, dass die Bildungs- und beruflichen Qualifizierungsmöglichkeiten in den USA für Ernst Papanek bei weitem attraktiver waren, als sie bei einer Remigration gewesen wären. Seine berufliche Karriere begann in Einrichtungen für delinquente Jugendliche, führte zu einer Professur für Pädagogik am Queens College, CUNY (1959–1971) und an der New School for Social Research New York (1968–1971) und zum Vorsitz in der International Society of Adlerian Psychology (1951–1969) (vgl. *Biographisches Handbuch* 549).

Nicht nur mit seiner Dissertation, die der Aufarbeitung der Wiener Schulreform galt (vgl. Papanek, *The Austrian School Reform*), schloss Ernst Papanek an seine (bildungs)politische Vergangenheit an: Er wurde 1941 Mitglied der American Socialist Party (ab 1956 im Vorstand) und arbeitete in österreichischen sozialistischen Gruppierungen mit (vgl. *Biographisches Handbuch* 549).

Wien war und blieb Heimat und Bezugspunkt: „Die Tätigkeit im Alös, die Arbeit in Spanien, die Arbeit mit den Flüchtlingskindern in Frankreich und die Arbeit in den USA sind weltanschaulich, pädagogisch und menschlich darauf aufgebaut, was ich in Österreich theoretisch, praktisch und weltanschaulich gelernt habe" (*Bericht* 18). In seinem Nachruf *Erinnerungen an Ernst Papanek* (am 5. August 1973 in Wien verstorben) schreibt Richard Berczeller: „Für uns nach Amerika verschlagene österreichische Sozialisten war Papaneks Wohnung unser Parteilokal. Dort, im Hause 1, West 64th Street, in Manhattan [...] versammelten sich die Genossen, und wir fühlten uns wie einst in Wien" (12).

Zusammenfassung

In den verschiedenen Vorstufen des eigentlichen Exils, das Ernst Papanek zusammen mit seiner Familie im September 1940 in den USA fand, setzte er seine
zuvor in Wien praktizierte politische und pädagogische Tätigkeit fort. Es wirkt
so, als ob er lediglich seinen Arbeitsplatz ins Ausland verlegt hat, allerdings
jetzt mit einem europaweiten Einsatzort. Obwohl er selbst als Flüchtling gefährdet war, engagierte er sich für die Rettung Tausender im Spanischen Bürgerkrieg und ungezählter Kinder vor der Verfolgung im Nationalsozialismus
und Faschismus.

Zitierte Literatur

Unveröffentlicht

Internationales Institut für Sozialgeschichte / Internationaal Instituut voor Sociale Ge-
schiedenis (IISG). Amsterdam: Ernst Papanek Collection, Inventory – August 1995
by Kristine Ann CasaBianca. www.iisg.nl/archives/en/files/p/10766022full.php.
Bericht Ernst Papaneks an Wolfgang Neugebauer vom 5. April 1968, Folder G-2, IISG.
Brief Ernst Papaneks an H. Steiner, Dokumentationsarchiv des österreichischen Wi-
derstands, vom 10. November 1966, Folder G-2, IISG.
Brief Ernst Papaneks an Wolfgang Neugebauer vom 7. Mai 1968, Folder E-19, IISG.
Briefe Ernst Papaneks an Gustav, Georg und Helene Papanek 1934–1937, Folder B-12,
B-13, B-14, B-15, und Taschenkalender 1937–1940, Folder B-1, B-2, B-3 und B-5, IISG.
Notizen Ernst Papaneks, Folder B-14, IISG.
Papanek, Ernst / Linn, Edward. *Outline for Non-Fiction Book: They were Not Expendable.*
(o. J., ca. Ende der 1960er Jahre), Folder A-6, IISG.

Veröffentlicht

Berczeller, Richard. „Erinnerungen an Ernst Papanek". *Zukunft*, Wien 20/21, November
1973, S. 11–12, Signatur: K5. 730800.1, IISG.
Biographisches Handbuch der deutschsprachigen Emigration nach 1933. Bd. 1: *Politik,
Wirtschaft, öffentliches Leben.* Hrsg. vom Institut für Zeitgeschichte und von der
Research Foundation of Jewish Immigration unter der Gesamtleitung von Werner
Röder / Herbert A. Strauss. K.G. Saur, 1980.
Hansen-Schaberg, Inge. „'Sie waren unentbehrlich' – Ernst Papanek und die Rettung
traumatisierter Kinder". *Bildung und Erziehung*, Jahrgang 62, Heft 1: Emigration und
Remigration in der Pädagogik, 2009, S. 105–121.
Internationale Pädagogische Information (I.P.I.). Oktober 1936–April 1938, Signatur:
ZO 6075, IISG.

Neugebauer, Wolfgang. *Bauvolk der kommenden Welt. Geschichte der sozialistischen Jugendbewegung in Österreich.* Europaverlag, 1975.

Papanek, Ernst. *Die Idee steht mir höher als das Leben. Ein Bericht über Josef Gerl und seine Freunde.* Karlsbad, 1935.

Papanek, Ernst. „Die *I.P.I.*" *Internationale Pädagogische Information,* Jahrgang 1, Oktober 1936, S. 18–19, ZO 6075, IISG.

Papanek, Ernst. „Die Kinderfürsorge der ‚OSE'. 500 Refugeekinder aus Frankreich wollen in die U.S.A". *Aufbau,* 7. Februar 1941, S. 8. Besitzende Institution: Deutsche Nationalbibliothek. Exilarchiv 1933–1945, Frankfurt a. M.

Papanek, Ernst. "They Are Not Expendable: The Homeless and Refugee Children in Germany". *Social Service Review,* Vol. 20, No. 3, September 1946, S. 312–319.

Papanek, Ernst. *The Austrian School Reform. Its Bases, Principles and Development – The 20 Years Between the Two World Wars.* New York, 1962.

Papanek, Ernst. *Die Kinder von Montmorency.* Europaverlag, 1980.

Papanek, Ernst. *Pädagogische und therapeutische Arbeit. Kinder mit Verfolgungs-, Flucht- und Exilerfahrungen während der NS-Zeit.* Hrsg. von Inge Hansen-Schaberg, Hanna Papanek, Gabriele Rühl-Nawabi. Böhlau, 2015.

Papanek, Ernst/Linn, Edward. *Out of the Fire.* William Morrow, 1975.

Papanek, Hanna. *Elly und Alexander. Revolution, Rotes Berlin, Flucht, Exil – eine sozialistische Familiengeschichte.* Mit einem Vorwort von Peter Lösche. Übersetzt von Joachim Helfer und Hannah C. Wettig, Vorwärts, 2006.

Papanek, Hanna. „Als Jugendliche in den OSE-Heimen: Geschichte und Geschichten zu Ernst Papanek". Papanek, Ernst. *Pädagogische und therapeutische Arbeit. Kinder mit Verfolgungs-, Flucht- und Exilerfahrungen während der NS-Zeit.* Hrsg. von Inge Hansen-Schaberg, Hanna Papanek, Gabriele Rühl-Nawabi. Böhlau, 2015, S. 173–270.

Samuel, Vivette. *Die Kinder retten.* Fischer Taschenbuch, 1999.

PART 4

*Dazwischen und Übergang / In-betweenness
and Transition*

∴

CHAPTER 10

"Between Nations, between Genders": Transgender and the Experience of Exile

Pamela L. Caughie

Abstract

In this essay, I draw on my research for a comparative scholarly edition of *Man into Woman* (1933), the life narrative of Lili Elbe, one of the first persons to undergo a surgical change in sex. This early trans memoir presents the experience of transition in terms of "the early stages of exile." While many transgender scholars resist analogizing the experience of transgender with the experience of exile because it risks re-territorializing the concept of gender, I want to ask instead why this analogy persists in trans memoirs from the 1930s to the 2010s. What is so compelling about the early experience of exile that it seems to capture the early stages of transition? What does reading these narratives in terms of exile studies bring to an understanding of the history of transgender? And what can transgender narratives tell us about the experience of exile?

My interest in the early experience of exile stems from my research for a comparative scholarly edition I am co-editing with Sabine Meyer of Berlin. *Man into Woman* (1933) is the life narrative of Lili Elbe, who, as Danish artist Einar Wegener, underwent one of the first surgical and hormonal changes in sex in 1930. Elbe's story is very much a German story insofar as Germany was the birthplace of gender reassignment surgeries as well as Lili's (but not Einar's) birthplace. Lili Elbe's life narrative was first published in Danish in 1931, shortly after Elbe's death. The Danish version was translated from the German typescript compiled by Ernst Harthern, who published the work under the pseudonym Niels Hoyer. The typescript was then re-edited and published in German in 1932, a version which differs from the Danish edition in significant ways. The German edition was then translated into English and published in Britain and the US in 1933, adding an introduction by British sexologist Norman Haire that erroneously presents the narrative as a case study rather than a fictionalized memoir. Reading Lili Elbe's life narrative in the context of early twentieth-century case histories by sexologists and more recent memoirs of and by transpeople brings into strong relief the way the experience of transgender, especially transsexuality, is analogous to the early experience of exile.[1] What does reading narratives of transsexuality in terms of exile studies bring to an understanding of the history and experience of transgender? What might narratives of transsexuality tell us about the experience of exile in its initial stages?

I begin with some background on Elbe's story. Around 1918 Einar Wegener (Andreas Sparre in the narrative) began to cross-dress as Lili to serve as a model for his wife, the artist and illustrator Gerda Wegener. His cross-dressing was one reason he and Gerda left their native Copenhagen in 1912 for Paris, where Gerda's "Lili" paintings depicting the modern girl were soon in high demand. Increasingly Einar began to live as Lili, spending days and weeks at a time in his cross-dressed persona. Eventually he came to feel that Lili was a separate being trapped inside his body. In 1930 he traveled first to Berlin, then to Dresden to undergo a series of operations to transition to Lili Elbe. Dresden became the birthplace of Lili, who, according to the narrative, chose her last name from the river that runs through that city. When Lili and Gerda returned to Denmark with the goal of having their marriage absolved, the narrative tells us that Lili felt a stranger in Andreas's native country and longed to return to Germany. After a scandalous article about her was published by a sensational journalist, disclosing her identity, Lili determined to leave Copenhagen as quickly as possible: "Now she knew that in Copenhagen she was outlawed" (239). Dislocation from what we might call her "native self" results in a feeling of no longer belonging in her native land. Lili eventually returned to Germany where she underwent a fourth, and fatal, operation. She died in Dresden in September 1931.

Lili Elbe is not the first transperson to leave her home country, or to feel an exile in her native land. As early as 1910 Hirschfeld's *Die Transvestiten* provides case studies of cross-dressing individuals, many of whom we would today call transgender, who tell stories of self-exile due to the discomfort, embarrassment, or rejection they feel from family and friends, not to mention the legal restrictions they faced in countries with laws against cross-dressing in public.[2]

---

1   The contemporary use of transgender, dating from the 1990s, generally refers to a range of gender variant presentations, lifestyles, and identities including, but not limited to, transsexuals, a term that came into popular use c. 1949 to specify those who desired to change sex through hormonal and surgical intervention. Magnus Hirschfeld, founder of the *Institut für Sexualwissenschaft* in Berlin, first used the term "transsexualism" in a 1923 article entitled "Die intersexuelle Konstitution" to distinguish those who identified as persons of the sex opposite to that assigned to them at birth from those who dressed as the opposite sex. He soon abandoned the new term, preferring to use "transvestite" for both.

2   In Germany, cross-dressing was outlawed as a form of "gross indecency," but it wasn't criminalized in the way homosexuality was through Paragraph 175 of the Prussian penal code

ILLUSTRATION 10.1
Lili Elbe, 1882–1931

So many transvestites were hassled on the streets by the police that Hirschfeld created a transvestite pass granting permission for certain individuals to appear in public wearing clothing that did not match their birth gender. Even within their homeland, trans individuals, then and now, can be exiled from the nation and its regime of justice by failing to fit into a binary system of gender codified by legal documents such as birth certificates, marriage licenses, and passports. Lili's surgeon in Dresden initially provided her with a new passport so she could travel home to Denmark unmolested, but in the narrative, Lili expresses her desire for a passport that records her "biological" age. "Don't forget," Lili tells a friend, "every time one books a room in an hotel, fills up a census paper, applies for a situation, or marries, one must always answer questions about age" (245), and Andreas's age could not be hers, she argued, because it did not correspond to her "physical development as a woman" (245). In the Danish and German editions of this narrative, Lili refers to the passport her

---

imposed in 1871 on a newly unified Germany. In the US and UK, cross-dressing was considered an act of fraud. See Sutton 335–338 and Beachy 46, 65–66.

ILLUSTRATION 10.2   Grave of Lili Elbe

surgeon gave her as "a Nansen passport," one created for those with no homeland. Issued between 1922 and 1938 and named for the Norwegian explorer,
Fridtjof Nansen, who created it, the Nansen passport protected people ren-
dered stateless by war and genocide, allowing them to cross borders. The use of
that term conveys the extent to which Lili felt stateless, an exile. She tells a
friend that she has "no home and no country" (249). Creating, as she expresses
it, a bridge "across that abyss which separates man and woman" (270), Lili finds

herself between nations and between genders. Denmark was Einar's past, Germany is Lili's present.

"It is a commonplace to speak of gender transition as a border crossing of sorts," writes Gayle Salamon in *Assuming a Body*. "The figuration of a transperson traversing a border in her passage from one gender to another is perhaps the most common trope used to describe transition in […] works […] written by transpeople and nontranspeople alike" (171–172). To be "an exile from gender" (182), Salamon writes, is to be perceived as having no gender because one is neither male nor female, and often having no identity papers for who one is. Much like one who is exiled, the transperson often must leave behind "personal effects, letters, photographs," whatever would reveal their former identity, and "disappear" into the new homeland, blend in, become "one of us," especially but not solely through the issuing of new identity documents with a new name and gender (187, 190). Salamon ultimately cautions against analogizing the experience of transgender with the experience of exile because it risks re-territorializing gender as a concept. Rather than take a position for or against this analogy, I want to ask instead why it persists in writings about transsexual experience—even in the face of changing notions of gender and transgender that understand these concepts in terms of practices, not identities; even as the trope of the "wrong body" wanes as a way of describing trans embodiment. What is so alluring about exile as an experience that it seems to fit the experience of transgender?

Some of the many parallels between these experiences are suggested by Salamon herself. In creating a new future, many transpeople choose to edit their past, she notes. But such self-editing, what Sandy Stone refers to as constructing a "plausible history" (166), provides no guarantee of safety. As Salamon observes, the US Social Security Administration sends what are called "no-match" letters to employers when the information they give about employees doesn't match what the administration has on file. "No-match" letters meant to target illegal immigrants end up targeting transpeople as well, turning "transgressions of citizenship" into "transgressions of gender" insofar as a transperson's gender designation may not align with the official paperwork (191). Here the analogy works most effectively to capture a generalized anxiety about crossing borders. "The primary anxiety today is not that transpeople will fail to pass," Salamon writes, "but that they will pass *too well*—that they will walk among us, but we will not be able to tell them apart *from* us, an anxiety that mirrors current apprehensions about nationality, border control, and the war on terror with uncanny precision" (192). The transsexual's body figures the threat posed to the body politic when policing borders fails.

"Transgender identity," writes Jessica Berman, "produces a kind of internal exile" (227), a feeling of not being at home in one's body, and the "wrong body" trope is, like border crossing, a staple of early transgender memoirs. Yet transgender frequently necessitates a literal exile from one's homeland as well, at least temporarily. In the early twentieth century, Germany was the only place where transgender surgeries were being performed, beginning in the 1920s at Hirschfeld's Institute for Sexual Science in Berlin. Not until the 1950s were such surgeries performed in other countries, such as Britain (Roberta Cowell was among the first) and Denmark (Christine Jorgensen was the most famous). Many transgender memoirs describe traveling to another country for surgery, such as Morocco and Thailand, today one of the most popular destinations for transsexual surgeries. In his essay, "Feminine Transformations: Gender Reassignment Surgical Tourism in Thailand," Aren Z. Aizura refers to these temporarily displaced people as medical or surgical travelers (425, 438). Travel is both a figure for transsexual transition and a literal journey (cf. Prosser 88). British travel writer Jan Morris remarks in her 1974 memoir, *Conundrum*, in reference to her "life of traveling in foreign places," "I have only lately come to see that incessant wandering as an outer expression of my inner journey" (101). Like many new exiles, pre-transition transpeople often suffer periods of despair, anxiety, and loneliness, affective responses that are only exacerbated when one is compelled to travel alone to another country to receive surgery. In the words of trans memoirist Juliet Jacques, "*Imagine being cut off from all support networks like that* [...]. *It must be heartbreaking*" (182, original emphasis).

Morris is one who had to travel for the surgery she can't get in Britain in 1972 without having to first divorce her wife, whom she married when living as James Morris many years earlier.[3] So Morris, then 45, traveled to Casablanca, as Lili Elbe traveled to Germany. The clinic Morris enters "was not as I imagined it," Morris writes, and records the "natal sounds" and "clamor of women's Arabic" as she waits to see the doctor (136–137). The velvety-curtained rooms and heavily perfumed air suggested "the allure of a harem" (137). Foreign scents, foreign sounds, even foreign soap—Morris, like many early transsexuals, endures the estrangement of the traveler, but one whose travel has been forced upon her by legal restrictions in her homeland. Morris is exiled in a foreign land, like Elbe, away from family and friends. Unlike Elbe who adopts her new country, Morris is repatriated to Britain following her surgery. Because genital reassignment surgery is costly, controversial, and even banned in many countries, many transsexual individuals, as surgical travelers, are self-exiles.

---

3   Until very recently, courts often voided marriages after one partner transitioned. Elbe's marriage was annulled by the King of Denmark following her surgery.

Although as Morris's memoir exemplifies, and as transgender scholars like Ai-zura and Jay Prosser have noted, travel narratives commonly figure the experience of transgender, the subgenre of exile, especially its early stages, conveys more strongly the political and psychological estrangement experienced by many transsexuals (cf. Aizura 426 and Prosser 92).

The trope of exile, so compelling for representing early transsexual experiences, persists into twenty-first century transgender memoirs. "Sometimes I think the best way to understand gender shift is to sing a song of diaspora" (113)—so writes Jennifer Boylan (born James) in her 2003 memoir, *She's Not There*. Given that Boylan is able to receive surgery in the U.S. in the early 2000s, with family and friends supporting her, the experience of exile is not literal, but it does aptly describe the emotional, psychological, and somatic experience of transitioning. While surgery has become more available and concepts of gender have changed since Morris was writing in the 1970s, the *embodied experience* of transgender has not altered dramatically for many transpeople. Boylan employs competing metaphors for transgender. At times she describes it as morphing, a subtle transformation of her embodied identity (cf. 137). But more often, and more emphatically, she employs the analogy of diaspora. Living abroad, still as Jim, in Cork, Ireland, and singing in pubs, Boylan says she preferred ballads, whose lyrics spoke to her because they voiced the "theme of emigration." Transgender, she writes, is like "making a difficult ocean crossing" and arriving in a new world, "the land of promise," though "never quite fitting in [...] always speaking with a trace of a foreign accent" (113). Hormones make one "see the world in a different way" (123), make one's brain function in a different way (125), and make one's voice sound different, though Boylan concedes "more from culture than biology" (125). The early exile undergoes a similar transition, leaning to see and think and talk differently, both from the immersion in a new language and culture, and from the pressure to fit in.

As much as British journalist Juliet Jacques's 2015 memoir entitled *Trans* deconstructs many popular tropes of transgender, presenting transgender not as a bridge between two shores or an ocean crossing from one gender to another, but as a space between male and female (85), Jacques still falls back on the territorial metaphor implicit in the analogy of early exile. Jacques has no desire to pass as a woman, to disappear into the land of femaleness and femininity, as do Lili Elbe, Jan Morris, Jenny Boylan, and Stefánie Faludi (discussed below), for that is, Jacques says, "the means by which the violence of assimilation takes place" (182). Jacques wants instead to see transgender as "challenging ideas of what it meant to be male [...] or female" (132). Even so, the territorial metaphor is powerful and alluring. Indeed, my title phrase, "between nations, between genders," comes from Jacques's memoir. Referring to the life of a transperson she knows, Jacques writes that it was "a journey in which she was constantly crossing borders, between nations, between genders" (143). For all Jacques's insistence on her difference from Jan Morris and an earlier generation of transsexuals, in part because Jacques never felt she had to be a "straight" man as did Morris, Boylan, and Faludi, she retains Morris's metaphor in saying "my *journey* has been quite different" from hers (168, emphasis added). Granted, "journey" connotes an excursion more than the experience of exile, and yet the metaphor of being between nations suggests the early exile's plight. Exile seems the appropriate narrative for the kind of instability, loneliness, and disorientation felt by many transpeople who, like Jacques, feel alienated from their embodied identities, and sometimes from their newly embodied ones as well. Although Jacques conceives being between genders positively, as a continual process of transition, a resistance to being located in any one embodied home, she tells friends in her "coming-out" email that with gender reassignment surgery she "will finally be comfortable in [her] new body" after "two decades of struggling" (159). The exile has come home.

Jessica Berman rightly cautions against "an all-inclusive or too-simple critical analogy" (219) between exile and transgender. For "the transgendered person's experience is not really 'like' anything," observes Boylan's friend Richard Russo (291). Analogies fail. Salamon criticizes the trope of border-crossing for "analogizing gender and nation" as territory or property (172). In the mid twentieth century and even into the twenty-first, Salamon notes, transpeople were advised to divest themselves of artifacts of their former identity, and thus, as transgender scholar Sandy Stone puts it, the transgendered subject was "programmed to disappear" (164, qtd. in Salamon 187), much as the exile must leave behind personal effects and "disappear" into the new homeland, as Boylan's wife "watched her husband disappear" (291). Some trans individuals wish for that; Jenny Boylan says to a student late in the memoir, "I'm transgendered—or ... I used to be" (271), meaning she is now fully assimilated into womanhood, and Stefánie Faludi remarks, "Before I was a transsexual. Now I'm a woman" (194). That view of transgender, as a form of assimilation, is one most contemporary trans scholars and writers reject. Still, the history of transgender does not follow a narrative arc of progression. As Jacques's memoir shows, the experience of exile still resonates for transpeople. Even assimilation, as Faludi's story suggests, can be a form of resistance.

One of the most compelling recent accounts of transsexuality is Susan Faludi's 2016 memoir of her father's transition late in life. The politics of Eastern Europe, Hungary in particular, in the 1930s and '40s is at the center of Faludi's narrative. István Friedman (Friedman István, in Hungarian) turned Steven Faludi turned Stefánie Faludi was born in Budapest to Jewish parents. For Susan

Faludi, understanding her father's past as a Hungarian Jew is crucial to understanding his transition from Steven to Stefánie, though she rightly resists positing any causal connection; for there are more pasts here that require editing than simply a Jewish one. "Anti-Semitism has many wellsprings," writes Susan Faludi, "but the Jewishness that threatened the modern fascist state wasn't only Jewishness as religion. It was also Jewishness as gender" (246). Jewish men were perceived to be feminine. As Otto Weininger wrote in *Geschlecht und Charakter* (*Sex and Character*) in 1903, a work widely read by German and British sexologists as well as by Nazi leaders, "the manliest Jew may be taken for a female" (qtd. in Faludi 247). When Nazi interior minister Wilhelm Frick introduced an anti-gay bill in the Reichstag in 1930, Faludi tells us, "he dubbed homosexuality 'that Jewish pestilence'" (246). Jewishness, as Sander Gilman observes, is as much a gender category as a racial one (cf. Faludi 246).

István's adolescence in fascist Europe had a profound effect on his sense of identity. His survival depended on the art of deception, changing personae and editing personal documents. It is a past Stefánie works hard to conceal against the relentless questioning of her inquisitive daughter, for example, regarding her identity: "[...] it's what society accepts for you. You have to behave in a way that people *accept*, otherwise you have enemies" (344). Criticizing the campy transsexuals at the Pest gay pride parade, Stefánie makes the connection explicit: "You have to do it [transsexuality] in a nice way, with a smile [...]. Otherwise, they are going to go behind your backs and say, 'Who the hell are these people!' It's like what they say about Orthodox Jews in their awful getup" (196). Trans and Jews. What more powerful figure for exile than the Jew of fascist Europe?

In the introduction to *Transgender Migrations: The Bodies, Borders, and Politics of Transition*, Trystan T. Cotton writes of Aizura's contribution, "The Persistence of Transgender Travel Narratives": "Aizura argues that persistent characterizations of transitioning as a journey outward that is (always already) a return home domesticates transsexuality's potential to disrupt and destabilize the binary" (6). But unlike travel, exile as a trope does not carry a guarantee of return, nor does it necessarily undermine transsexuality's resistance to the binary. Interviewing Mel, one of Stefánie's friends who, as Melanie, ran a resort for post-op transsexuals in Phuket, Thailand, Susan Faludi learns that Mel/Melanie didn't find Stefánie "sensitive enough about the niceties of being a woman" due to her dominating personality. Susan thinks, "I was somehow pleased that, whoever my father had become on the operating table, whatever category she'd hope to join, she was already, incorrigibly, defying the template" (163). Stefánie tells Susan she was role-playing as a man but not as a woman. Susan asks, "Because this is who you were all along? This is your true self?"

Stefánie responds with her characteristic expression of impatience, "Waaall, it's who I am *now*" (381, original emphasis). The emphasis on *now* voices a more contemporary understanding of trans as "a general instability of identity" (Halberstam 50) and undermines any notion of a final destination. Her return home from surgery may be to the country of her birth, but it is one she returned to only late in life after decades of living as an exile; it is the country that drove her into exile as a Jew, and later forced her into temporary exile as a transsexual since gender reassignment surgery was not available in Hungary. Nobody knows better than the assimilated European Jew of the mid twentieth century that disaster threatens when, as Faludi puts it, "a fluid system becomes binary" (204): Magyar or Jew, German or Jew, man or woman. Transpersons and Jews both have historical reasons to destabilize the binary.

Keeping in mind Berman's admonition against too facile an analogy, I want to end by returning to my opening questions. What does this comparison between exile, especially its early stages, and transgender tell us about exile studies? For one, it urges us to acknowledge, as Berman notes, the centrality of gender embodiment to concepts of national belonging and the significance of transgender theories of embodiment to our understanding of the experience of exile (cf. 218). Halberstam provides one example in his recent book, *Trans**. Writing on an independent film directed by Angelina Maccarone and released in Germany in 2005 under the title *Fremde Haut*, Halberstam articulates the way the film frames asylum in terms of trans experience. *Fremde Haut*, which translates "foreign skin," is, Halberstam tells us, "the UN term for asylum seekers" who are said to be "in orbit" because they can find legal residence nowhere (39). The title "places the emphasis on motion, transition, flight, precariousness, and inbetweenness" (40)—in short, in terms of the early experience of exile. Halberstam writes of the film's protagonist, an Iranian lesbian woman who is denied asylum in Germany and who takes on the persona of a dead man, a fellow Iranian, who has been granted temporary asylum: "Balanced as s/he is between nations, identities, and legibility, the asylum seeker traces a trans* orbit as s/he moves passes [sic.] back and forth between legal and illegal, man and woman, citizen and foreigner. By naming this space inbetween as trans*, we begin to see the importance of mutual articulations of race, nation, migration, and sexuality" (40).

What can exile studies teach us about the experience of transgender? For one, it can displace the first-world, heteronormative, class-privileged narrative of so many early transsexual memoirs framed as travel narratives. Exiles do not have the privileges of travelers. For another, it can remind us that for all our theorizing about gender as fluid and performative, not an essential trait of a person's identity, gender *is* necessarily embodied and felt in ways that can

make the experience of transgender as disorienting, disenfranchising, and dis-
ruptive as the early stages of exile. In his exploration of the trope of travel,
Prosser asks how to read an account of transition that doesn't end in finding a
new home, one that presents the subject as traumatized by even having to
make a gender transition ("Exceptional" 107). Wendy Pearlman's description of
the stages of exile in her 2018 NASES paper, "Alienation in and from the Homeland," provides one model. Exile is a staged process beginning within the
homeland, she said, with estrangement from one's own self and a feeling of
hopelessness produced by the authoritarianism of certain political regimes, as
the estrangement of the transperson stems from social opprobrium, legal restrictions, and limited cultural repertoires of gender. "Exile inside the homeland is exile from human existence," Pearlman adds, in that there are no laws
to protect you, and thus, like Faludi's Jewish family, one suffers a loss of citizenship. That loss can lead to flight, a "transformative liberation" from one's earlier
sense of alienation as one forms alliances with others, and/or to flight, physical
separation from the homeland, which means starting life anew, reinventing
the homeland in a new land. At this stage the exile must make meaning of their
movement, Pearlman continues, by creating a narrative that bridges "then"
and "now," "there" and "here," which can explain why so many transsexuals
write memoirs. But there is no *one* story to tell. Both the political situation in
the homeland, Pearlman noted, and the policies of the asylum country affect
the exile's status and their view of exile, an uneven process that alters over
time. Indeed, one might question, as did the exhibit "Exile: Experience and
Testimony" on display at the NASES conference, whether exile, or transition,
ever ends.

    Exile is one narrative that can give meaning to the trajectory of transgender,
if we don't assume, as Berman says, that comparison means equivalence (cf.
220). The persistence of exile as a trope in transgender narratives underscores
the evocative appeal of being banished from one's homeland as a metaphor to
convey the experience of feeling estranged from one's body. Thinking exile and
transgender together may help us re-conceptualize borders of all kinds—
between nations and genders, the exile and the citizen, cisgender and transgender. The desire to fit in, to be accepted, and the nostalgia and longing that
desire can induce for a past left behind, surely both the early exile and the
transperson reveal our common humanity. As Richard Russo reminds readers
in his afterword to Boylan's memoir, "we [all] make our way through the world
in awkward bodies that betray us at every turn" (299).

    In June 1931, Lili Elbe returned from Copenhagen to Dresden for one last
surgery. The words on her gravestone—"Geboren in Dänemark, Gestorben in
Dresden"—suggest she died in exile. Yet transgender complicates that reading.

Elbe embraced Germany as her native land. "My love for Germany, for Berlin, and above all for Dresden, is easy to understand," she wrote to a friend. "Here I have merely to fight for my future from the basis of the present, unburdened by the painful past of another person" (276). While I suggest above that Elbe felt estranged from her native land (Denmark), it might be more accurate to say that her transition, her fourteen-month life as a woman, allowed her to cast off the stigma of exile and to accept a new land as homeland.

Works Cited

Aizura, Aren Z. "Feminine Transformations: Gender Reassignment Surgical Tourism in Thailand." *Medical Anthropology* 29.4 (November 2010), pp. 424–443.

Aizura, Aren Z. "The Persistence of Transgender Travel Narratives." In: Cotten, pp. 139–156.

Beachy, Robert. *Gay Berlin: Birthplace of a Modern Identity.* Vintage Books, 2014.

Berman, Jessica. "Is the Trans in Transnational the Trans in Transgender?" *Modernism/ modernity* 24.2 (April 2017), pp. 217–244.

Boivin, Jean. *Beauty's Scapel.* Trans. Eileen Bigland. Jarrolds Publishers, 1958.

Boylan, Jennifer. *She's Not There: A Life in Two Genders.* Broadway Books, 2003.

Cotten, Trystan T., ed. *Transgender Migrations: The Bodies, Borders, and Politics of Transition.* Routledge, 2012.

Faludi, Susan. *In the Darkroom.* Metropolitan Books, 2016.

Halberstam, Jack. *Trans*: A Quick and Quirky Account of Gender Variability.* U of California P, 2018.

Hirschfeld, Magnus. "Die Intersexuelle Konstitution." *Jahrbuch für sexuelle Zwischenstufen* (16 März 1923), pp. 3–27.

Hirschfeld, Magnus. *Transvestites: The Erotic Drive to Cross Dress.* Trans. Michael A. Lombardi-Nash. Prometheus Books, 1991.

Hoyer, Niels, ed. *Man into Woman: An Authentic Record of a Change of Sex.* Trans. H.J. Stenning. E.P. Dutton & Co., Inc., 1933.

Jacques, Juliet. *Trans: A Memoir.* Verso, 2015.

Morris, Jan. *Conundrum.* 1974. The New York Review of Books, 2002.

Pearlman, Wendy. "Alienation in and from the Homeland: Narratives of the Lived Experience of Exile among Syrian Refugees in Germany and Beyond." NASES Conference, Chicago, May 18–19, 2018.

Prosser, Jay. "Exceptional Locations: Transsexual Travelogues." In: *Reclaiming Genders: Transsexual Grammars at the Fin de Siècle.* Ed. Kate More and Stephen Whittle. Continuum, 1999, pp. 83–114.

Prosser, Jay. *Second Skins: The Body Narratives of Transsexuality*. Columbia UPE, 1998.

Salamon, Gayle. *Assuming a Body: Transgender and Rhetorics of Materiality.* Colombia UP, 2010.

Stone, Sandy. "The *Empire* Strikes Back: A Posttransexual Manifesto." *Camera Obscura* 2.29 (1992), pp. 150–176.

Sutton, Katie. "'We Too Deserve a Place in the Sun': The Politics of Transvestite Identity in Weimar Germany." *German Studies Review* 35.2 (2012), pp. 335–354.

CHAPTER 11

Seher Çakır: Poetry Framed by Exile

Sarah Voke

Abstract

This essay focuses on the writer Seher Çakır and examines the exilic voice of her poetry. Çakır's writing expresses memories of her early life in Turkey, her journey and
arrival in Austria, as well as her search for a literary form capable of housing her exilic
experience. Her lyrical poetry reveals the impact the early stages of exile have had on
her life, namely stirring a sense of uprootedness, separation, and a profound duality.
Her poetry is framed geographically between homes and two languages. The theme of
'in-betweenness' surfaces as well as the sense of void and death, but also the healing
process gained from the act of writing, providing a form of rebirth that overcomes the
dichotomy of life and death, here and there, now and then. This article also points to
how her poetry has been framed by the context of "Migrationsliteratur" and reflects on
the reception of authors writing in German who have foreign backgrounds.

Seher Çakır was born in 1971 in Istanbul. In 1983 she emigrated with her parents
and sister as a twelve-year old from Turkey to Austria. She grew up bilingual in
Vienna, where she has resided ever since her arrival. She has established herself as a writer with several publications to her name: a collection of poems
titled *Mittwochgedichte* (2005) and two collections of short stories, *Zitronenkuchen für die 56. Frau* (2009) and *Ich bin das Festland* (2012). She has also published numerous short stories in various anthologies. Furthermore, Çakır was a
founding member of the German-Turkish journal *Öneri* and is also the 2005
recipient of the Austrian literary prize "Schreiben zwischen den Kulturen." In
2008/9 she received an Austrian state grant for literature. In all the critical
work, interviews and reviews that have focused on her work, her writing has
predominantly been associated to and read through the prism of her personal
background, thus tracing it back to the early stages of exile she experienced. In
other words, she has been linked to what has often been termed "Migrantenliteratur" or "Migrationsliteratur," among other terms. Even though her texts
don't explicitly use the word "exile," they clearly deal with the lasting implica-
tions of its early stages.

It is not altogether surprising that literary critics have associated her writing with her biography. Indeed, the author has stated that she has often been inspired by her own life: "Ich lass mich vom Leben inspirieren—von meinem eigenen und dem der anderen" (Çakır, "In zwei Kulturen"). For example, the first four stories of the collection *Ich bin das Festland* ("Hatice," "Die Plakate," "Die Schatzkiste," and "Der Tipp des Arztes") are inspired by autobiographical events and are grouped together under the title "Aus Seldas Welt" (7–32). In various ways they suggest the movement of the early stages of exile. The collection opens with a story set in Turkey and retraces a bus journey undertaken by Selda, a thirteen-year old girl, and her family from Turkey to Vienna. The stories of these early stages of exile are narrated from the young girl's point of view and reveal the first contact with the foreignness of a new city, a puzzling new language, a new house, a school with different dress codes, comparisons between "home" in Turkey and this place of arrival that is to become a new home. In the same way as teenage years mark the divide between childhood and adulthood, so too the journey from Turkey to Vienna creates a divide between the familiar and the unfamiliar, tracing a border between a before and an after. These narratives reveal a sense of an initial clash, a consciousness of entering

ILLUSTRATION 11.1 Seher Çakır

a new space and the realisation of being different, of needing to adapt and to understand this new world. This transition left an indelible mark on the author's sense of identity as we shall examine later in this essay. It is interesting to note that Çakır chose to revisit this pivotal time in her life through the eyes of a young girl, as though these early stages of exile had caused a wound that never completely healed and had determined so much in her life.

Precisely the poet's experience of migration as a teenager has particularly shaped the way her writing has been received in Austria. It is interesting to think in terms of 'hospitality': not only to raise the question of the hospitality of language for exilic experiences, but also the hospitality toward "foreign" texts within literary canons and publication houses. Holger Englerth has indicated that Çakır's writing has exclusively been received as arising out of a context of migration (cf. 171–200), while Stefanie Grubich has noted that Çakır's texts are often more closely linked to a sociological framework than a literary one (Grubich). This topic has also been studied in depth by Wiebke Sievers in her work *Grenzüberschreitungen: Ein literatursoziologischer Blick auf die lange Geschichte von Literatur und Migration* (cf. 10–38). In sum, a form of persistent exclusion has framed writers with migratory backgrounds.

Starting around the 1990s, a conscious dynamic to include such writers through various initiatives has arisen (cf. Sievers 30). One such example is the "Exilzentrum" that has existed in Vienna since 1988. Its intention is to promote writers and artists who come from another language and culture, and who currently live in Austria and write in German. In their own words, they support writers from ethnic minorities who would otherwise encounter difficulties in finding a place within the art and literary scene in Austria and to fight against racism (cf. Literaturhaus). The centre initiated for instance a yearly award called "Schreiben zwischen den Kulturen." As mentioned above, Çakır was awarded this prize in 2005 and has clearly stated that it helps writers to become known: "Aber wenn es sie nicht gäbe, wenn es diese Förderungen nicht gäbe [...]. Ich weiß nicht, ob ein Dimitré Dinev, eine Julya Rabinowich, eine Anna Kim oder auch eine Seher Çakır entdeckt worden wäre" ("Ich mache Literatur und Punkt!"). This centre also provides a publication house called "exil edition," and both of Çakır's collections of short stories were published there. More than simply supporting minority writers, this centre highly values the literary quality of their work, for these texts bring a unique consciousness to language, often using it in a creative and new way, thereby stretching its traditional boundaries.

The "Exilzentrum" is not the only initiative in Austria to support such writers. In fact, many anthologies of minority writers were assembled to raise awareness of the diversity within Austria. Çakır contributed, for example, to the following anthologies: *Die Fremde in mir: Lyrik und Prosa der österreichischen Volksgruppen und Zuwanderer* (1999), *Eure Sprache ist nicht meine Sprache: Texte von Migrantinnen in Österreich* (2002), *Heim.at: Burgaz Projekt, Gedichte von Migrantinnen und Migranten aus der Türkei in Österreich* (2004), or *andernWOrts* (2007). Without even delving into the content and poetic form of these texts, one grasps that the unity of these texts is founded upon the authors' backgrounds and their experiences of displacement.

However, Çakır has struggled with the categorisation of "Migrantenliteratur." Silke Schwaiger in her work titled *Über die Schwelle* has detailed the way in which authors have been viewed as migrant writers and has focused on concepts such as cultural identity, canonisation, as well as the important role that the "Exilzentrum" has played for these writers in a context that hasn't systematically favoured their publication. The term "Migrantenliteratur" is felt as derogatory and exclusionary—outside of German literature. It underlines the fact that Çakır does not have an obvious place within Austrian literature, nor in fact does she have a natural place within Turkish literature: "In der türkischen Literatur fühle ich mich eigentlich gar nicht richtig heimisch" ("Zitronenkuchen und Mittwochgedichte"). The position of an outsider that she first experienced upon arrival in Vienna has followed her ever since. She stands on an in-between threshold, neither fully Austrian nor Turkish, half-in and half-out at the same time, and this is precisely an aspect of early stages of exile.

Hence, it has become crucial to think beyond such categories that underline differences and generate either inclusionary or exclusionary dynamics. Literary critics and publication houses play an immensely influential role in the reception and understanding of texts, and the terms they employ reveal an entire literary and political culture. Which terms are sufficiently broad to embrace the uniqueness of each author, and how can literary critics analyse texts without speaking louder than the text itself, without tainting its reception, all the while respecting authors' wishes and accompanying the internal structures of the text? What is a respectful balance between the text and the author's biography? Regarding such methodological questions, the term "exile" and its early stages as the focus of this volume as they are beginning to be used is noteworthy. First and foremost, this supposes that the term can pertain to a context wider than the period leading up to and between 1933–1945 as it has traditionally been used within the context of German Studies and include migration dating from after the war up to the current migratory movements to the German-speaking world.

Within this vein of thought, it is useful to consider the French term "exiliance" coined by Alexis Nouss, which can be defined as

> [...] the existential core that is common to every experience of migrant
> subjects regardless of the historical periods, cultures and circumstances
> which welcomes or provokes them. Exiliance is comprised of the condi-
> tion and the consciousness of exile, both don't necessarily coincide: one
> can feel in exile without concretely being in exile (consciousness); one
> can concretely be in exile without feeling it.
>
> *La condition de l'exilé* 65

Exiliance thus bridges the path from the traditional definition of "exiled writers" within the German Studies context to current writers who have an experience of geographic mobility. It further allows the comparison between the
early stages of exile that take place even before leaving one's country (consciousness of exile) and the condition of exile itself. In this sense, other essays
in this volume shed light on the term exiliance since some deal with the condition of exile, namely authors who fled National Socialism, such as Guy Stern,
Egon Schwarz, Thomas Mann, or Stefan Zweig, while others present aspects of
a consciousness of exile, for instance in the case of Pamela Caughie's essay on
the transgender experience. Moreover, the term exiliance appears an accurate
term for it erases the negative and over-mediatised image of migration, which
is above all an economic term. In addition, talking about migration movements omits a personal and human experience that exiliance includes.

In light of the biographical details previously given, it is clear that Çakır
presents the condition of exile and has chosen to reveal certain aspects of this
experience. However, let me move away from the condition of exile and toward
questions of aesthetics: Does her writing also present a consciousness of exile?
More specifically, have the early stages of exile left a print upon her writing as
such? If so, how has she translated an experience of an initial stage of exile and
it ensuing impact on her life into a poetic creation?

The aforementioned poetry collection titled *Mittwochgedichte* is a short collection of 67 pages with 28 poems. It is characterised by direct poetic structures that paint different scenes, at times mundane, always with an imagist
quality. The free verse contributes to the desire of capturing scenes as they
appear, without the weight of rhymes, codified versification, punctuation, and
capital letters, thus translating a desire for freedom. The poet also pays close
attention to space. Geographical spaces for instance root the first poem within
Vienna, a familiar setting as well as natural or urban settings ("In der Mittagshit-
ze eines Sonntags / Am Ufer des Donaukanals" 11). The space on the page is also
central in poetry, for this genre above all others perhaps is defined by the dia-
logue between content and form. The visual space in Çakır's verse includes a
lot of emptiness, and its bilingual form exhibits a double heritage. Her poetry
is one of movement, abounding in verbs, shifting weather details and vibrant

colours. Her poetry also expresses a strong and perceptible voice that speaks in the first person, and which truly centres around the "lyrisches Ich," voicing deep and personal emotions through the use, for example, of many adjectives. The theme of identity is absolutely central and seems to drive the work as a whole. In this regard, numerous body parts are included: eyes, ears, arms, lips, body, naked, etc. What defines exilic identity here?

Above all, Çakır's poetry reveals a sense of profound duality that follows an experience of being uprooted and migrating to a new place. A duality lies between geographical spheres (Turkey and Austria), points in time (before and now), languages (Turkish and German), and sides of the page. This sense of duality is characteristic of early stages of exile, since one still feels close to the place that was left behind and has not fully arrived in the new culture. Yet, this in-between position may never be completely surmounted and as such, the early stages of exile have a durable presence. In this regard, the poem "Stühle" is interesting to analyse. It reads as follows:

> Lange
> Saß ich zwischen den Stühlen
> Bis
> Ich
> Es satt hatte
> An diesem Tag beschloss ich
> Einen weiteren Stuhl
> Zwischen die Stühle zu schieben
> Zum einen
> Habe ich mir eine Verbindung geschaffen
> Zum anderen
> Endlich einen bequemen Sitz
> > *Mittwochgedichte* 29

In this simple twelve-line poem, Çakır expresses the position she finds herself in as a result of her exilic experience. The image of chairs symbolises each culture and country she is a part of. They don't smoothly fit together and create an uneven surface, an in-betweenness. The assonances in the second line ("Saß ich zwischen den Stühlen") suggest the sound of pushing chairs around. The poet sits in this uncomfortable position, until it finally becomes too oppressive. The solution found is to add a chair in the middle. This conscious action is highlighted by the use of the pronoun "Ich" as well as active verbs ("schieben," "geschaffen"). It's not a question of omitting one chair, but rather of making the connection smoother by adding something new that overlaps both, by considering this third space. One can draw a parallel here with Homi Bhabha's concept of "third space" as described in *The Location of Culture* (53–56). Çakır's image is an expressive way of picturing the work accomplished by exilic poets: writing as a way of uniting two places and overcoming the duality of early exile.

The uneasy duality is further exemplified in the bilingual German and Turkish version of the collection, both of which Çakır wrote. Each version remains on separate pages, unable to co-exist within the same space of a page and thus depicts the apparent divide that lies between them. This fault line is visible through the crack of the page, through the very materiality of this collection which could be viewed as an object of exile that resembles a painting that the readers study and frame as a whole, travelling from one side to the other, in an attempt to compare. Questions regarding the possibility of translation arise here: What is lost and what survives during translation, during an exilic experience? How will a poet work out a path to welcome into a language something that doesn't usually fit and which disturbs? In this regard, Çakır explained in an interview that the image of chairs is a known and widely understood metaphor in German but not in Turkish (cf. "Polyphonie"). Yet, she chose to translate this poem literally and thus stretches the Turkish language in order for this picture to exist in both languages. This particular Turkish poem thus reflects an otherness; one can see and hear a foreign print on it.

The theme of an empty space and separation is inherent in the experience of exiliance and surfaces over and over throughout Çakır collection of poetry with empty, arid landscapes, absent objects, and a sense of being invisible. The double absence she experiences—while in Austria, the Turkish part of her self is absent; in Turkey, certainly the Austrian part of her would be absent—leads to sadness and melancholy (a notion that could be linked to the sociologist Abdelmakel Sayad's work in *Double absence*). In that context, she uses the words "Sehnsucht," "Saudade," and "Hüzün" (the Turkish equivalent) in her work. Exile is also likened to an experience of loss and of death. The theme of death creeps into this collection, for example, in the poem titled "Wüstenasche":

Asche geworden
Mit Sehnsucht Wüste
Getrocknete Lippen aufgerissen
Körper gebrochen
Sehnsucht ist Sonne
Die aufgeht
Langsam brennt sie alles nieder
Und jeden Tag sterbe ich in deiner
Abwesenheit
Sonne
Mittwochgedichte 23

The image of fracture, of a broken body, dying, and absence is very telling. There seems to be a deathly fear of losing a core identity while standing in this empty middle space, an angst-ridden threshold space. In another poem, "Wieder der Tod," she talks of that fear more explicitly: "Ich weiß / Meine Angst ist unbegründet / Meine Angst / Meine Angst vor dem Tod" (*Mittwochgedichte* 45). In "Ein Stück Leben" we read of death: "In einem Leben / Der Tod / Immer auf der Lauer / Immer hinter dir" (*Mittwochgedichte* 25). There also lurks a risk of forgetting: "Er ist nass geworden/ Er hat es vergessen/ Vergessen wie es ist nicht nass zu sein / Vergessen wie es ist zu sein" (*Mittwochgedichte* 27), adding a fear of not existing. Incidentally, the collection opens with a poem about memories of nothing: "Erinnerungen an nichts" (*Mittwochgedichte* 11).

Yet, one would be mistaken to think that the exilic experience, such as it comes through Çakır's writing, is limited to this state of mourning and loss. Just as much as death is an intrinsic part of the experience, so too is the presence of life. Let's turn back to the poem "Stühle." Within the action of adding a third chair lies a vital quality. The act of writing enables a healing process that allows a comfortable position, and this therapeutic poet-identity is claimed in the final poem of the collection with the title "Schreiber": "Schreibe / Streiche durch die Nacht / Sitze in der Tiefe / Schreibe / Meine Lieben / Dich / Mich / und die Ängste" (cf. *Mittwochgedichte* 67). In this sense, one could talk of life-writing in that she not only writes about her own life, but also in that the act of writing enables renewed life. Her poems point to a desire to draw a self-portrait, to turn a mirror onto who she is and to create the space to exist entirely and freely. The poem "Nachruf" reads as follows:

> Als ich in den Spiegel sah
> Heute
> In der Früh
> Sah ich in der Ausgeweintheit meiner Augen
> Tiefe
> Leere
> Trauer
> Jetzt
> Schaue ich, sehe nichts
> Die Leute, so viele Leute!
> Ob die mich sehen?
> *Mittwochgedichte* 13

A link can here be made with Simone Weil's notion of roots and uprootedness. The twentieth-century philosopher advanced that "to be rooted is the perhaps the most important and least recognised need of the human soul" (41). Writing is the means for the poet Çakır to root herself, to see herself and to be seen, and to claim her dual identity. In this sense, the poet is truly writing between cultures, as Homi Bhabha theorises, and exemplifies the Exilzentrum's prize "Schreiben zwischen den Kulturen." The power of poetry is a welcoming space to weave together two sides, two cultures, two languages, multiplicity, resulting in a truly mixed poetic. In this regard the term exiliance is undoubtedly a most interesting term. Indeed, all other terms ('migrant,' 'immigrant,' 'emigrant,' 'exile' etc.) focus on various points of the experience (leaving, arriving, the journey), while exiliance includes the experience as a whole on an individual and subjective level. Nouss states the following: "an exilic experience joins both [the place that is left, the place of arrival], thus creating and outlining a sense of belonging to multiple places" (*Enjeu et fondation des études exiliques* 222).

In conclusion, Seher Çakır's writing results in a multilingual and multicultural poetry that roots itself both in Turkish and Austrian landscapes, that reveals how the themes of life and death are closely intertwined and never quite disappear, and above all how vital it is to root oneself and to claim one's unique and personal voice. One notices in her case that even when the early stage of exile, the initial experience of uprooting occurred at a young age, the wound carries on well in adulthood. There is something never-ending in the process of exile, something that is never fully resolved, and the borders between the early stages of exile and exile itself are fluid. Finally, Çakır is not an entirely unique case. Indeed, there is an entire generation of poets, of women poets, from diverse cultures and languages, who are raising similar questions of identity, who are mourning the loss and fracture that follows exile and who are finding a sense of rebirth through the process of writing.

Works Cited

Primary Sources
Çakır, Seher. *Mittwochgedichte*. Hans Schiler Verlag, 2005.
Çakır, Seher. *Zitronenkuchen für die 56. Frau*. Edition Exil, 2009.
Çakır, Seher. *Ich bin das Festland: Erzählungen*. Edition Exil, 2012.

Anthologies
Ballauff, Karin. *Eure Sprache ist nicht meine Sprache: Texte von Migrantinnen in Österreich*. Milena-Verlag, 2002.
Dağdevir, Yeliz. *Heim.at: Burgaz Projekt ; Gedichte von Migrantinnen und Migranten aus der Türkei in Österreich*. EYE Literaturverlag, 2004.

Die Fremde in mir, Lyrik und Prosa der österreichischen Volksgruppen und Zuwanderer, ein Lesebuch. Hermagoras/Mohorjeva Verlag, 1999.

Verein für Kultur Inzing. *andernWOrts. Anthologie.* Skarabäus, 2008.

Interviews

Çakır, Seher. "Polyphonie Mehrsprachigkeit Kreativität Schreiben Interview Datenbank." Interview by Michaela Bürger-Koftis. Vienna, Hotel de France, 04/12/2015, Leitfadeninterview, 66 minutes. http://www.polyphonie.at/?op=interviewdatabase.

Çakır, Seher. "In zwei Kulturen beheimatet." Interview by Stefan Beig. *Wiener Zeitung,* 10/08/2010. https://www.wienerzeitung.at/nachrichten/kultur/mehr_kultur/39750 _In-zwei-Kulturen-beheimatet.html.

Çakır, Seher. "Ich mache Literatur und Punkt!" Interview by Meri Disoski. *Der Standard,* 15/02/2010.

Çakır, Seher. "Zitronenkuchen und Mittwochgedichte." Interview by Elke Ritzlmayr und Paula Graf. *Textfeld Suedost.* https://www.textfeldsuedost.com/gespr%C3%A4che -und-portraits/seher-%C3%A7ak%C4%B1r/, 07/12/2015.

Secondary Sources

Englerth, Holger. "Vom Ausloten der Freiheit: Seher Çakır." In: Wiebke Sievers, *Grenzüberschreitungen: ein literatursoziologischer Blick auf die lange Geschichte von Literatur und Migration.* Böhlau Verlag, 2016.

Grubich, Stefanie. *Lange saß ich zwischen den Stühlen: eine postkoloniale Literaturanalyse mit intersektionalem Ansatz anhand der Werke von Seher Çakır,* 2013. http://othes.univie.ac.at/26139/.

Nouss, Alexis. *La condition de l'exilé.* Éditions de la Maison des sciences de l'homme, 2015.

Nouss, Alexis. "Enjeu et fondation des études exiliques ou Portrait de l'exilé." *Socio,* no. 5, 2015, pp. 241–268.

Sayad, Abdelmalek. *La double absence, Des illusions de l'émigré aux souffrances de l'immigré.* Éditions du Seuils, 1999.

Schwaiger, Silke. *Über die Schwelle: Literatur und Migration um das Kulturzentrum »exil«.* Praesens Verlag, 2016.

Sievers, Wiebke. *Grenzüberschreitungen: ein literatursoziologischer Blick auf die lange Geschichte von Literatur und Migration.* Böhlau Verlag, 2016.

Sievers, Wiebke, Ilker Atac, Philipp Schnell. "Editorial: Turkish migrants and their descendants in Austria, Patterns of exclusion and individual and political response." *Migration Letters,* Volume 11, no. 3, September 2014, pp. 263–274.

Vlasta, Sandra. *Contemporary Migration Literature in German and English: A Comparative Study. Internationale Forschungen zur Allgemeinen und Vergleichenden Literaturwissenschaft*, vol. 187. Brill Rodopi, 2016.

Weil, Simone. *The need for Roots: Prelude to a Declaration of Duties Towards Mankind.* Ark, 1987.

Website

Literaturhaus Wien. http://www.literaturhaus.at/.

PART 5

Diskriminierung in der Theaterwelt und schauspielerische Überlebensfähigkeiten / Discrimination in the Theater World and Acting Skills of Survival

∴

Die „Affäre Ophüls" und die Diskriminierung jüdischer Theaterkünstler vor 1933

Helmut G. Asper

Abstract

Already long before the planned expulsion of Jewish theater artists by National Socialists in 1933, they were discriminated against in Germany and Austria and prevented from carrying out their professions. As early as 1926, the "Genossenschaft deutscher Bühnenangehöriger" published extensive factual material about such discrimination since the Jewish theater artists themselves hardly went public for fear of negative consequences for their careers. An exception was the young director Max Ophüls who resisted his early dismissal for anti-Semitic reasons from the Burgtheater in Vienna and informed the press. With the "Ophüls Affair" and the anti-Semitic experiences of the young actor Walter Wicclair as the point of departure, the entire extent of anti-Semitic harassment will be explored. This essay will show that the radical persecution of theater artists by National Socialists was the consistent continuation of years of discrimination. It by no means emanated just from the National Socialists but was also backed by several political parties as well as broad strata of the population. This discrimination can also be seen within the context of the early stages of exile.

In den Wiener Tageszeitungen wurde Ende April 1926 tagelang unter den Schlagzeilen „Das antisemitische Burgtheater" oder „Das ‚christlich-germanische Kulturideal'. Warum der Burgtheaterregisseur Ophüls gehen muß" über die vorzeitige Kündigung des Regisseurs Max Ophüls[1] aus antisemitischen Gründen berichtet (Asper, „Die Affäre Ophüls" 135). Ophüls war seit September 1925 für drei Jahre am Burgtheater als Regisseur und Schauspieler engagiert mit der üblichen Kündigungsoption zum Spielzeitende. Noch Anfang Februar 1926 hatte der damalige Burgtheaterdirektor Franz Herterich dem jungen Regisseur

---

1   Max Ophüls (eigentlich Oppenheimer, 1902–1957) hatte seine Karriere als Schauspielschüler am Staatstheater Stuttgart begonnen, war als Schauspieler an den Stadttheatern Aachen und Dortmund engagiert, wo er erstmals Regie führte und 1924/25 als Schauspieler und Regisseur an den Vereinigten Stadttheatern Barmen-Elberfeld engagiert (Asper, *Max Ophüls* 45–101).

versichert, dass er weiter engagiert bliebe, worauf Ophüls Angebote dreier renommierter deutscher Bühnen abgelehnt hatte. Aber nachdem Ophüls in seiner Inszenierung des Dramas *Maria Orlowa* von Otto Zoff, auf Drängen Herterichs auch als Schauspieler aufgetreten war, änderte dieser seine Meinung, wie Ophüls der *Wiener Morgenzeitung* schilderte und teilte ihm brieflich mit, „dass er zu seinem größten Bedauern von seinem Kündigungsrecht Gebrauch machen müsse, da [Ophüls] für eine gute Spielleitung noch nicht die nötigen praktischen Erfahrungen besitze." Als Ophüls ihn zur Rede stellte, habe Herterich ihm erklärt: „Es war ein großer Fehler von Ihnen [...], dass Sie in *Maria Orlowa* aufgetreten sind. Maßgebende Persönlichkeiten haben nämlich gesehen, dass Sie Jude sind. Sie wissen ja, wir leben in einem christlich-sozialen Staat und ich muss mich danach richten." Auf Ophüls' Antwort, „[d]as kann doch unmöglich der Standpunkt des Burgtheaterdirektors sein, der muss doch künstlerische Gesichtspunkte im Auge haben!", erwiderte Herterich: „Es ist nun einmal so und daran kann man nichts ändern"(Asper, „Die Affäre Ophüls" 135 f.).

Ophüls hatte zunächst vergeblich versucht, eine Rücknahme der Kündigung zu erreichen, an die Öffentlichkeit wandte er sich erst, nachdem er an das Neue Theater in Frankfurt engagiert worden war, „um nicht den Anschein zu erwecken, dass ich auf dem Wege einer Zeitungskampagne ein neues Engagement erreichen wolle" (Asper, „Die Affäre Ophüls", 136). Herterich dementierte die Vorwürfe natürlich, worauf Ophüls durch seinen Rechtsanwalt die Anschuldigungen wiederholte und in der *Neuen Freien Presse* erklärte, er sei „jederzeit bereit" seine Aussage „vor Gericht unter Eid zu erhärten" (Asper, „Die Affäre Ophüls" 136). Zu dieser gerichtlichen Klärung kam es nicht, der Skandal verlief im Sande. Doch nach Studium der erhaltenen Dokumente (Asper, *Max Ophüls* 116–120) gibt es keinen Zweifel an der Richtigkeit von Ophüls' Darstellung, die auch der damals am Burgtheater engagierte Schauspieler Willy Eichberger in einem Interview 1985 dem Verfasser bestätigt hat (Asper, Interview). Die christlich-soziale Regierung Österreichs war antisemitisch geprägt und sah im Burgtheater ein nationales Kunstinstitut, das vor ‚Überfremdung' geschützt werden sollte. Deshalb hatten Bundestheaterverwaltung und Unterrichtsministerium Herterichs Kompetenzen bei seiner Personalpolitik beschnitten, er musste sich tatsächlich den mehrfach zitierten „maßgebenden Persönlichkeiten beugen" (Asper, „Die Affäre Ophüls" 138 f.). Diesen Vorwurf von Ophüls hat Herterich auch nie dementiert.

Ophüls hatte Mut, den Skandal öffentlich zu machen, denn andere jüdische Schauspieler, die damals aus antisemitischen Gründen an deutschen und österreichischen Theatern gekündigt wurden, scheuten sich, an die Öffentlichkeit zu

gehen, aus Angst, dann erst recht boykottiert zu werden. Der Regisseur und
Schauspieler Walter Wicclair[2] hat erst in seinen Erinnerungen berichtet, dass
auch ihm 1929 in Münster nach einer Spielzeit aus antisemitischen Gründen
gekündigt worden war, obwohl der neue Intendant ihm erst versichert hatte,
„dass mein Vertrag für ein weiteres Jahr verlängert werde. Ganz beiläufig fragte
er nach meiner Religion – und der Vertrag wurde nicht verlängert" (55). Anders
als Ophüls war Wicclair schon 1923 mit massivem Antisemitismus konfrontiert
worden, als er für die Sommerspielzeit nach Borkum verpflichtet worden war.
Noch auf dem Bäderschiff drückte jemand ihm eine Ansichtskarte mit dem be-
rüchtigten Borkum-Lied in die Hand und forderte ihn auf, „kräftig mitzusingen.
Dem Sinne nach lautete er etwa so: ‚Und wer uns naht mit platten Füßen, mit
Nasen krumm und Haaren kraus, der darf nicht unsern Strand betreten, die Juden müssen alle raus" (46).[3] Wicclair sollte den Erbprinzen Karl-Heinrich in
Alt-Heidelberg spielen, aber ihm wurde ob dieser Begrüßung „himmelangst, und
ich machte mich aus dem Staube. Mit meiner Nase konnte ich in Borkum einfach nicht spielen" (46).

Seine sofortige Flucht bewahrte ihn vor den gewalttätigen Anpöbeleien, die
andere Badegäste erlitten, die das wüste antisemitische Treiben auf der Insel
kritisierten, denn Borkum war in der Weimarer Republik „zeitweise zum antisemitischen Tollhaus" geworden, „das reichsweit Aufsehen erregte" (Bajohr 73).
1923 bekam Wicclair immerhin noch ein neues Engagement: „Mein Agent
reichte mich an das Truppentheater in Munsterlager weiter. Dort musste ich
dann doch den Karl-Heinz spielen [...]. Mit weißen Strichen auf der Nase mim-
te ich einen ‚arischen' Prinzen mit gerader Nase" (46 f.). Nach seiner Kündigung
1929 bekam Wicclair jedoch kein vergleichbares Engagement mehr. Denn als
Folge der Wirtschaftskrise hatten zahlreiche Theater schließen müssen, und
die Zahl der arbeitslosen Schauspieler war sprunghaft angestiegen: „Um Tarife
und Engagements wurde erbittert gekämpft. Nazis erhielten in Stadtverwal-
tungen Einfluss auf die Theaterpolitik. Wenn man von einer Agentur vermittelt wurde, spielten Parteibuch und Religion eine ausschlaggebende Rolle. Ich
besaß weder ein Parteibuch noch die richtige Religion" (57). Wicclair schlug
sich durch mit kurzfristigen und unsicheren Engagements bei Zirkus- und
Wanderbühnenunternehmungen. Schließlich gründete er mit finanzieller

---

2   Walter Wicclair (eigentlich Weinlaub, 1901–1998) begann seine Karriere als Schauspieler 1920
    am Stadttheater Gleiwitz. Er änderte im Exil in der Tschechoslowakei seinen Namen in Wie-
    lau, 1938 in den USA in Wicclair.

3   Zum mehrfach geänderten Text des öffentlich gesungenen und auch von der Kurkapelle ge-
    spielten Borkum-Lieds vgl. Bajohr 73–88 und 171–174.

ILLUSTRATION 12.1
Der Schauspieler Walter Wicclair ca. 1923, als er
noch Walter Weinlaub hieß

Unterstützung seiner Eltern Anfang 1932 das erste stehende Theater in seiner
Heimatstadt Kreuzburg, das jedoch nur eine Spielzeit erleben durfte, weil sein
Gründer von den Nazis gewaltsam vertrieben wurde (Asper, *Walter Weinlaub*
32–37).

Auch die Karriere von Ophüls erlitt einen Knick durch den Rauswurf am
Burgtheater, der eine Vorstufe des Exils war. Denn nach dem öffentlichen
Skandal wurde der Regisseur nicht mehr an städtischen und staatlichen Bühnen engagiert, sondern nur noch an privaten Theatern, die von jüdischen Direktoren geleitet wurden. Die Konfrontation mit dem Antisemitismus führte
aber auch dazu, dass der freireligiös erzogene Ophüls sich erstmals bewusst
mit jüdischer Kultur auseinandersetzte und sich gegen die stärker werdenden
reaktionären Kräfte engagierte. Im Neuen Theater inszenierte er 1926 geradezu
programmatisch als erstes Stück *Dybuk* von An-Ski, das in dem im Frankfurter
Westend gelegenen Privattheater beim Publikum erfolgreich war (vgl. Asper,
Max Ophüls 122–125), wohingegen 1930 das *Dybuk*-Gastspiel des Moskauer He-
bräischen Theaters in Würzburg unter Polizeischutz gestellt werden musste.
Trotzdem hat eine von der örtlichen NSDAP aufgeputschte Menge vor dem
Theater die Besucher als „Saujuden" beschimpft und misshandelt (vgl. Oden-
wald 98 f.). Ophüls inszenierte auch weiterhin ganz bewusst zahlreiche Stücke
jüdischer Autoren. 1930 trat er in Breslau mit seiner Inszenierung von Hans
Rehfischs Dokudrama *Die Affäre Dreyfus* dem wachsenden Antisemitismus

entgegen, was wiederum zu Protesten in der rechten Presse gegen den Regisseur führte (vgl. Asper, *Max Ophüls* 165–168).

Die Kündigungen von Ophüls und Wicclair aus antisemitischen Gründen waren jedoch keine Einzelfälle. Vielmehr sind sie nur zwei Beispiele für die Diskriminierung und Verfolgung, die jüdische Theaterkünstler in Österreich und der Weimarer Republik vor 1933 ertragen mussten, wie der Tatsachenbericht „Jüdische Schauspieler und antisemitische Direktoren" zeigt, den die Genossenschaft Deutscher Bühnen-Angehöriger (GDBA) 1926 in ihrem Organ *Der neue Weg* veröffentlichte:

> In letzter Zeit laufen beim Präsidium der Deutschen Bühnengenossenschaft zahlreiche Beschwerden ein. Es beklagen sich jüdische Bühnenangehörige darüber, dass der Antisemitismus unter den Theaterleitern und den staatlichen und städtischen Theater-Aufsichtsbehörden außerordentlich zunimmt. Selbst tüchtige jüdische Künstler könnten oft kein Engagement finden. Die Bühnengenossenschaft, die zu ihren Mitgliedern Angehörige aller Konfessionen und Weltanschauungen zählt, durfte diese Mitteilungen, die ihr von vertrauenswürdiger Seite zukommen, nicht unbeachtet lassen. Sie sieht sich daher gezwungen, das wichtigste Tatsachenmaterial, das diese unerfreulichen Verhältnisse beleuchtet, der Oeffentlichkeit zu unterbreiten".
>
> *Der neue Weg 1926,* 295

Der Bericht führte zahlreiche Fälle an, zu denen der GDBA Dokumente und Aussagen vorlagen. So bekannte sich der Intendant einer „sehr bekannten Bühne" (295) ganz offen zum Antisemitismus und lehnte es prinzipiell ab, jüdische Schauspieler und Regisseure zu engagieren. Noch skandalöser war, dass mehrere Direktoren besonders im Osten und im Norden Deutschlands von den vorgesetzten städtischen Behörden gezwungen wurden, keine Juden zu engagieren. Das deckt sich mit Wicclairs Einschätzung der Situation in Münster: „In der streng katholischen Stadt brütete die Reaktion und ich nehme an, dass der Intendant bei Einstellungen für die Spielzeit 1929/30 nicht mehr sein eigener Herr war" (55). Weiter heißt es im Bericht der GDBA, dass „eine ganze Gesellschaft von Intendanten und Direktoren [...] sich offen oder in passivem Widerstand weiger[t], Schauspieler zu engagieren, die nur jüdisch aussehen" (295). Auch Ophüls war sein Aussehen zum Verhängnis geworden, denn ihm wurde gekündigt, nachdem sein „semitisches Ponem" aufgefallen war, über das er in einem Brief an seine Schwester wenige Wochen zuvor noch gescherzt hatte (Asper, *Max Ophüls* 111). Die GDBA hatte die „dokumentarischen Beweise über diese Tatsachen [...] protokollarisch innerhalb der Bühnengenossenschaft

ILLUSTRATION 12.2   Der Schauspieler und Regisseur Max Ophüls ca. 1925

festgelegt und deponiert" (295),[4] nannte jedoch in ihrem Bericht keine Namen – mit Ausnahme des Bühnenvolksbunds (BVB) und seines Generaldirektors Gerst, der

> [...] in der gesamten Provinz auf die Boykottierung der jüdischen Schauspieler hinwirkt. Es bestehe da ein sehr klar erkennbares System, dass es z.B. jüdischen Schauspielern geradezu unmöglich mache, in den Städten an der Wasserkante ein Engagement zu finden. Genau so schlimm stehe es in Schlesien, in Pommern und in Teilen Ostpreußens. Die Theateragenturen seien dem Antisemitismus dieser Direktoren und Intendanten gegenüber vollkommen machtlos. Doch übertreibe man nicht, wenn man die Ursache für diese verhängnisvolle Engagementspolitik mit in der Tätigkeit des Generaldirektors Gerst suche. (295)

---

4   Leider sind diese Dokumente und Protokolle im Archiv der GDBA durch Kriegseinwirkung verloren. Auskunft des Präsidenten der GDBA, Jörg Löwer, an den Verf. v. 23.1.2018.

Konfrontiert mit den Vorwürfen, bestritt der Theaterfunktionär Wilhelm Carl Gerst (1887–1968) jegliche antisemitische Politik, doch war der von ihm 1919 mitgegründete BVB, der gegen den „volksfremdem Geist und die Herrschaft eines bedenkenlosen Vergnügungsgeschäfts" kämpfte und das Theater wieder „zur geistigen Heimat unseres Volkes" machen wollte (*Wille und Werk* 3 f.), eindeutig antisemitisch eingestellt, wie die Formulierung der Ziele ebenso verrät wie die Parole „Bekämpft die Entartungserscheinungen des deutschen Theaters! Unterstützt die christliche Theaterbewegung", mit der neue Mitglieder geworben wurden (abgedruckt bei Boetzkes/Queck 705). Der BVB war eine Sammlungsbewegung christlich-nationaler Kräfte; zahlreiche führende Mitglieder standen dem Zentrum, der Deutschen Volkspartei und der Deutschnationalen Volkspartei nahe und vertraten deren theaterpolitische Interessen. Zwar war der BVB nie so mitgliederstark wie die von ihr bekämpfte sozialistische Volksbühne, aber mit über 200.000 Mitgliedern und den mit öffentlicher Unterstützung eingerichteten sechs eigenen Landestheatern vor allem in der Provinz eine Macht im Theaterwesen der Republik und nachweislich ein Vorreiter antijüdischer Engagementspraktiken. Der BVB engagierte in seinen eigenen Theatern keine jüdischen Schauspieler, und namentlich die norddeutschen Landes- und Ortsgruppen drängten die von den Einnahmen des Besucherrings abhängigen Theater dazu, keine Juden zu beschäftigen (vgl. Kannberg 36–38).

Es blieb auch nicht bei Diffamierungen und Kündigungen der jüdischen Schauspieler. Wie die GDBA berichtete, waren diese „sogar in letzter Zeit einer körperlichen Gefahr ausgesetzt gewesen, wenn sie ihre Pflicht tun wollten" (295). Bei der Uraufführung des 1919 erschienenen Weltkriegsdramas *Die Sands und die Kotzebues* des deutschnationalen Schriftstellers Franz Frobert Kaibel wurde ein jüdischer Schauspieler von Stahlhelm-Mitgliedern tätlich angegriffen, die die Premiere mit Gewalt sprengten und alle „Schauspieler in die Flucht" jagten (295). Die GDBA sah in dieser „skandalierenden Klassen- und Rassenpolitik" ganz zu Recht einen „drohenden Kulturkampf", den sie mit der Veröffentlichung des Berichts „von Beginn an abzustoppen" versuchte (295).

In Wirklichkeit hatte dieser Kulturkampf in Wahrheit schon 1919 begonnen und das Theaterleben der Weimarer Republik und Österreich in den Metropolen und in der Provinz von Beginn an erschüttert. Bereits 1920/21 bei den Skandalen um die *Reigen*-Aufführungen in Berlin, Wien und München hatten sich antisemitische Organisationen mit christlich-nationalen, nationalliberalen und nationalistischen Kräften verbündet und gemeinsam gegen den angeblichen Schmutz und Schund gekämpft, den nach ihrer Meinung jüdische Dramatiker und Theaterdirektoren über die deutschen Bühnen ausgeleert hätten. Gemeinsam mobilisierten sie das sogenannte gesunde Volksempfinden und inszenierten massive Störungen der Aufführungen, um ein Verbot wegen Gefährdung der öffentlichen Ordnung zu erreichen. Die Direktoren der Theater, die den *Reigen* aufführten, wurden in den *Deutschvölkischen Blättern* als „jüdische Geschlechtsspekulanten" denunziert (Pfoser Bd. 2, 148), und der im Berliner *Reigen*-Prozess mitangeklagte Co-Direktor des Theaters, Maximilian Sladek, berichtete, dass er in Briefen als „dicker, fetter, schwarzer, osteuropäischer Jude" und als „galizischer Jude" beschimpft und bedroht worden sei (Pfoser Bd. 2, 147).

Dabei ging es keineswegs nur um die Aufführung des *Reigen*, der zum „Symbol des Judentriumphes über die in den Staub geworfene christlich-nationale Kultur" geworden war, wie das Wiener Hetzblatt *Volkssturm* pathetisch formulierte (Pfoser Bd. 1, 366), sondern um die Säuberung des deutschen Theaters von allen „jüdischen Schweineliteraten und -direktoren, Schieberschweine(n) und Lüstlinge(n)" (Pfoser Bd. 1, 348), kurz, von allem „Undeutschen" und von aller „Überfremdung" (Odenwald 50). Diese eindeutig antisemitisch aufgeladenen Kampfbegriffe tauchen immer wieder auf auch bei den zahlreichen Protesten gegen Stücke von Ernst Toller, Carl Zuckmayer, Friedrich Wolf und Julius Hay (vgl. Odenwald 85 ff.). Das deutsche Theater sollte gänzlich von der „jüdisch-negroiden Kultur" (Fischer 240) befreit werden. Bei der Uraufführung seiner Oper *Johnny spielt auf* wurde dem Komponisten Ernst Krenek sogar Propagierung von Rassenschande auf der Bühne vorgeworfen. Der scheinbar groteske Vorwurf erklärt sich durch den verbreiteten Hass auf die farbigen französischen Besatzungstruppen, denen allgemein Vergewaltigungen deutscher Frauen nachgesagt wurden.[5] Auf die angebliche „jüdisch-negerische Besudelung" (Fischer 241) der deutschen Oper durch *Johnny spielt auf* verweist noch 1939 die rassistische Karikatur der Titelrolle mit dem Judenstern auf Ausstellungsplakat und Titelblatt der Broschüre *Entartete Musik* (vgl. Dümling/Girth 127).

Dieser radikale Antisemitismus und Rassismus war keineswegs auf die Nationalsozialisten beschränkt, sondern weit über die NSDAP hinaus auch bei christlich-sozialen und deutsch-nationalen Gruppen und Parteien verbreitet, deren antisemitische Rhetorik von der der NSDAP nicht zu unterscheiden ist. So hetzte die Deutschnationale Volkspartei (DNVP) jahrelang im Preußischen Landtag gegen den Intendanten des Preußischen Staatstheaters Leopold Jessner und beschuldigte die Schauspieler Fritz Kortner und Elisabeth Bergner,

---

5   Vgl. dazu die rassistische Karikatur auf der Titelseite der Nr. 22 des *Kladderadatsch* vom 30. Mai 1920, auf der ein schwarzer Gorilla mit französischer Uniformmütze eine weiße Frau wegschleppt. Die Unterschrift lautet: „Der schwarze Terror in deutschen Landen (Frei nach ‚Der Gorilla' von [Emmanuel] Frémiet)" (http://digi.ub.uni-heidelberg.de/diglit/kla1920/0317/ image).

die „aus dem alten Ghetto von Wien" stammten, als Hintermänner Jessners „die neupreußische Ghettokunst an sein Staatstheater" zu importieren und das deutsche Theater unter die Herrschaft der Juden zu bringen (Brand 173 f.). Vor allem Fritz Kortner, meist nur ‚Kortner-Cohn' genannt, war einer der Hauptfeinde der antisemitischen Rechten, auch weil er demonstrativ in Theater und Film mehrfach Judenrollen übernahm, u.a. 1930 Schnitzlers *Professor Bernhardi*, den Bankier Danieli in Alfred Neumanns *Das Haus Danieli* und den Hauptmann Dreyfus in Richard Oswalds gleichnamigem Film 1930, in dem der wachsende Antisemitismus angeprangert wurde. Doch war Kortners Kampf vergebens, denn die jahrelange Hetze hatte schließlich Erfolg: Der Schauspieler wurde von den Theatern und vom Film boykottiert, unternahm deshalb Auslandstourneen, begann Drehbücher zu schreiben und Filmregie zu führen. Kortner erkannte im Rückblick, dass dies bereits eine Vorstufe zum Exil war und kommentierte in seinen Erinnerungen seine Situation in den letzten Jahren der Weimarer Republik: „Aber erst, als man anfing sich zu scheuen, mein Gesicht auf der Leinwand zu zeigen, vertraute man mir eine Regie an. Der Name war immer noch attraktiv, mein Gesicht aber schon ‚rassefremd' geworden" (416).

Erfolgreich war auch das „Kesseltreiben" auf Jessner (Heilmann 410), das Anfang 1930 zu dessen vorzeitiger Entlassung als Intendant führte. Eine gescheiterte Silvesterpremiere „wurde zum Vorwand, um Jessner endgültig los zu werden" (Heilmann 409), der nur noch als Regisseur arbeiten konnte. Weil Regieverträge nicht eingehalten wurden und die ursprünglich zugesagten Gagen durch die Notverordnungen drastisch gekürzt wurden, geriet Jessner schon vor seiner Emigration 1933 in wirtschaftliche Not. Auch der ebenfalls von rechts heftig angefeindeten Elisabeth Bergner wurde im November 1932 am Preußischen Staatstheater auf Grund eines neuen Gesetzes (s. weiter unten) eine Vertragsverlängerung verweigert. Daraufhin fuhr Bergner zu einem bereits geplanten Arbeitsbesuch nach England, von dem sie nicht mehr nach Deutschland zurückkehrte. Es war ihr erster Schritt in die Emigration (vgl. Völker 190).

Trotz der Warnung der GDBA 1926 hatten sich die Probleme für jüdische Künstler seitdem mit der Erstarkung des Nationalsozialismus nur noch verschlimmert. Schon im Juni 1928 beklagte Max Berges in der Genossenschaftszeitung *Der Neue Weg* erneut, dass sich leider die „städtischen Theaterausschüsse [sogar mehren], die ihren Theaterleitern Engagements jüdischer Schauspieler untersagen" (270). Von der rasant steigenden Arbeitslosigkeit der Schauspieler, 1928 ca. 4.000 bis 1932 ca. 6.000, waren die jüdischen Schauspieler besonders betroffen, denn nach dem ‚Preußenschlag' vom 20. Juli 1932 hatte die NSDAP im Preußischen Landtag ein Gesetz durchgesetzt, dass die Staatstheater keine „nichtdeutschstämmigen" Künstler mehr beschäftigen durften (vgl. Rübel 228 f.). Die GDBA protestierte zwar in scharfer Form gegen diese „Einteilung nach politischen oder gar rassepolitischen Grundsätzen" (Rübel 229), war aber letztlich machtlos, weil sie den Theaterleitern keine Vorschriften bei Engagements machen konnte. Das Gesetz bedeutete das Aus für Juden und Ausländer und war ein fatales Signal auch für die Stadttheater. Während viele erwerbslose Schauspieler „wenigstens in der Theorie die Chance [haben] eines Tages doch wieder" ein Engagement zu bekommen, „gilt das nicht mehr für Juden und Halbjuden" konstatierte Hilde Walter noch im Januar 1933 in der *Weltbühne*:

> Wenn die nationalsozialistischen Stadtväter in der Provinz ihre Subventionen von der Judenreinheit des Theaters abhängig machen, so wagen es eine Reihe von Intendanten und Theaterleitern nicht mehr, jüdische Schauspieler zu beschäftigen. Und wenn nicht genug Antisemiten im Stadtparlament sitzen, genügt unter Umständen ein kleiner Theaterskandal, den das Publikum bestreitet. (185 f.)

Es ist festzuhalten, dass die antisemitische Propaganda gegen jüdische Theaterkünstler bereits in der Weimarer Republik erfolgreich war. So schrieb 1928 auch ein Gegner des Antisemitismus, der liberal-demokratische Politiker und Wissenschaftler Willy Hellpach, in seinem Buch *Politische Prognose für Deutschland*, dass sich das Verhältnis von Juden und Nichtjuden „in den Theatern und Konzertsälen vielfach auf 1:25 oder gar auf 1:10 und noch darüber hinaus" verdichte (368). Hellpach führte dies auf die bei Juden „sehr ausgeprägte Sippenhilfe" zurück (369) und warnte, dass durch „ihr sippenweise gehäuftes Auftreten [...] Abwehrreaktionen [...] versteift" würden (369). Doch waren die Behauptungen, dass Juden im Theater überproportional vertreten seien, nicht-jüdische Künstler von ihnen unterdrückt und verdrängt würden und die deutschen Theater ‚verjudet' seien, nachweislich falsch: 1930 waren im gesamten deutschen Theater- und Musikbereich lediglich 2,4 % Juden tätig (vgl. Hermand 32) – aber diese Fakten zählten nicht. Die Hetze gegen alles ‚Undeutsche', gegen die ‚Judenrepublik', gegen die ‚Judenkultur' und den angeblich von Juden „verschuldeten Schandfrieden" (Pfoser Bd. 1, 159) schürte bei den durch den verlorenen Krieg und dessen Folgen verunsicherten Bürgern die Angst, dass die Juden auch noch die Theater besetzen und die deutsche Kultur zerstören wollten. So wandte sich 1921 eine *Versammlung christlicher Arbeiter* in einem *Offenen Brief* gegen die *Reigen*-Aufführung mit den Worten:

> Viele von uns sind Heimkehrer. War unser Kampf und unser Blut nicht mehr wert, als mit einer republikanischen Freiheit zu solcher Auffassung

belohnt zu werden. Manche von uns möchten sich einen Hausstand gründen und können es nicht, da die ortsfremden Wucherer noch immer ungestört ihre Zimmerfluchten bewohnen dürfen. Sollen jetzt diesem Gesindel auch unsere Kunststätten vollends ausgeliefert werden?

PFOSER Bd. 1, 341 f.

Weil sich breite Bevölkerungsschichten von allem Fremden – und dazu gehörten trotz aller Assimilationsbestrebungen auch die deutschen Juden – in ihrer Existenz bedroht fühlten, stieß die Hetze gegen die im Rampenlicht stehenden jüdischen Theaterkünstler auf allgemeine Zustimmung, so dass sie bereits in der Weimarer Republik diskriminiert, bedroht und nachhaltig in ihrer Berufsausübung behindert wurden – es war bereits eine Vorstufe des Exils. Die massenhafte Vertreibung der jüdischen und ausländischen Theater- und Filmkünstler sofort nach der Machtübernahme der Nationalsozialisten war die konsequente Fortsetzung dieser Diskriminierung, Bedrohung und Behinderung vor 1933. Etwa 7.000 Theaterkünstler wurden aus rassistischen und politischen Gründen verfolgt und vertrieben (vgl. Trapp 5). Der Dirigent Herbert Zipper, dessen Vertrag in Düsseldorf nicht verlängert wurde, erinnerte sich, dass er gemeinsam „with a large number of other artists whose contracts had expired" im Juni 1933 zurück nach Wien fuhr: „At every stop more artists would board the train; it was a strangely grim reunion among many friends and acquaintances of Zipper" (Cummins 61 f.). Auch der an den Städtischen Bühnen Essen engagierte Regisseur P. Walter Jacob war schon Ende 1932 kaltgestellt worden und wurde am 29. März 1933 vorzeitig wegen der „zur Zeit vorhandenen Stimmung weiter Volkskreise" vom Oberbürgermeister entlassen (Naumann 40). Er flüchtete nach mehreren Zwischenstationen schließlich nach Argentinien, wie Robert Kelz in seinem Beitrag „Theater on the Move: Routes to Buenos Aires" in diesem Band ausführt.

Auch Max Ophüls und Walter Wicclair wurden 1933 aus Deutschland vertrieben: Wicclair wurde im Februar 1933 von SA-Schlägern im Theater überfallen, brutal misshandelt und schwer verletzt. Nach seiner Genesung floh er in die Niederlande, von dort in die ČSR, wo er bis kurz vor dem Einmarsch der Nazitruppen getarnt als Walter Wielau am Theater in Leitmeritz als Schauspieler und Regisseur wirkte und 1938 schließlich in die USA ging, wo er die Freie Bühne Los Angeles gründete. Max Ophüls musste im März 1933 Proben im Berliner Komödienhaus abbrechen, nachdem Rosenbergs *Kampfbund für deutsche Kultur* das Theater übernommen hatten und exilierte zum zweiten Mal, diesmal nach Frankreich. Seine Emigration habe sich „unheldisch" vollzogen. „Fliehen ist keine Tat" schrieb Ophüls in seinen Erinnerungen (135). In Frankreich wurde er 1938 eingebürgert und musste als französischer Soldat am Krieg

ILLUSTRATION 12.3   Verfolgte und nicht-verfolgte Schauspieler am Stadttheater Leitmeritz
                     1938. Von links nach rechts stehend: Walter Wielau (Wicclair,
                     emigriert), Emil Koch, Walter Kent-Kohner (emigriert), Mary Ronald;
                     sitzend: Irma Laufer († 1942 KZ), Gisela Werbezirk (emigriert)

ILLUSTRATION 12.4
Max Ophüls als französischer Soldat (1939)

teilnehmen. Nach der Niederlage Frankreichs exilierte Ophüls 1941 zum dritten Mal in die USA, wo er erst nach jahrelanger Arbeitslosigkeit wieder als Regisseur arbeiten konnte.

Zitierte Literatur

Anonym. „Jüdische Schauspieler und antisemitische Direktoren". *Der neue Weg,* Jg. 55, Nr.17/18 (1926), S. 295.

Asper, Helmut G. „Die Affäre Ophüls. Antisemitismus am Wiener Burgtheater 1926". *TheaterZeitSchrift,* H. 22 (1987), S. 135–142.

Asper, Helmut G. Interview des Verfassers mit Willy Eichberger/Carl Esmond am 27. März 1985 in Brentwood, CA.

Asper, Helmut G. *Walter Weinlaub und die Gerhart-Hauptmann-Bühne. Eine Dokumentation zum 90. Geburtstag von Walter Wicclair am 24. Januar 1991.* Universität Dortmund Forschungsstelle Ostmitteleuropa, 1991.

Asper, Helmut G.: *Max Ophüls. Eine Biographie mit zahlreichen Dokumenten, Texten und Bildern.* Bertz, 1998.

Bajohr, Frank. *„Unser Hotel ist judenfrei". Bäder-Antisemitismus im 19. und 20. Jahrhundert.* 3. Aufl. Fischer, 2003.

Berges, Max. „Antisemitismus und Theater". *Der Neue Weg,* Jg. 58, Nr.14 (1929), S. 270.

Boetzkes, Manfred/Marion Queck. „Die Theaterverhältnisse nach der Novemberrevolution". *Theater in der Weimarer Republik.* Hg. Kunstamt Kreuzberg und Institut für Theaterwissenschaft der Universität Köln, 1977, S. 687–715.

Brand, Mathias. *Fritz Kortner in der Weimarer Republik.* Schäuble, 1981.

Cummins, Paul F. *Dachau Song.* Lang, 1992.

Dümling, Albrecht/Peter Girth. *Entartete Musik. Zur Düsseldorfer Ausstellung von 1938. Eine kommentierte Rekonstruktion.* Landeshauptstadt Düsseldorf, 1988.

Fischer, Jens-Malte. „Die ‚jüdisch-negroide Epoche.' Antisemitismus im Musik- und Theaterleben der Weimarer Republik". *Theatralia Judaica. Emanzipation und Antisemitismus als Momente der Theatergeschichte. Von der Lessing-Zeit bis zur Shoah.* Hrsg. Hans-Peter Bayerdörfer. Max Niemeyer, 1992, S. 228–243.

Heilmann, Matthias. *Leopold Jessner – Intendant der Republik. Der Weg eines deutsch-jüdischen Regisseurs aus Ostpreußen.* Theatron. Studien zur Geschichte und Theorie der dramatischen Künste, Bd. 47. Max Niemeyer, 2005.

Hellpach, Willy. *Politische Prognose für Deutschland.* S. Fischer Verlag, 1928.

Kannberg, Gregor. *Der Bühnenvolksbund. Aufbau und Krise des Christlich-Deutschen Bühnenvolksbundes 1919–1933.* Ralf Leppin, 1997.

Kortner, Fritz. *Aller Tage Abend.* Kindler, 1959.

Naumann, Uwe (Hrsg.). *Ein Theatermann im Exil: P. Walter Jacob.* Ernst Kabel Verlag, 1985.

Odenwald, Florian. *Der nazistische Kampf gegen das ‚Undeutsche' in Theater und Film 1920–1945.* Münchener Universitätsschriften Theaterwissenschaft, Bd. 8. Herbert Utz, 2006.

Ophüls, Max. *Spiel im Dasein. Eine Rückblende.* Mit einem Vorwort von Marcel Ophüls und einem Nachwort von Hilde Ophüls. Hrsg. u. kommentiert v. Helmut G. Asper. Alexander, 2015.

Pfoser, Alfred/Kristina Pfoser-Schewig/Gerhard Renner (Hrsg.). *Schnitzlers ‚Reigen'. Zehn Dialoge und ihre Skandalgeschichte. Analysen und Dokumente. Bd. 1: Der Skandal; Bd. 2: Die Prozesse.* Fischer, 1993.

Rübel, Joachim. *Geschichte der Genossenschaft Deutscher Bühnen-Angehörigen.* Bühnenschriften-Vertriebs-GmbH, 1992.

Trapp, Frithjof/Werner Mittenzwei et al. (Hrsg.). *Handbuch des deutschsprachigen Exiltheaters 1933–1945. Bd. 1: Verfolgung und Exil deutschsprachiger Theaterkünstler.* K.G. Saur, 1999.

Völker, Klaus. *Elisabeth Bergner. Das Leben einer Schauspielerin.* Edition Hentrich, 1990.

Walter, Hilde. „Judenreines Theater". *Weltbühne*, 29. Jg., Nr. 5 (1933), S. 185–186.

Wicclair, Walter. *Von Kreuzburg bis Hollywood.* Henschelverlag, 1975.

Wille und Werk. Ein Handbuch des Bühnenvolksbundes. Hrsg. Arbeitsgemeinschaft in der Reichsgeschäftsstelle des Bühnenvolksbundes. Unter Leitung von Wilhelm Karl Gerst. Bühnenvolksbundverlag, 1928.

CHAPTER 13

Thespians in Transit: Exile and Emigration to Buenos Aires

Robert Kelz

Abstract

During the late 1930s German emigrants in Buenos Aires, Argentina, founded the Nazi German Theater and its antifascist adversary, the Free German Stage. This paper focuses on the preliminary stages of emigration from Europe to South America of two actors—Paul Walter Jacob, founder of the Free German Stage, and his counterpart and opponent, Ludwig Ney, at the German Theater. Director and manager of a successful touring ensemble funded by the Strength through Joy organization in Germany, Ney abruptly emigrated to Argentina in 1937. Shifting to Jacob, this paper then reconstructs his final years in Germany before fleeing from Nazism in 1933 as a Jewish actor. Although these artists formed sharply hostile alliances, during the preliminary stages of emigration they honed overlapping survival skills and then deployed surprisingly similar tactics to prosper in Buenos Aires.

1   Introduction

In the late 1930s, German emigrants in Buenos Aires, Argentina, founded both the Nazi German Theater and its antifascist opponent, the Free German Stage. Funded by Joseph Goebbels's Ministry of Propaganda, the hitherto unstudied German Theater performed the German Classics to sold-out audiences at the grand Argentine National Theater. In a strategy of retaliation, the next year German-speaking Jewish refugees founded the Free German Stage, which became the only exilic theater worldwide to stage regular performances throughout World War II. Intense competition between these communities and their theaters continued for decades after 1945. Both stages performed regularly until the mid-1960s and, eventually, referred to themselves as emigrant theaters.

Covering the period from 1932 to 1936, this essay focuses on the last years in Germany of Ludwig Ney, founder of the German Theater, and his adversary at the Free German Stage, Paul Walter Jacob. Although his choice to emigrate

ILLUSTRATION 13.1
Portrait of Ludwig Ney in 1940

from Germany in 1936 is anomalous among adherents of Hitlerism, Ney was no dissident. He was not sent to Argentina by the Nazi regime, however both in Germany and Argentina Ney actively collaborated with Nazi officials and purposefully contributed to the dissemination of National Socialist ideology. Jacob, by contrast, was a vocal antifascist and a victim of Nazi anti-Semitism. The case of Ney and Jacob demonstrate the breadth of the term, "emigration," invoked by Egon Schwarz earlier in this book. While both men were emigrants, only Jacob was a refugee in exile. Despite their sharp political differences, the crucial preliminary stages of emigration prepared both Ney and Jacob for professional success across the Atlantic on dramatic stages in Argentina. Therefore, alongside the diverse contributions to this volume, the present inquiry into the opposing worlds of Nazi and antifascist theater reveals intersecting elements of the emigration experience, however dissimilar the participants may be.

2   Ludwig Ney: "A Soldier of Art"

Ludwig Ney was born into a German military family in Landau on May 29, 1901. Like his rival in Buenos Aires, Paul Walter Jacob, Ney faced vehement opposition

ILLUSTRATION 13.2   The ensemble of the Free German Stage following its debut season in 1940

from his family toward his decision to become an actor. He had to flee home, living as a pauper before being admitted to the Mannheim School of Theater and Music. In 1922, he joined the cast of a small theater in Sonneberg, Thuringia. It was a humble start. Ney had to study his lines during intermissions because, with thrice weekly premieres, it was impossible to prepare well for each performance. He even had to fashion his own costumes because of the theater's tight budget and the scarcity of props in the rural area. Later, Ney claimed that these conditions prepared him for South America, because they taught him optimism, resilience, and improvisation (cf. "Gespräch" 10).

Ney got his break in 1927 when Hanns Niedecken-Gebhard contracted him to collaborate on Händel's scenic oratorios in Münster, and then again in subsequent years at the renowned cultural festivals held annually at the Heidelberg Castle. Esteemed by Joseph Goebbels, who entrusted him with artistic oversight for the opening ceremony of the 1936 Olympic Games in Berlin and performances honoring the German capital's 700th anniversary in 1937, Niedecken-Gebhard reported to the Reich Theater Chamber that Ney's innovative vision would help to fill a palpable void in the theater landscape in Germany (cf. "Deutsches Theater"). In the same article, the *Deutsche La Plata Zeitung* noted that these activities later garnered Ney a teaching position at the prestigious Folkwang School in Essen. In this city he coincided with a young conductor and director at the municipal theater—his future foe in Argentina, Paul Walter Jacob. Eventually they were reunited in Buenos Aires, but in Essen

Jacob and Ney had very divergent trajectories. In March 1933, the city's most widely read newspaper derided the Jewish Jacob as a stain on German art and forced him into exile (cf. "Randbemerkungen"). Whether or not Ney read of Jacob's dismissal, the scandal clearly signaled that his own acting career was contingent on the goodwill of Nazi authorities. Shortly thereafter, together with his former student and future wife, Irene Winkler, Ney left the Folkwang School to work full-time as an actor and director. In Berlin he founded a group called the Romantic Cabaret, which gained funding from the Strength Through Joy (*Kraft durch Freude*) organization and toured throughout Germany from 1934 to 1936. Its lifespan thus coincided with National Socialists' efforts to consolidate their domination of German cultural life.

A branch of the German Labor Front, Strength Through Joy had the self-declared goal of creating a National Socialist people's community while facilitating the perfection and refinement of the German people (cf. Baranowski 40–42). Perhaps best known for its activities in the tourism sector, Strength Through Joy also provided the German working class affordable access to cultural events, such as concerts and theater. The primary goal of such performances, as articulated in the theater journal *Die Bühne*, was to cultivate ethnic unity through shared experiences of German cultural heritage (cf. Strobl 52). In addition to theater ensembles, critics were also conscripted into this endeavor. Pressured by the *Reich Press Chamber* and the 1933 Editors' Law, critics had the task of assisting—or impelling—theaters to inculcate citizens with Nazi values (cf. Ruppelt 116). In the Romantic Cabaret's theater programs, Ney affirmed the National Socialist agenda of achieving a cohesive citizenry through cultural heritage by declaring his group's aspiration to reinforce the timeless virtues of the German race through art (cf. "Romantische Kleinkunstbühne Program" 3). As a self-described "soldier of art," he exhorted his entire cast to devote themselves completely to this objective (cf. "Gespräch" 10).[1]

On September 8, 1934, the Romantic Cabaret debuted at the well-known Tingel Tangel Theater, a political cabaret venue founded in 1931 by the Jewish composer Friedrich Hollaender in the cellar of the Theater of the West in Berlin. By 1934, Hollaender already had fled to Paris, and coordination of the venue to Nazism was underway.[2] Ney's debut garnered approving reviews from local media. The *Berliner Zeitung* praised Ney as the "heroic father of the

---

1   All translations in this essay are by the author.
2   Remnants of the political program at the Tingel Tangel Theater persevered until 1935, when the Gestapo arrested actors Walter Gross, Günther Lüders, and Walter Lieck for subversive remarks during performances. The venue's reputation notwithstanding, there appears to have been no subversion in Ney's debut.

group," and lauded his troupe's performance. Their repertoire spanned from canonical figures, such as Hans Sachs and Matthias Claudius, to lesser known regional folk songs from Mecklenburg and Franconia, many of which Ney had unearthed himself during his travels throughout Germany. Reviewers across Germany commended Ney for utilizing the cabaret genre to revitalize obscure works from the rich tradition of Germanic song, dance, theater, and poetry: "the director draws from the reservoir of history—German history" (cf. "Romantische Kleinkunstbühne" 1934). Asserting that the presentation represented the soul of unadulterated German folklore, the *Würzburg General Anzeiger* reflected that the Romantic Cabaret's greatest accomplishment was to have created cabaret-style ditties that cultivated and informed Germans' sense of national identity (cf. "Ein heiter-besinnlicher Abend"). Reviewing the ensemble's performance at the Residence Theater in Wiesbaden on December 13, 1935, the *Landeszeitung für Rhein-Main* praised the ensemble for sculpting theatergoers' sense of German cultural history in the image of National Socialism (cf. "Romantische Kleinkunstbühne" 1935). Yet, this performance proved to be the Romantic Cabaret's swansong.

Months later, Ney and his co-thespian and partner, Irene Winkler, abruptly abandoned Europe and sailed for South America. Most emigrants from Nazi Germany were victims of Hitler's tyranny who sought safety abroad, but not Ney. Although it abstained from bellicose depictions of German history and occasionally incorporated multicultural accents into its performances, in the last analysis the Romantic Cabaret was a propagandistic theater that strongly upheld Nazism. Furthermore, Ney stood to gain from Hitlerism. The mass exodus of persecuted artists opened opportunities for racially and politically unobjectionable actors such as himself. Rainer Schlösser's Reich Theater Chamber recruited and funded artists for German stages and, as an experienced thespian and pedagogue, Ney was in fine position to profit from these programs. He had collaborated with major figures in the Nazi German theater milieu, such as Niedecken-Gebhard, and already was the director of his own ensemble with funding from the influential Strength Through Joy organization. His future under the swastika appeared bright, but he decided to leave Germany with no arrangements for continued support by National Socialist authorities in distant Paraguay. So why, with so much in his favor, did Ney voluntarily emigrate and join the thousands of persecuted refugees fleeing Europe?

Answers to this question are elusive. Cornelia Ney told me that her father was enticed by an invitation to a friend's plantation in Paraguay, which is possible but seems simplistic and fails to convince because corroborating evidence is lacking (cf. Ney interview). An alternative theory might be that the Nazi government could have contracted Ney to establish a German theater in South America. Indeed, when Ney launched the German Theater in Buenos

Aires in 1938, it was sponsored by the Argentine branch of Strength Through Joy. However, Ney's arrival in Paraguay and yearlong sojourn there before moving to Buenos Aires do not align with this scenario. Strength Through Joy did not exist in Paraguay, and reports of Ney's theatrical activities there do not mention any association with German institutions (cf. "Die Pfingstkutsche" 12 and "Deutsche Review" 16). All sources agree that Ney's cooperation with Strength Through Joy and the German Embassy in Argentina originated at some point after he had arrived in South America. Despite interviews with Ney's former colleagues and his family, as well very extensive archival research, no compelling narrative has emerged to clarify why he left Europe in the first place (cf. "Gespräch" 10–11, Majian 70, and Knepler 2). A final possibility is that his partner, Irene Winkler, had Jewish ancestry. Her maiden name, Winkler, can indicate Jewish genealogy. Such lineage could have motivated her and Ludwig Ney to emigrate, a decision which otherwise resists explanation. However, there is no hard proof to support this hypothesis; it is limited to conjecture.

Whatever his motivation, Ney's experiences in Germany functioned as a preliminary phase of emigration that prepared him well for Argentina (cf. "Zusammenarbeit"). His abilities as a pedagogue and director were valuable in Buenos Aires, where some members of his cast were not professional actors. Additionally, in rural Germany, Ney had learned to achieve a maximum artistic effect with minimal resources (cf. "Ein heiter-besinnlicher Abend"). Perhaps most importantly, as he reflected in a 1938 interview with the magazine, *Teutonia*, his passion for theater eclipsed whatever challenges he faced: "It is the greatest happiness to have a profession that is a source of happiness in itself. In this situation, difficulties do not really matter" (cf. "Gespräch" 11). Under the auspices of the Nazi embassy and Strength Through Joy, Ludwig Ney's inaugural performance in Buenos Aires took place on May 19, 1938 (cf. "Deutsche Kleinkunstbühne"). Success was instantaneous. Estimates placed attendance for his theater's official productions during the 1939 theater season at 18,000, and in 1942 his group began performing at the Argentine National Theater, which had capacity for 1,155 spectators (cf. "Deutsches Theater" and "Theater Abonnement"). Ney would continue to be a prominent player on stages in Argentina for the next thirty-four years.

3   Paul Walter Jacob: Theater in Times of Crisis

Paul Walter Jacob was born to a middle-class orthodox Jewish family on January 26, 1905. He attended the Hessian Secondary School in Mainz and simultaneously studied music at the Paul Schumacher Conservatory. When he completed his studies, Jacob decided to pursue a career as an actor or musician, which enraged his family. His mother even lashed him with a dog whip and insisted he become a merchant like his father (cf. Naumann 23). Similar to Ney, this conflict discloses a reserve of willpower essential to Jacob's perseverance as an exilic artist. It also reveals that his family groomed him for a career in business. Both in Europe and South America, Jacob's achievements are attributable to his ability to marry creative talent with business acumen. In 1923, Jacob enrolled at Max Reinhardt's acting school at the German Theater in Berlin. After working as assistant conductor at the Berlin State Opera, from 1930 to 1933 he was a conductor, director, and actor in Koblenz, Lübeck, Wuppertal, and Essen. Scholars have argued that he developed competencies as a theater director and entrepreneur already during the European part of his exile in Luxemburg, France, and Czechoslovakia. However, Jacob's memoirs show that these skills—which would prove to be vital in Argentina—stem from his work in pre-1933 Germany (cf. Lemmer 18 and Naumann 61).[3]

At provincial German stages and later in Buenos Aires, Jacob was confronted with the challenge of managing theaters in politically volatile environments with unstable, insufficient finances, incomplete and traumatized ensembles, and a small, beleaguered public. In 1931, his first season at the Wuppertal Municipal Theater, financially strapped local authorities threatened to close the theater the following year. Management had to rapidly refashion the stage into a solvent business enterprise while maintaining its cultural value. As the representative of the German Actors Guild in Wuppertal, Jacob played a leading role in this effort. The core of the Wuppertal theater's predicament was dwindling audiences. According to Jacob, the theater was failing because it had neglected its obligations as a community institution. Consequently, it had grown estranged from spectators, a potentially fatal development. The theater had to recover its historical, emotional, and moral appeal while also negotiating the harsh economic climate of 1932. Jacob defined three steps to surmount this challenge: (1) establish a close and direct rapport between residents and their theater; (2) increase its pull and profile as a popular entertainment option through an aggressive, modernized advertising campaign, and (3) reform the

---

3 In 1935, Jacob was engaged by Walter Eberhard for the newly founded Luxemburg touring theater, The Comedy. Anne Lemmer and Uwe Naumann have claimed that Eberhard was Jacob's mentor but, in fact, Jacob tried to advise his older colleague on personnel and budgeting, futilely exhorting him to maintain a small ensemble to reduce costs. When the stage went bankrupt in 1936, its cast was left penniless and unemployed. The actors even had to sue Eberhard for unpaid wages. In Buenos Aires, Jacob took every precaution to ensure that the Free German Stage did not repeat the fiasco of Luxemburg (cf. Jacob to Eberhard 1935 and 1936, and Jacob to Arndt).

repertoire to suit the tastes of theatergoers in such turbulent times (cf. Jacob, "Denkschrift" 2–7 and Jacob, "Bemerkungen" 1–2). To its details, Jacob's successful strategy for rescuing the Wuppertal theater laid the groundwork for the program he followed at the Free German Stage in Buenos Aires. Meanwhile, at the nationalist German Theater, Ney copied Jacob's tactics.

Jacob believed the crises of 1932 could strengthen the bond between the stage and its community. Writing in the local newspaper, *Bergische Heimat*, Jacob presciently described 1932 as a grave hour on the threshold of a dark, menacing future. Against this backdrop of shared struggle, he depicted Wuppertal's theater as a cultural edifice, constructed with sacrifice over generations. Its cast faced a ruinous fate should the stage close, so Jacob exhorted his readers: "Rescue art and artists! Save culture from its downfall!" (cf. Jacob, "Bevölkerung" 22). His appeal evoked empathy for local artists while simultaneously empowering citizens to protect and preserve their cultural traditions.

The relationship between theater and city, Jacob stressed, was interdependent. Amidst economic and social tumult, just months before the National Socialists' victories in the Reichstag elections of 1932, Jacob claimed its stage would strengthen and unite Wuppertal: "In times of distress, German theater has always given you solidarity and edification!" (cf. Jacob, "Bevölkerung" 22). Jacob's admonishment that the arts were an essential source of guidance in times of crisis, intersects with Ottmar Ette's concept of literary studies as a survival science. A dynamic und highly regenerative repository of knowledge for living, literature provides audiences a vast store of accumulated wisdom, moral support, and guidance (Ette 5). Dramatic performances, then, test these ideas in a fictional laboratory and enable theatergoers to hone survival strategies for precarious external environments. Crucially, Jacob noted, live theater is a shared experience imbued with a vitalizing social dimension that transcends the typically solitary act of reading (cf. Jacob, "Bevölkerung" 22). Moreover, the communal commitment required to sustain the theater fortifies the social union that each performance engendered. In Buenos Aires, too, both antifascist and nationalist immigrant blocs asserted that the theatrical experience would consolidate their local community as well as inform and inspire its efforts to withstand crises during the Nazi and postwar periods. Victims and supporters of Nazism agreed that German theater had a pivotal role to play in the tenuous transition from despair to prosperity.

In tandem with these goals, Jacob elaborated a pragmatic business model that he followed closely in Wuppertal and Buenos Aires. Despite its status as a sacrosanct German cultural institution, the stage was subject to the same competition as any business enterprise and had to formulate corresponding marketing tactics (cf. Jacob, "Bemerkungen" 2). Failure to do so amounted to suicidal snobbery. One of Jacob's maxims was: "The theater has no future unless it wins over the youth" (cf. Jacob, "Denkschrift" 5). Hence, in Wuppertal, Jacob presented dramas targeting younger audiences, put on workshops for school pupils, and offered discounted ticket packages for educational institutions. Both he and Ney would do the same in Buenos Aires. Another tactic was to utilize local news outlets as a means of connecting with the community. Anticipating the Free German Stage's cooperation with the antifascist *Argentinisches Tageblatt* and the German Theater's relationship with the pro-Nazi *Deutsche La Plata Zeitung*, respectively, Jacob envisioned thorough previews, personalized anecdotes from backstage, reports on social and economic issues facing the theater, and essays about works being prepared for performance. By emphasizing offstage communication between the audience and ensemble, both Jacob and Ney aimed to forge a community identity centered around theater.

Jacob also reformed the repertoire. A quicker rotation of dramas would best exploit promotional activities by staging plays closer to the time of the publicity and before it had been forgotten (cf. Jacob, "Bemerkungen" 2). While this would limit rehearsals, Jacob insisted that the foundation of any marketing must be the quality of the performance itself (cf. Jacob, "Denkschrift" 8). For this reason, his plans were contingent on seasoned thespians working under a director who knows them well and understands how to distribute roles for each piece. The Free German Stage would draw exiled actors from across South America, several of whom had worked with Jacob in Europe and understood how to implement this strategy.[4] Finally, more premieres would encourage habitual theatergoers to attend a greater number of productions, thus improving ticket sales and cultivating a closer relationship between audiences and actors.

Polemically, Jacob argued that the cultural theater had to attract a broader public by balancing the Classics and highbrow contemporary drama with simple, lighthearted comedies, operettas, and even farces. The core of the repertoire had to be literary dramas, but these would be carried by popular, profitable lighter genres (cf. Jacob, "Denkschrift" 8). A firm and much-debated policy at the Free German Stage in Buenos Aires (cf. Bab, Pohle, 47–48, Trapp 118–137), Jacob had already formulated this plan in Germany in 1932, theorizing that in times of social and political crisis, the lighter muse could allay audiences' hardships by offering respite from a troubled reality (cf. Jacob, "Bemerkungen" 1).

Jacob's strategy helped to save the Wuppertal Municipal Theater and was a blueprint for his success with the antifascist Free German Stage in Argentina. Furthermore, Ney incorporated many of his ideas at the rival Nazi German

---

4   Some of these thespians included Jacques Arndt from Uruguay, Ernst Wurmser and Georg Braun from Bolivia, and Wolfgang Vacano from Chile.

Theater. Despite divergent or, in the case of Buenos Aires, bitterly conflictive audiences, each enterprise took a remarkably similar approach to community building, marketing, and the composition of its repertoire. The survival of all three stages lends credence to Jacob's tactics and marks common ground between him and Ney as they strove to establish emigrant theaters in South America.

4   Conclusion

Politically antithetical, Paul Walter Jacob and Ludwig Ney were linked by a mutual, unrelenting passion for the dramatic stage. Despite their obvious differences, these men of the theater had overlapping backgrounds, including their country of origin, language, vocation, professional experiences, and the mutual challenge of prospering as immigrants thousands of miles from their homeland. In Argentina, they underwent similar processes of adaptation and reinvention that Egon Schwarz has identified as germane to the evolution from emigrant to immigrant: the struggles to establish financial stability, learn a new language, construct social and professional networks, and contend with the new customs and moral norms of a foreign culture (cf. Schwarz 18). The preliminary, preparatory stages of emigration that Paul Walter Jacob and Ludwig Ney experienced in Germany taught them essential survival skills for professional success and personal perseverance as immigrant thespians in Argentina. Therefore, this comparison of two very distinct individuals highlights the intersections between contrasting forms of migration. In the case of Ludwig Ney and Paul Walter Jacob, the survival skills acquired before exile or emigration closely resemble each other. Their story underscores the universality of the challenges inherent to migration, and how to confront them.

Works Cited

Bab, Julius. "Deutsches Theater in Argentinien." *Sonntagsblatt: Staats-Zeitung und Herold*, 16 May 1948.

Baranowski, Shelley. *Strength through Joy: Consumerism and Mass Tourism in the Third Reich*. Cambridge UP, 2004.

"Das Theater Abonnement." *Deutsche La Plata Zeitung*, 1 March 1942.

"Die Pfingstkutsche." *Deutsche Zeitung für Paraguay*, 20 May 1937, p. 12.

"Deutsche Review in San Bernardino, Paraguay." *Deutsche La Plata Zeitung*, 30 May 1937, p. 16.

"Deutsches Theater." *Deutsche La Plata Zeitung* 10 March 1940.

"Ein heiter-besinnlicher Abend." *Würzburg General Anzeiger*, 7 February 1935.

Ette, Ottmar. "Literaturwissenschaft als Lebenswissenschaft: Eine Programmschrift im Jahr der Geisteswissenschaften." *Lendemains*, vol. 125, 2007, pp. 7–32.

"Gespräch mit Ludwig Ney." *Teutonia*, September 1938, pp. 10–11.

Jacob, Paul Walter. "An die Bevölkerung Wuppertals." *Bergische Heimat*, January 1932, p. 22.

Jacob, Paul Walter. "Bemerkungen zu Theateretat." Paul Walter Jacob Archive (PWJA) IV c) 253, Hamburg.

Jacob, Paul Walter. "Denkschrift zur Frage Theaterbewerbung." PWJA IV c) 253, Hamburg.

Jacob, Paul Walter to Jacques Arndt. 23 January 1941. PWJA Correspondence, Hamburg.

Jacob, Paul Walter to Walter Eberhard. 17 December 1935. PWJA Correspondence, Hamburg.

Jacob, Paul Walter. 26 January 1936. PWJA Correspondence, Hamburg.

Lemmer, Anne. *Die "Freie Deutsche Bühne" in Buenos Aires 1940–1965*. Hamburger Arbeitsstelle für deutsche Exilliteratur, 1999.

Knepler, Guillermo. "Ludwig Ney: 70. Geburtstag – 50. Bühnenjubiläum." *Argentinisches Tageblatt*, 3 June 1971, p. 2.

Majian, Rosa. "Cuando empiezan a ser argentinos: una familia alemana." *La Nación*, 2 April 1961.

Naumann, Uwe. *Ein Theatermann im Exil: P. Walter Jacob*. Ernst Kabel Verlag, 1985.

Ney, Cornelia. Personal interview. 3 February 2009.

Pohle, Fritz. "Paul Walter Jacob am Rio de la Plata: Der Kurs der FDB – eine exilpolitische Gratwanderung." *Exil*, 7, no. 2, 1987, pp. 34–58.

"Randbemerkungen." *Essener National Zeitung*, 26 March 1933.

"Romantische Kleinkunstbühne." *Landeszeitung für Rhein-Main*, 13 December 1935.

Romantische Kleinkunstbühne Program. 1 July 1935. Collection of Cornelia Ney, La Cumbre, Argentina.

"Romantische Kleinkunstbühne." *Berliner Zeitung*, 8 September 1934.

Ruppelt, Georg. *Schiller im nationalsozialistischen Deutschland. Der Versuch einer Gleichschaltung*. Metzler, 1979.

Schwarz, Egon. "La emigración de la Alemania nazi." *Paul Zech y las condiciones del exilio en la Argentina*, edited by Regula Rohland de Langbehn. Universidad de Buenos Aires, 1999, pp. 13–28.

Strobl, Gerwin. *The Swastika and the Stage: German Theatre and Society, 1933–1945*. Cambridge UP, 2007.

Trapp, Frithjof. "Zwischen Unterhaltungsfunktion und der Erwartung politischer Stellungnahme. Spielplan und künstlerische Konzeption der Freien Deutschen Bühne

Buenos Aires." *Exiltheater und Exildramatik 1933–1945*, edited by Frithjof Trapp. Koch, 1991, pp. 118–137.

"Zusammenarbeit mit einem Künstler." *Deutsche La Plata Zeitung*, 5 January 1941.

PART 6

Literarische Prozesse / Literary Processes

∵

CHAPTER 14

Das Tagebuch der Hertha Nathorff 1933–1945: Versuche der Selbstvergewisserung innerhalb der zentrifugalen Gewalten von Ausgrenzung und Terror, Vertreibung und Exil

Friedericke Heimann

Abstract

The diary of the German-Jewish doctor Hertha Nathorff possesses special meaning both as an historical document as well as a space for self-assurance in the midst of the centrifugal movements of dissolution during her experience of Nazi Germany. On the basis of the diary entries, the various early stages of exile in National Socialist Germany up to Nathorff's emigration to the United States can be illustrated. In the process, her medical profession can be seen both as a means of emancipatory accomplishment as well as loss of that independence due to persecution and exile.

Im Januar 1940, ziemlich genau in der Mitte ihres Lebens, notiert die 45-jährige Hertha Nathorff (sie wurde 98 Jahre alt) „in einer dürftigen Kammer in einer Vorstadt von London" folgende Worte: „Doch eines habe ich gerettet: lose, zerrissene Blätter aus meinem Tagebuch, das ich trotz Angst und Gefahr immer noch zu führen wagte" (Nathorff 13).

Die Berliner Ärztin war im Frühjahr 1939 mit ihrem Mann und dem 14-jährigem Sohn aus dem nationalsozialistischen Deutschland zunächst nach England geflohen, wo die Familie nun schon seit Monaten auf ihre Visa zur Weiterreise in die USA wartete. Während Nathorff die ihr verbliebenen Tagebuchnotizen noch einmal durchgeht und in eine Ordnung zu bringen sucht, bemerkt sie des Weiteren, dass diese Blätter zugleich dokumentieren „wie ich aus beglückendem Leben in Arbeit und Frieden gequält, verfolgt, bedroht und langsam zu Grunde gerichtet wurde mit Mann und Kind. Eine von vielen, die nichts anderes verbrochen, keine andere Schuld auf sich geladen hat, als dass sie lebt, geboren aus jüdischem Blute" (13). Es ist eine Notiz, die in wenigen Worten ein äußerst komplexes Exilschicksal umreißt und zugleich auf mehrere entscheidende Aspekte hinweist, um die es im Folgenden gehen soll.

Abgesehen davon, dass sie in ihrem letzten Satz selbst bereits auf das Exemplarische ihres Schicksals hinweist, befindet sich Nathorff in ihrer Transitsituation in London an genau jenem Punkt, an dem die im nationalsozialistischen Deutschland erfahrenen Vorstufen des Exils zu einer realen Situation des Exils geworden sind, das auch mit der schließlich geglückten Ankunft in New York im März 1940 keineswegs beendet sein wird.

In seinem Essay „Wir sind alle im Exil" spricht der seit 1989 selbst im amerikanischen Exil lebende rumänische Schriftsteller Norman Manea über den „konfliktträchtigen Widerspruch zwischen zentrifugaler Modernität und zentripetalem Bedürfnis nach Zugehörigkeit", der sich im Tumult unserer Epoche aufs äußerste zugespitzt habe (7). Auch Nathorffs Geschichte ist von solch einer äußersten Zuspitzung zwischen den Zerstreuungsbewegungen von Vertreibung und Flucht und der fortwährenden Sehnsucht nach einem Ort von Zugehörigkeit bestimmt. Auf den vielen Stationen sukzessiver Entwurzelung und traumatischer Bedrohung, die sie nach 1933 als deutsche Jüdin durchleben musste, bedeutete der performative Akt des Tagebuchschreibens, das regelmäßige Notieren und Reflektieren des Erfahrenen, immer wieder auch das Bemühen, für sich einen zentripetalen Ort der Sammlung und Identitätssicherung innerhalb der zentrifugalen Gewalten drohender Selbstauflösung und gänzlichen Selbstverlustes herzustellen: „Wieder flüchte ich mich zum Schreiben, die jagenden Gedanken zu ordnen" (Eintrag vom 28. April 1939 auf der Überfahrt nach England, 163). Immer wieder geht es darum, der zunehmenden Gefahr der Ich-Auflösung ein Bewahrendes im Akt des Schreibens entgegen zu setzen oder, wie Norman Manea dies ausführt, „im Schreiben nach Kraft gegen die äußeren Zwänge" zu suchen, denn „in einer totalitären Umgebung, wo der Druck der äußeren Umstände jederzeit die Oberhand gewinnen konnte", sei vielleicht gerade der innere Rückzug auf das Selbst „der Ort, an dem sich die zentripetale Notwendigkeit, die eigene Identität unter geheimem Verschluss zu halten, und die zentrifugale Tendenz zur Flucht kreuzen" (8).

Dabei bietet „Das Tagebuch der Hertha Nathorff" nicht nur detaillierte Einblicke in äußere und innere Prozesse der Veränderung aufgrund der Erfahrungen von Ausgrenzung, Vertreibung, Flucht und Exil, sondern es kann überdies – wie sein Herausgeber Wolfgang Benz es einmal bezeichnet hat – als „eine historische Quelle ersten Ranges" angesehen werden (Nathorff 17). Bei den Aufzeichnungen 1933–1939 handelt es sich bereits um eine rekonstruierte und überarbeitete Version, da Teile des Originaltagebuchs mit der Verschickung nach New York verloren gegangen waren. Anfang 1940 unternahm Nathorff daher mithilfe noch vorhandener Blätter und geretteter Notizen eine Neuschrift, auch um diese anschließend bei einem Schreibwettbewerb an der Universität Harvard einzureichen. Hierfür hatte sie noch einen zusätzlichen Prolog in Form eines autobiographischen Rückblicks auf ihre Kindheit und

Jugend in Süddeutschland angefügt. Zwar gewann sie für ihr Manuskript sogar einen Preis, doch verschwand dieses anschließend „unveröffentlicht und wirkungslos – in den Archiven der berühmten Universität" (Ziegler 190). Eine Kopie davon befindet sich heutzutage im Leo Baeck Institut in New York. Fast fünfzig Jahre später wurde es im Jahr 1987 nach ebendieser Vorlage – unter Einbeziehung noch weiterer Tagebuchnotizen aus der Ankunftszeit in Amerika bis zum endgültigen Ende des Zweiten Weltkrieges im August 1945 – von dem Historiker Wolfgang Benz in Zusammenarbeit mit der damals noch lebenden Autorin als Buch in Deutschland herausgegeben und damit zum ersten Mal einer größeren Öffentlichkeit zugänglich gemacht. Es lässt sich also von drei unterschiedlichen Tagebuchteilen ausgehen: Erstens, dem autobiographischen Rückblick im Prolog; zweitens, den überarbeiteten Aufzeichnungen von 1933–1939; und drittens, den fortgesetzten Eintragungen nach ihrer Ankunft in New York bis Sommer 1945. Mithin handelt es sich bei diesem Text um eine Mischung von alltäglichen, diaristischen Notizen und im Rückblick geschriebenen autobiographischen Ausführungen.

Zur Erschließung und zum genaueren Verständnis des Tagebuchs sind nun verschiedene Herangehensweisen möglich. Zunächst lässt es sich historiographisch gesehen als ein Dokument der Zeitzeugenschaft auffassen. Unter diesem Gesichtspunkt wäre insbesondere das Spannungsverhältnis von Individual- und Zeitgeschichte oder – anders gesagt – der „hermeneutische Zirkel" von Mikro- und Makrogeschichte zu untersuchen (vgl. Sepp 15).

Dies trifft sich mit einigen Überlegungen des Historikers Reinhart Koselleck, der von der Behauptung ausgeht: „Geschichte ist und bleibt eine Erfahrungsgeschichte" (30). Dabei sei die erste „Erfahrungsart" immer „so singulär wie unwiederholbar", und damit überraschend und einmalig. Gleichwohl entstehen Erfahrungen nicht nur, „indem sie gemacht werden", sondern ebenso, „indem sie sich wiederholen", das heißt sie akkumulieren sich in einer generationsbedingten gemeinsamen „Erfahrungsfrist" (35). In einem dritten Schritt führt dieser „Erfahrungsgewinn" schließlich zu einem langfristig schleichenden oder auch schubweisen „Erfahrungswandel", dem die historische Erklärung zu gelten hat (38 und 45).

Die Zeugnisse jener ersten unmittelbaren Erfahrungen können sowohl aus mündlichen Befragungen hervorgehen, als auch aus persönlichen Aufzeichnungen wie Tagebüchern, Briefen, autobiographischen Berichten oder Ähnlichem (vgl. Koselleck 43). Dies vorausgesetzt, stellt sich die Frage, inwiefern sich die singulären Erfahrungen Nathorffs, die anhand ihrer Notizen nachvollziehbar werden, als exemplarisch innerhalb der „Erfahrungsfrist" ihrer Generation verstehen lassen und zu welchen weiteren Erkenntnissen dies auch im Sinne eines „Erfahrungswandels" aus historischer Sicht schließlich führen wird.

Ein derartiges Vorgehen wäre noch durch einige Überlegungen zur Textexegese zu ergänzen. Zwar besteht das Besondere von Tagebucheintragungen gerade in einer auf die alltägliche Gegenwart bezogenen Schreibsituation, doch kann ein Tagebuchwerk – wie Hartmut Steinecke einmal erwähnt hat – nicht einfach nur als ein „authentisches Dokument" angesehen werden (Einleitung, Aloni, 28 und 29). In jedem Schreibprozess, auch dem diaristischen, wird gefiltert, ausgelassen, verdichtet oder auch hinzugefügt, sodass die Position der Schreibenden stets mit zu bedenken ist und ebenfalls einer gezielten Interpretation bedarf. Wird das diaristische Schreiben außerdem als „Methode einer Selbstkonstruktion" oder auch als eine „kulturelle Technik zur Erzeugung von Identität" aufgefasst, so erlaubt die textexegetische Analyse dieser Eintragungen zugleich „sich lebensgeschichtlichen Konstruktionen des [oder der] Schreibenden zu nähern" (vgl. Sepp, 81 und 83). Unter diesem Gesichtspunkt gerät in den Aufzeichnungen Nathorffs als eine zentrale identitätsstiftende Konstruktion unübersehbar ihr Beruf als Ärztin in den Fokus der Aufmerksamkeit.

Hertha Nathorff wurde 1895 unter dem Familiennamen Einstein (Albert Einstein war ein entfernter Onkel von ihr) in Laupheim, einer kleinen süddeutschen Stadt, als älteste Tochter einer alteingesessenen, akkulturierten jüdischen Kaufmannsfamilie geboren. Mit der Erfahrung ihrer späteren Karriere als Ärztin war für sie zugleich ein doppelter Emanzipationsprozess verknüpft, der einerseits ihre Situation als Frau und andererseits ihre Situation als deutsche Jüdin betrifft. Für ihre Generation war die weibliche Ausübung des Arztberufes noch alles andere als selbstverständlich, sondern eher die Ausnahme. Noch Anfang der Dreißigerjahre stellten Ärztinnen eine zahlenmäßig eher kleine, gleichwohl durchaus bemerkenswerte Gruppe innerhalb der Ärzteschaft Deutschlands dar. So wurden Atina Grossmann zufolge 1932 in Berlin 722 Ärztinnen gezählt, darunter mindestens 270 jüdische (140).

Aus ihrem autobiographischen Lebensrückblick wie zahlreichen weiteren Einträgen im Tagebuch tritt immer wieder deutlich hervor, wie stolz Nathorff selbst auf diese Errungenschaft, ja auf ihren gesamten Bildungsweg ist, der zu jener Zeit nur über den Besuch einer normalerweise Jungen vorbehaltenen Lateinschule möglich war. Noch im Rückblick aus dem Jahr 1940 erwähnt sie begeistert, dass ihr Weg schon in frühester Jugend „in neuartige Bahnen gelenkt wurde" (21). „Alle Türen öffneten sich mir", fährt sie enthusiastisch fort, ja sie habe „niemals in all diesen Jahren zu spüren bekommen, dass ich etwa nicht dazu gehörte oder weniger galt als die anderen, weil ich Jüdin war" (22). Einmal aber traf es sie dann doch. Denn Nathorff hatte sich in einen ehemaligen Mitschüler verliebt, „ein ernster, kluger, tief philosophisch veranlagter Mann" (22), wie sie schreibt, der die Absicht hatte, Offizier zu werden, und der sie am liebsten gleich nach ihrem Abitur 1914 hätte heiraten wollen, allerdings nur unter der Bedingung, dass sie sich taufen ließ. Ein Ansinnen, das Nathorff zutiefst verletzt zurückweist und das zum ersten Mal bei ihr den Wunsch entstehen ließ, ihr Land zu verlassen und nach Amerika zu gehen, „um nichts zu sein als ein freier Mensch unter freien Menschen" (23).

Stattdessen bricht der Erste Weltkrieg aus und Nathorff versucht nun, wie viele deutsche Juden dieser Zeit, mit aller Kraft ihre Vaterlandsliebe unter Beweis zu stellen: „Des Kaisers Worte: ‚Ich kenne keine Parteien mehr, ich kenne nur noch Deutsche', drangen in mein Herz, waren Balsam für meinen jungen Schmerz. Ich war deutsch, deutsch und nichts anderes, welcher Religion ich auch angehörte" (23). Nun will sie nur noch helfen, ihren Beitrag leisten und sich mit ganzer Kraft für ihr Land einsetzen. Aufopferungsvoll widmet sie sich der Versorgung der Kriegsverwundeten und muss erkennen, dass ihr hier oft die nötigen Kenntnisse fehlten: „Helfen wollte ich, richtig helfen, den Gedanken, mit dem ich oft heimlich gespielt hatte, ich musste ihn verwirklichen: Ärztin musste ich werden, um jeden Preis" (23). Noch im Jahr 1914 beginnt Nathorff in Heidelberg Medizin zu studieren und sich zur Ärztin ausbilden zu lassen. Während ihrer späteren Assistenzzeit in Freiburg sieht sie sich dann ein weiteres Mal mit antisemitischen Vorurteilen konfrontiert. Und auch hier wird sie erneut jene Grundhaltung einnehmen, durch gesteigerte Tüchtigkeit das diskriminierende Verhalten in ihrer Umgebung entkräften zu wollen (vgl. Nathorff, 25)

Trotz der spätestens seit Kriegsende in jeder Hinsicht geltenden jüdischen Emanzipation war die Akkulturation der deutschen Juden oft längst nicht so umfassend, wie häufig angenommen wird, sondern eher ein vielfältiger, differenzierter Prozess, in dem die jüdische Identität in unterschiedlichem Maße beibehalten wurde. So traf auch für Nathorff in gewisser Weise zu, was Paul Mendes-Flohr einmal als die „Verwirrung" der deutschen Juden beschrieben hat, die sich ihm zufolge daraus ergab, dass sie einerseits oftmals „entgegen ihren eigenen Vorstellungen noch immer an ihre ursprüngliche Kultur und Identität gebunden" waren, während sie zugleich „eine feste Position in der deutschen Kultur und Gesellschaft" suchten (55). Voll und ganz als eine Deutsche akzeptiert zu sein und doch das eigene Judentum nicht leugnen zu müssen, war auch für Nathorff ein sehnsüchtig angestrebtes Ziel. Dabei vollzog sich eine identitätsstiftende Integration dieser zwei Zugehörigkeiten vor allem und ganz besonders in ihrer beruflichen „Selbstkonstruktion" einer unermüdlichen, hingebungsvollen Ärztin. „Ich will doch Ärztin sein und nichts anderes", formuliert sie noch nach ihrer Ankunft in den USA in ihrem Prolog zum Tagebuch (30) – ein für ihr Selbstverständnis absolut zentrales Motto, das gleichsam metonymisch für ihren Aufstieg und Fall zu stehen scheint. Es gilt daher, sich besonders auf diesen Aspekt zu konzentrieren, um die verschiedenen Stadien bis zur endgültigen Emigration genauer zu veranschaulichen.

Den beruflichen Erfolg, der sich zusehends einstellt, genießt Nathorff über alles, und nach ihrem Wechsel ins liberale Berlin, findet sie eine offene und aufgeschlossene Umgebung vor, in der sie sich angenommen und zugleich angekommen fühlen kann. Sie heiratet den Arzt Erich Nathorff, führt trotz baldiger Mutterschaft eine gleichberechtigte Ehe mit fortgesetzter Berufstätigkeit, leitet über Jahre eine Frauenklinik, übernimmt ehrenamtlich eine der ersten Ehe- und Familienberatungsstellen und wird standespolitisch in verschiedenen Funktionen ärztlicher Verbände aktiv. Noch in ihrem späteren Tagebuch aus dem Jahr 1938 erwähnt sie eine wiederentdeckte Eintragung vom 13. Juli 1923: von „damals", als sie „eine glückliche Braut" war, als sie gerade die Leitung jenes Entbindungs- und Säuglingsheims des Deutschen Roten Kreuzes übernommen hatte und von ihren Patienten aufgrund ihrer freundlich zugewandten Art liebevoll „Sonnendoktorchen" genannt worden war (111). Es ist eine Notiz, die Nathorff sich nun rückblickend in Erinnerung ruft, zu einem Zeitpunkt, als all dies längst gründlich anders geworden war.

Mit der Machtübergabe an die Nationalsozialisten im Januar 1933 wandelte sich die immer schon schwelende Unsicherheit hinsichtlich einer unhinterfragten deutschen Zugehörigkeit zu der traumatischen Erfahrung einer brutalen Verstoßung. Ein erster, alles erschütternder Einschnitt ereignete sich für Nathorff mit dem sogenannten Juden-Boykott vom April 1933 und dem damit einhergehenden „Gesetz zur Wiederherstellung des Berufsbeamtentums". Fortan war es ihr als Jüdin verboten, weiterhin als Kassenärztin zu praktizieren. Fassungslos kommentiert sie in einem Eintrag vom 25. April 1933 die ihr zugestellte Aufforderung, ihre „Tätigkeit als leitende Ärztin der Frauen- und Beratungsstelle" einzustellen: „Fast 5 Jahre habe ich diese Stelle geleitet, groß und bekannt gemacht, und nun? Aus, aus – ich muss es mir immer wieder sagen, damit ich es fassen kann" (41).

Das Berufsverbot kommt Nathorff vor, als würde sie ihr „eigenes Begräbnis" erleben, und dem anfänglichen Schock folgt schnell ein Gefühl ansteigender Verzweiflung bis hin zu Suizidgedanken (46). Zwar bleibt ihr noch die gemeinsam mit ihrem Mann in den Nachmittagsstunden betriebene Privatpraxis, doch ist eine erste irreparable Zäsur in ihrem Verhältnis zu Deutschland und ihrer eigenen Identifikation damit eingetreten. Mit dem Ausschluss per Gesetz aus einer bislang als unverbrüchlich und sicher angesehenen Ordnung setzen nun tiefe Bedrohungs- und Verunsicherungsgefühle ein. Immer wieder finden sich jetzt im Tagebuch Notizen einer sich steigernden Angst vor Verfolgung, Bespitzelung und Denunziation, manches Mal einhergehend mit dem Vorsatz, dies alles zu verlassen. Dem steht allerdings nach wie vor der Wunsch entgegen,

ILLUSTRATION 14.1   Das Ehepaar Hertha und Erich Nathorff 1936 in Berlin

trotz derartig eingeschränkter Bedingungen auch weiterhin ihren Beruf ausüben zu können (vgl. z.B. Nathorff, 56, 60 und 87).
Wie Marion Kaplan hervorhebt, kann der Grund für diese „Zwiespältigkeit",
mit der „Juden in den Jahren vor 1938 reagierten", gerade in den erstaunlichen
persönlichen und beruflichen Erfolgen gesehen werden, die diese „inmitten

und trotz des Antisemitismus im Kaiserreich und in der Weimarer Republik"
erzielt hatten, was mit dazu führte, dass sie sich an die widersprüchlichen
Signale „klammerten", „die vom Regime selbst und von nichtjüdischen Freunden wie von Fremden ausgingen" (14). Gleiches gilt für Nathorff, deren Absicht,
schnellstmöglich nach Amerika auszuwandern und die damit einhergehenden Schwierigkeiten auf sich zu nehmen, immer wieder von der Angst einge-
holt wird, dann nicht mehr als Ärztin arbeiten zu können. Das einzige, was sie
noch in Deutschland halte, notiert sie Ostern 1934, ist: *„Mein Beruf,* den ich
liebe, der mir Lebensinhalt ist und den ich drüben nicht ausüben zu können
befürchte!" (56).

Hinzu kommt, dass auch bei Nathorff, ähnlich wie dies Steven E. Aschheim
bei Victor Klemperer analysiert hat, eine Strategie der Aufsplitterung im Tagebuch nachvollziehbar wird. Die Gleichzeitigkeit gegenüber ihrem „Deutsch-
tum" als einem positiv besetzten, geistigen und regulativen Ideal und dessen
Desillusionierung mit seinen realen Nazi-Manifestationen existiert noch über
lange Zeit Seite an Seite (vgl. Aschheim 88). Am 16. April 1933, nach dem Ausschluss aller Jüdinnen aus der Versammlung des Bundes deutscher Ärztinnen, hält Nathorff in ihrem Tagebuch fest: „Ich bin so erregt, so traurig und
verzweifelt, und ich schäme mich für meine ‚deutschen' Kolleginnen" (40).
Doch schon am 2. Juni 1933 äußert sie sich dann fast mütterlich verzeihend:
„Wie dumm und doch wie gut ist dieses Volk im Grunde" (45). Sie fühlt sich als
aufrechte, wahre Deutsche und schämt sich dafür, was aus Deutschland geworden ist. Immer wieder nimmt Nathorff aus dieser Perspektive die Nazis als
schamlose Verbrecher wahr, die ein armes, geschundenes und oft sogar hilflo-
ses Volk durch Propaganda und Strafandrohungen verführen und beherrschen.

Dies änderte sich spätestens mit den Nürnberger Gesetzen vom September
1935 und den darin festgelegten Rasseverordnungen, mit denen die Trennung
zwischen jüdischen und nichtjüdischen Deutschen unwiderrufliche Realität
wird. „Die Nürnberger Gesetze führten zur endgültigen Zerstörung vieler
Beziehungen sowie zur Verhaftung von Juden und Nichtjuden, die enge
Freundschaft miteinander pflegten", resümiert Kaplan (73). Auch die Nathorffs
müssen erleben, dass frühere nichtjüdische Bekannte, ja sogar Freunde sich
offen von ihnen abwenden, auf der Straße nicht mehr grüßen und die Begeg-
nung meiden. Sie reagieren darauf mit einem äußerlichen wie innerlichen
Rückzug. Sie gehe „schon nirgends mehr hin", schreibt Nathorff am 9. Oktober
und, wie aus Selbstschutz die zu erwartende Reaktion vorwegnehmend, ergänzt sie: [...] „soll ich mir und den anderen Ärger machen?" (75). Einige
Wochen später, am Silvesterabend 1935, wird sie schließlich erklären: „Täglich
bröckelt ein Stückchen ab, auch ein Stückchen von meiner Jugend" (78).

Mit der Einführung dieser Gesetze, „einem ‚trockenen Pogrom,‘ wie aus Exilkreisen nun oft zu hören ist" (von Soden 80), hatten die Nazis die längst bestehende Kluft zwischen den Juden und den übrigen Deutschen als unüberbrückbar festgeschrieben. Auf jüdischer Seite setzt damit verstärkt ein Prozess der Distanzierung, ja Dissimilation von der einst geliebten deutschen Heimat ein, der unausweichlich in den Zustand einer inneren Emigration führt. Alles sei ihr „fremd geworden", notiert Nathorff im Tagebuch, „es ist nicht mehr meins" (91). Entsprechend nehmen die Ausreisepläne zu. Doch tritt auch hier immer wieder hemmend die Angst vor dem endgültigen Berufs-verlust dazwischen, die nun noch dadurch verstärkt wird, dass die Frist für die Anerkennung deutscher Ärztezulassungen durch den Bundesstaat New York im Oktober 1936 abgelaufen war (vgl. Grossmann 143). Eine weitere Erschwer-nis entsteht im Februar 1938 durch den Umstand, dass alle Juden ihre Pässe abzugeben hatten und nur noch bei gesicherter Ausreise eine offizielle Reise-genehmigung erhalten konnten.

Den endgültigen Bruch aber, ihr „Todesurteil" (113), wie Nathorff es bezeich-net, erlebt sie als sie im August 1938 vom Entzug der Approbation für alle jü-dischen Ärzte und Ärztinnen erfährt. Für sie selbst bedeutet dies nun das voll-ständige Berufsverbot, während ihr Mann als sogenannter „Judenbehandler"

ILLUSTRATION 14.2   Familie Nathorff/Einstein, aufgenommen 1936 in Laupheim. Ausen links Hertha Nathorff, neben ihr Erich Nathorff, in der Mitte der Sohn Heinz

noch eingeschränkt weiterpraktizieren darf. Darin zeigt sich eine geschlechts-
spezifische Aufteilung, die – wie Stefanie Schüler-Springorum in ihrer Studie
Geschlecht und Differenz ausgeführt hat – durchaus symptomatisch war, denn
die antijüdische Politik des NS-Regimes übte in den Dreißigerjahren „in viel-
facher Weise einen massiven Druck auf die Geschlechterverhältnisse aus". So
sei in der allgemeinen Notlage „Männern auf allen Gebieten deutlich der Vor-
rang eingeräumt" worden, waren diese auf der anderen Seite jedoch „den Bru-
talitäten des Regimes in sehr viel stärkerem Maße ausgesetzt". Demgegenüber
schränkten sich die sozialen und beruflichen Spielräume für Frauen noch weiter ein, sodass sie sich schließlich zurückgeworfen „auf traditionelle weibliche
Rollen, Tätigkeitsbereiche und Anforderungen" sahen (Schüler-Springorum
118). Auch Nathorff blieb nichts anderes übrig, als ihrem Mann fortan als
Sprechstundenhilfe zu assistieren. „Eine furchtbare Seelenmarter", wie sie im
Tagebuch schreibt (118).

Doch erst die Reichspogromnacht, wenige Wochen später, führte zur endgültigen Entscheidung fortzugehen. Sowohl ihr Mann, der mehrere Wochen
im KZ Sachsenhausen verbringen musste, als auch sie selbst, die völlig schutzlos in der eigenen Wohnung überfallen, bedroht und ausgeraubt wurde, erleben während dieser Tage schwere Traumatisierungen. Jetzt werden alle nur
erdenklichen und noch so beschwerlichen Anstrengungen unternommen, die
nötigen Papiere zu beschaffen, um nur möglichst schnell fortzukommen. Der
14-jährige Sohn Heinz kann noch im März 1939 mit einem Kindertransport
nach England geschickt werden. Wenige Wochen später folgen ihm auch die
Eltern dorthin, wo sie über lange ungewisse Monate gemeinsam auf eine Wei-
terreisemöglichkeit nach Amerika warten. Als völlig mittellose Flüchtlinge
kommen die drei Nathorffs schließlich am 22. Februar 1940 in New York an.

Obwohl es dem Ehepaar gelingt, sich nach einer sehr entbehrungsreichen
Anfangszeit im neuen Land wieder eine Existenz aufzubauen, Erich Nathorff
dort bald wieder als Arzt praktizieren kann und Hertha Nathorff durch eine
Vielzahl sozialer wie kultureller Aktivitäten allmählich wieder gesellschaftli-
ches Ansehen und persönliche Wertschätzung gewinnt, kann sie sich dennoch ihrem neuen Leben gegenüber nicht mehr innerlich öffnen. Zwar wird
sie nach dem frühen Tod ihres Mannes noch mit 59 Jahren einen Berufsab-
schluss als Psychotherapeutin absolvieren, doch ist sie nicht mehr in der
Lage, das Zertifikat für den Arztberuf zu erwerben. Damit steht sie keineswegs allein da, denn wie Grossmann nachgewiesen hat, gelang circa zwei
Dritteln aller emigrierten Ärztinnen die Rückkehr in den ehemaligen Beruf
später nicht mehr (148). Die dafür notwendigen Examina waren schwer, setzten ausgezeichnete Sprachkenntnisse voraus, kosteten Geld und gerade den

Frauen wurde von vornherein mit vielen Vorbehalten begegnet. Allzu viele
der Geflüchteten konnten diesen Beruf vorweisen, man fürchtete geradezu
eine Ärzteschwemme, was die Lage keineswegs erleichterte. In der Regel
wurde den Männern der Vortritt gelassen, zumal viele Frauen, wie auch
Nathorff, zunächst alle Hände voll damit zu tun hatten, die Familie mit Arbeiten jeglicher Art möglichst über Wasser zu halten, was noch zusätzlich
kaum Zeit für irgendwelche Examensvorbereitungen ließ. Für Nathorff,
deren positives Selbstwertgefühl stets unauflösbar mit ihrer Tätigkeit als Ärztin verwoben gewesen war, kam der endgültige Verlust dieser Berufsmöglich-
keit jedoch einem vollkommenen persönlichen Scheitern gleich. Dass sie
nicht mehr als Ärztin arbeiten durfte, war gleichsam das Symptom dafür,
dass es kein wirkliches Ankommen mehr im neuen Land geben konnte.

Noch an ihrem letzten Abend vor der Abreise aus Berlin hatte sie am 27.
April 1939 in ihrer nun gänzlich leeren, ausgeplünderten Wohnung in ihr Tagebuch geschrieben: „Ein letztes Kerzenstümpfchen flackert in meiner Hand [...]
ein paar Stündlein noch und alles ist überstanden. Alles? Ich kauere in der
dunklen Ecke meines alten Sprechzimmers – ich sehe das Kerzchen langsam
erlöschen, ein heißer Tropfen fällt brennend auf meine Hand. Das Licht ist aus.
Hier war ich einst Ärztin, hier war ich einst glücklich – hier war ich daheim...“
(160). Ein äußeres und zugleich inneres Licht wird hier metaphorisch aufei-
nander bezogen, das in diesem Moment für die Schreibende endgültig erlischt.
Noch Jahrzehnte später wird Hertha Nathorff, in ihren weitergeführten Tagebuchnotizen an diese Metaphorik anknüpfend, davon sprechen, dass sie es
zwar „nach außen geschafft habe“, aber nun „leer, ausgebrannt“ da stehe
(Koerner 223). Und noch im hohen Alter bekennt sie, dass trotz allem ihr „Herz
ein Archiv deutschen Gefühls“ geblieben sei, doch sie ergänzt: „Sie haben meine Seele verbrannt, mein Leben zerstört, meine Jugend, meinen Frohsinn,
mein ganzes Ich ausgelöscht“ (Benz 135). So leidet Nathorff schließlich an jener „Krankheit Exil“, von der Hilde Spiel einmal als einer unablässig spürbaren
Wunde gesprochen hat (Deutschlandfunk). „But the recovering of a new personality is as difficult [...] as a new creation of the world“, behauptet Hannah
Arendt über die Flüchtlingserfahrung (117). Es koste die Exilierten sehr viel,
einen „Ort“ in der neuen Gesellschaft zu finden, erklären dazu passend León
und Rebecca Grinberg, die ihr eigenes Exilschicksal psychoanalytisch reflek-
tiert haben: [...] „denn sie können unter den neuen Bedingungen nicht das
wiederherstellen, was für sie die Achse des Lebens“ gewesen war (183). Auch
Hertha Nathorff konnte jene untergegangene, alte Welt nie wirklich loslassen,
weshalb kein innerer Raum für die neue Welt zu entstehen vermochte, anders
als Guy Stern es in seinen Ausführungen in diesem Band beschrieben hat, der

bereits vierzehnjährig als Flüchtling in die USA kam. Trotz seiner großen Trauer um die verlorenen Angehörigen in Deutschland und trotz seines heftigen Heimwehs, konnte er sich am Ende positiv mit seiner neuen Heimat identifizieren und dort wieder ein glückliches Leben führen, möglicherweise unter anderem auch deshalb, weil er noch jung genug dafür war und sein ganzes Leben noch vor ihm lag.

Bis ins hohe Alter setzte Hertha Nathorff ihre Tagebuchaufzeichnungen fort: „Hunderte und Aberhunderte loser Blätter", stets bedroht von zentrifugaler Auflösung und Verstreuung, die sie in Umschlägen, Plastiktüten und Kartons in ihrer New Yorker Wohnung verstaute. Einen erheblichen Teil davon übergab sie noch 1991, zwei Jahre vor ihrem Tod, Miriam Koerner bei einem Besuch (vgl. Koerner 221). Inzwischen lagert ihr Nachlass als ein weiteres Beispiel jener Schicksale, von denen Sylvia Asmus in ihrem Beitrag in diesem Band spricht, im Deutschen Exilarchiv in Frankfurt am Main. Es handelt sich um Dokumente, die aufschlussreich Zeugnis ablegen: Zum einen über die verschiedenen Vorstufen des Exils, vom Zustand einer geglückten Integration als Ärztin in Deutschland, über das traumatische Erleben einer abrupten Verstoßung durch die radikale Veränderung der politischen Verhältnisse, zu einem anwachsenden Zustand innerer Emigration bis zum endgültigen Verlassen der ehemaligen Heimat. Zum anderen aber auch über die Ankunft in einem Exil, das trotz äußeren Erfolgs kein innerer Ort der Zugehörigkeit mehr werden konnte.

Zitierte Literatur

Aloni, Jenny. *Ich muss mir diese Zeit von der Seele schreiben. Die Tagebücher 1935–1993: Deutschland – Palästina – Israel.* Herausgegeben und eingeleitet von Hartmut Steinecke. Verlag Ferdinand Schöningh, 2006, S. 11–30.

Arendt, Hannah. „We Refugees". *Altogether Elsewhere. Writers in Exile.* Faber and Faber, 1994.

Aschheim, Steven E. *Scholem, Arendt, Klemperer. Intimate Chronicles in Turbulent Times.* Indiana UP, 2001.

Benz, Wolfgang. „Das gelebte Unglück des Exils: Hertha Nathorff". *Deutsche Juden im 20. Jahrhundert. Eine Geschichte in Porträts.* Verlag C.H. Beck, 2011, S. 123–142.

Grinberg, León und Rebecca. *Psychoanalyse der Migration und des Exils.* Aus dem Spanischen übersetzt von Flavio C. Ribas. Psychosozial-Verlag, 2016.

Grossmann, Atina. „‚Neue Frauen' im Exil. Deutsche Ärztinnen und die Emigration". *Deutsch-jüdische Geschlechtergeschichte. Studien zum 19. und 20. Jahrhundert.*

Herausgegeben von Kirsten Heinsohn und Stefanie Schüler-Springorum. Wallstein Verlag, 2005, S. 133–156.

Kaplan, Marion. *Der Mut zum Überleben. Jüdische Frauen und ihre Familien in Nazideutschland.* Aufbau Taschenbuch Verlag, 2003.

Koerner, Miriam. „Central Park West, New York". *Das Exil der kleinen Leute. Alltagserfahrungen deutscher Juden in der Emigration.* Herausgegeben von Wolfgang Benz. C.H. Beck Verlag, 1991, S. 215–231.

Koselleck, Reinhart. *Zeitschichten.* Studien zur Historik. Suhrkamp Verlag, 2000, 5. Auflage, 2018.

Manea, Norman. *Wir sind alle im Exil.* Essays. Aus dem Rumänischen übersetzt von Georg Aescht, Roland Erb, Paul Schuster, Eva Ruth Wemme und Ernst Wichner. Carl Hanser Verlag, 2015, S. 7–12.

Mendes-Flohr, Paul. *Jüdische Identität. Die zwei Seelen der deutschen Juden.* Wilhelm Fink Verlag, 2004.

Nathorff, Hertha. *Das Tagebuch der Hertha Nathorff. Berlin – New York. Aufzeichnungen 1933 bis 1945.* Herausgegeben und eingeleitet von Wolfgang Benz. Fischer Verlag, 1987.

Schüler-Springorum, Stefanie. *Geschlecht und Differenz.* Verlag Ferdinand Schöningh, 2014.

Sepp, Arvi. *Topographie des Alltags. Eine kulturwissenschaftliche Lektüre von Victor Klemperers Tagebüchern 1933–1945.* Verlag Wilhelm Fink, 2016.

Soden, Christine von. „*Und draußen weht ein fremder Wind...*" Über die Meere ins Exil. Aviva Verlag, 2016.

Spiel, Hilde. „Das Exil ist eine Krankheit". Kalenderblatt zum 100. Geburtstag von Hilde Spiel, Christian Lindner, Deutschlandfunk, 19.10.2011.

Ziegler, Edda. „Vom Sonnenkind zur Dirty Refugee: Hertha Nathorff". *Verboten Verfemt Vertrieben. Schriftstellerinnen im Widerstand gegen den Nationalsozialismus.* Deutscher Taschenbuchverlag, 2010, S. 190–197.

CHAPTER 15

Heimatlos and *en exil*: Adamov's Language of Exile

Julia Elsky

Abstract

Between 1932 and 1941, Arthur Adamov radically altered his translation of Rilke's *Book of Poverty and Death*, the third book of *The Book of Hours*, from the German into French in an expression of entering into a new exile in his adopted country of France. As opposed to a reading of Rilke, this essay reconstructs Adamov's understanding of Rilke in his translations as well as his burgeoning theories of language and the absurd in his other wartime text, *The Confession*. Adamov has been considered one of the founding playwrights of the postwar Theater of the Absurd in France. However, I argue that we find in his wartime translations and writings his first reflections on language and alienation. These issues have become the hallmark of the postwar absurd, but they are already present in Adamov's wartime theory of language and translation.

1   Adamov's Exiles

Between 1932 and 1941, Arthur Adamov radically altered his translation of Rilke's *Das Buch von der Armut und vom Tode* (*The Book of Poverty and Death*), the third book of *Das Stunden-Buch* (*The Book of Hours*), from the German into French in an expression of his entering into exile in his adopted country of France. It was an early stage of a new exile. As opposed to a reading of Rilke, this article reconstructs Adamov's own understanding of Rilke in his translations. The very month that Adamov published his revised translations, he was arrested and imprisoned in two internment camps in France. After his release he wrote parts of *L'aveu* (*The Confession*), a series of short texts in which he lays out his theory of language and alienation in the war, underscoring his theory of translation. Adamov has been considered one of the founding playwrights of the postwar Theater of the Absurd in France. However, I argue that we find in his wartime translations and writings his first reflections on language and alienation in the war. These issues have become the hallmark of the postwar absurd, but they are already present in the burgeoning writer's wartime theory of language and translation.

Although Adamov was a stateless refugee in France since the 1920s, he entered a new phase of exile in France in 1938 and during the early years of the Second World War, while he was writing his translations of Rilke. Adamov (*né* Adamian) was born in 1908 in Kislovodsk in the North Caucasus region of the Russian Empire. From his earliest years he spoke Armenian, German, and Russian, as well as the prestige language French. In the summer of 1914, the Adamians were vacationing in Germany. When war broke out, they moved to the Russian colony in Geneva. After moving back to Germany in the early 1920s and attending the *Lycée français* of Mainz, he immigrated with his family to Paris in 1924. Although they had been extremely wealthy, his family began a steady decline into poverty during their emigrations. In Paris, Adamov befriended and collaborated on theater and poetry projects with émigré writers and artists like Benjamin Fondane and Victor Brauner, as well as more established French-born writers like Antonin Artaud. Amidst these movements and language changes, in 1932 he started to translate Rilke, publishing a short excerpt of the beginning of *Das Buch von der Armut und vom Tode* in the journal *Esprit* (cf. Rilke, "Le livre" 388–395). But the late 1930s and early 1940s would mark a change not only in his rewriting of his translations of Rilke, but also of his position in France. In January 1939, he was imprisoned for one month and fined 100 francs for his failure to legalize his status as a refugee under the May 2, 1938 Decree that pushed against the presence of illegal foreigners in France ("ADA-MIAN Arthur dit ADAMOV"). It was Daladier's government's response to thousands of refugees fleeing to France from Austria, Germany, and Spain, and it added new restrictions that increased the severity of penalties for any infraction ("Décret").[1]

After the French defeat in June 1940 and the beginning of the Occupation, like so many Parisian intellectuals, Adamov fled southward toward Marseille. It was another displacement, now within France and under the greatest risk as a stateless person. The Surrealist André Masson, one of people in the same circles as Adamov now displaced in Marseille, described this phrase of the war in Marseille as "a premonition of exile" (64). At this time, Adamov published an excerpt of his translations of Rilke along with a preface in the Algerian journal *Fontaine*, which was edited by Max-Pol Fouchet, and was one of the major publications of the intellectual resistance (cf. 281–282). In May 1941, the Éditions Charlot in Algeria published the translation as a book. After his release from the camps, he revised his *L'aveu*, further developing a theory of language and the absurd, theories he had first brought to light through his translations of Rilke.

---

1 Cf. Caron's discussion of this decree and its context in chapter 8 of *Uneasy Asylum*.

2   "Je suis perdu dans un abîme illimité": Translating Rilke

In his translator's note to the 1941 Charlot edition, Adamov gives insight into
his theory of translation. At the beginning of his career as a translator, he had
already translated Carl Jung, and after working on Rilke, he would go on to
translate nineteen works of literature into French from the Russian, German,
and Swedish. In this text, he expresses that transposing poetry from one language to another, using the verb *transposer*, is the most difficult task he has
undertaken ("Translator's Note" 18). His use of the term *to transpose* instead of
the more typical verb *to translate* (*traduire*) merits attention. Rather than
framing his text as a traditional translation, he writes that his work adapts,
transforms, or converts the original German text. It also highlights an almost
spatial element of the act of translation, as the first definition of *transposer*
also relates to moving the position of an object. Indeed, Adamov admits that
after much hesitation he took liberties with the text, ones he knows people will
criticize. He deleted words that were untranslatable into French, even remov-
ing entire passages; he did not always work with precision. Yet he says he does
not regret a thing, for "Traduire littéralement, c'eût été trahir l'Esprit" [to translate literally would have been to betray the Spirit] ("Translator's Note" 18).[2]
Adamov plays on the well-known proximity of the words *traduire* (to translate)
and *trahir* (to betray). A translator should not merely transcribe literal defini-
tions word for word, but instead write out the spirit of a text. My claim about
Adamov's translation is simple: during the war he made changes to Rilke's text
by translating words in a way that points to loss and exile. He reads Rilke's
text—the spirit of the text—in terms of exile and alienation, transposing it
onto the period of the Occupation. This is furthermore reflected in his changes
to his own translations made between 1932 and 1941.

Rilke's poem of 41 sections, first published in German in 1905, addresses
alienation in the city and takes the form of a prayer to the Poor One, God, who
represents a spiritual vow of poverty. His composition of the book came soon
after an enriching but also lonely stay in Paris. *Das Buch von der Armut und vom
Tode* opens with geological depth; the speaker stands within the mountains,
which are either away from the city or perhaps they are the city itself, in a moment that is both claustrophobic in its closeness and agoraphobic in its vast-
ness. The beginning of the poem features an almost entombment that obscures
any visible end: "und bin so tief, daß ich kein Ende sehe" [I am so deep that

---

2   All translations from the French are my own. English translations of Rilke from the German
     are Annemarie S. Kidder's, unless otherwise specified.

I see no end anymore] (Rilke, *The Book* 164–165).[3] It is a moment in which the speaker first calls to the Poor One. The notion of depth comes up numerous times in Rilke's *Buch*. When the speaker prays to God for one man to become closer to God beyond the misery of the teaming city, he asks to give through this man "was keines Menschen Tiefen noch betrat" [what no human depth has ever trod] (Rilke, *The Book* [2001] 176–177; Rilke, *The Book* [1995] 92).[4] Depths seem to relate to a special space, both internal and external, of spiritual knowledge that is vast and profound as opposed to the more surface-level life and death of the teaming cities.

Adamov's translations of Rilke's first stanza announce significant changes he would make throughout the translation that turn the original text towards a reflection on physical displacement. In 1932, Adamov translates the first quote faithfully as "et je suis si profond que je ne vois aucune fin" [and I am so deep that I see no end] (Rilke, "Le livre" 388). However, in 1941 Adamov changes his own translation to: "Je suis perdu dans un abîme illimité" [I am lost in an infinite abyss] (Rilke, *Le livre* 21). We find a similar change a few lines later in the poem, in the speaker's address to the mountain "Geh ich in dir jetzt?" [Am I walking inside you now?] (Rilke, *The Book* 164–165).[5] Adamov translates this line in 1932 as "Vais-je en toi maintenant?" [Do I go in you now?] (Rilke, "Le livre" 388). But in 1941, he translates it as "Me suis-je enfin perdu en toi" [Am I finally lost in you?] (Rilke, *Le livre* 21). The poem now relates not going into the depths in a moment of prayer but rather being lost in an abyss. There is even one important mistranslation from 1941, in which Adamov transforms the line quoted above, "was keines Menschen Tiefen noch betrat," to "où il ira plus loin qu'on n'a jamais été" [where he will go further than anyone ever has] (Rilke, *Le livre* 26). Human internal depth in Rilke has become instead the physical space of travel, and an alienating and lonely voyage.

Later in the poem, Adamov more explicitly turns Rilke's Poor One into a figure of exile. In 1941, he translates the German "Du bist der leise Heimatlose,/ der nichtmehr einging in die Welt" [You are the quiet one without a land,/ not entering the world anymore] (Rilke, *The Book* 190–191) into French: "Tu es en exil, tu n'as pas de patrie/ aucune place ici–bas n'est la tienne" [You are in exile, you have no fatherland/ No place here below is yours] (Rilke, *Le livre* 33). Through the use of *patrie* (fatherland), Adamov's version explicitly addresses a loss of citizenship as well as exile from one's nation. *Heimatlos* could also refer to a displaced person; but elsewhere in *Das Buch von der Armut und vom Tode*,

---

3 I have adapted Kidder's translation in order to stay closer to the German original.
4 I have adapted Kidder's and Stevie Krayer's translations.
5 I have adapted Kidder's translation.

especially in *Das Buch von der Pilgerschaft* (*The Book of Pilgrimage*), which Adamov did not translate but perhaps read, it is a kind of metaphysical homelessness.[6] But the word *patrie* is much more concretely related to a national homeland. It reflects a political reality, and one not so far removed from the dangerous position of statelessness at the beginning of the Occupation.

Adamov makes further changes in the text concerning two specific similes among many about poverty in Rilke's poem, again shifting the poem to talk about exile: he depicts the prisoner and the homeless person as lost figures in exile. First, he alters Rilke's depiction of the prisoner. In the original German, Rilke compares the Poor One to a dream that prisoners have: "und wie ein Wunsch, wenn Sträflinge ihn hegen/ in einer Zelle, ewig ohne Welt" [and like a dream that prisoners have,/ in a cell, forever without the world] (Rilke, *The Book* 190–191).[7] Adamov, however, writes: "et comme le seul vœu chéri d'un prisonnier/ au fond de sa cellule à jamais hors du monde" [and like the only treasured wish of a prisoner at the back of his cell forever outside the world] (Rilke, *Le livre* 32). In Adamov's version, the prisoner is not like someone without (*ohne*) a world but rather someone outside (*hors du*) the world. It is not that no world exists, but that the Poor One is separated from the existing world in an exilic removal.

The second simile that Adamov changes relates to Rilke's description of the homeless being invited in:

> Und wenn man sich sie in die Stube lädt,
> sind sie wie Freunde, die sich wiederbringen,
> und gehn verloren unter dem Geringen
> [And when one invites them over,
> they are like friends who have returned;
> they disappear among all that's small]
>   RILKE, *The Book* 192–193

Adamov changes the scene to read: "et quand au hasard des chemins un foyer les accueille / ils y prennent place humblement comme des visages familiers" [and when by chance from the road a home welcomes them / They humbly take their place like familiar faces] (Rilke, *Le livre* 33). In Adamov's version, the poor come like haphazard guests—*like* familiar faces—rather than returning like friends. This is an even further removed simile; they are not like friends

---

6 See "ein Unbekannter" (a stranger) and "Hergereister" (one from out of town) (Rilke, *The Book* 122–123); "ein Ausgestossner" (one expelled) (ibid., 144–145).

7 I have adapted Kidder's translation.

coming over, but when they come over they are like familiar faces. Although their faces are *like* familiar ones, they are not even within the simile of familiar ones. This added distance recalls their removal from the world.

Adamov's changes to simile in particular in these two cases is significant in a poem that, as Patrick Greaney has argued in *Untimely Beggar: Poverty and Power from Baudelaire to Benjamin*, has an overwhelming presence of simile. According to Greaney, it serves to demonstrate the impossibility of representing the poor. The entire text of *Das Buch von der Armut und vom Tode* reads as a series of similes that compare God to the poor, and the poor to other things; Gottfried Benn called Rilke, not in praise, "a great LIKE-poet" (quoted in Greaney 105). Greaney continues that Rilke uses simile to show that there is a distance between the speaker and the poor, and that language is inadequate to represent the pain of poverty, indicating that he is not aestheticizing poverty: "simile belongs to a progressive impoverishment of the central figure, because the simile assigns characteristics and, at the same time, emphasizes the estrangement from them with its 'like' that separates vehicle and tenor. The simile creates more distance between vehicle and tenor even as it asserts their similarity" (102). Adamov does not remove the simile but changes the vehicle. This change is not only an example of how he alters the text to address loss, separation, and exile, but it is also an emblem of his philosophy of translation as transposition. To capture what Rilke is saying, Adamov has to write *like* what he is saying, showing the spirit of the text. For Adamov, that spirit is exile and makes it such an important text to revise in 1941 in particular.

In his 1941 preface to the translation, Adamov firmly anchors his reading of Rilke's poetry in the historical present. He refers to the cataclysmic moment of his own time in which his contemporaries have ceased to be anchored to the world: "Parce qu'en nos temps d'horreur, l'homme a dénoué les liens qui le reliaient au monde, qui lui donnaient la preuve de sa propre inexistence" [Because in our time of horror, man has undone the ties that linked him to the world, that gave him the proof of his own inexistence] (Adamov, "Avertissement" 13). Adamov continues that man stands outside the world, echoing his translation of "ewig ohne Welt" [always without a world] as "toujours hors du monde" [always outside the world]. Furthermore, according to Adamov this separation means that man "a perdu le sens de la vie" [has lost the meaning of life] (Adamov, "Avertissement" 13). Adamov uses the word *sens*, which can mean both meaning and direction; he is lost, in a way that recalls the disorientation in an abyss in Rilke's poem.

In the teeming city of *Das Buch von der Armut und vom Tode*, no one owns their own death, or chooses it. Adamov makes a clear link between this notion of death in the poem and in his own times. In Rilke's poem, one of the key aspects of alienation in the city is that the poor are robbed even of their own death. They have a "small" death that is not their own but rather one that takes them as a foreign death. But the speaker begs for a higher notion of death: "Dort is der Tod … ihr eigener hängt grün und ohne Süße / wie eine Frucht in ihnen, die nicht reift" [And death is there … their own, hanging in them like a fruit / unripening, and green, and lacking sweetness] (Rilke, *The Book* 170–173). As opposed to the meaningless death in the city, the greater death is one that comes from within. In Adamov's preface, he writes that the higher idea of death has been lost for modern man, living "dans nos temps d'horreur" [in our time of horror]: "Le grand mal de notre civilisation est moins un crime contre la vie qu'un crime contre la mort" [The great evil of our civilization is less a crime against life than a crime against death] (Adamov, "Avertissement" 11). Chillingly, he describes his age as: "ce monde avili où la mort en série est seule 'légale'" [this debased world where only standard death is "legal"] (Adamov, "Avertissement" 12). *La mort en série* can refer to standard, serial, or mass death. This explicit moment in his introduction to the translation sets the stage for a reading of death in Rilke's poem through the lens of the Occupation. There is also a constant tension in his work, in which he both talks about his own specific exile and alienation, and turns it into a more generalized exile in the war for all of society.

After his new edition of *Das Buch von der Armut und vom Tode* was printed in Algiers, Adamov spent five months in the camps of Argelès and Rivesaltes. According to him, he was arrested for having been overheard criticizing Philippe Pétain, the new head of the authoritarian French state now based in Vichy ("La politique" 39). The French government opened Argelès in 1939 as a camp for Spanish Republican refugees of the Spanish Republican Army after its defeat, although it became a holding place for Jewish people, Roma, Germans on French soil, and other immigrants and stateless people in France before it closed in 1941 (cf. Caron 243). The second camp, Rivesaltes, was originally a transit site for French military troops leaving for the colonies, which then served as an internment camp for German refugees starting in October 1940. It also became a holding place for other stateless people residing in France like Adamov. Around the time Adamov was in the camp, during the period of mid-May ("Document 1") through the end of October 1941 ("Document 2"), there were 8,000 inmates living in deplorable, unhygienic conditions. Deportations to concentration camps began in the summer of 1942. Adamov describes the stifling heat and dirty conditions in Argelès: "C'était un camp épouvantable. Simplement il n'y avait pas les fours crématoires. La seule différence avec les camps allemands était là, il n'y avait pas de fours crématoires" [It was a horrendous camp. Only it had no crematoria. That was the only difference with German camps, it had no crematoria] ("La politique" 41). Jean-Jacques Champenois, of the American Friends Service Committee in Marseille, tried to help Adamov, imploring his colleagues to take personal care of him as he was completely distraught ("Letter"). Years after the war, Adamov would say that his experience in these camps awakened him to political realities but, as he bitterly regretted, did not teach him enough, for he always blamed himself for not joining the Resistance ("La politique" 39 and 41). After he was liberated, with the aid of the American Friends Service Committee, he remained in Marseille for another year before returning to Paris. There he published excerpts of *L'aveu* in which he continued to write about the notions of separation and exile that he had translated in Rilke.

3   Language, Exile, and the Absurd

Adamov's *L'aveu* goes further than his translation, creating a link between the degradation of language in his time and a sense of alienation. Adamov wrote *L'aveu* over the course of the years 1938 to 1943, publishing excerpts during the Occupation and the full edition in 1946.[8] Martin Esslin, the critic of the Theater of the Absurd, reads *L'aveu* as "a brilliant statement of the metaphysical anguish that forms the basis of Existentialist literature and of the Theatre of the Absurd" (93). In *L'aveu*, Adamov demonstrates that language and alienation are inextricably linked. In one of the earliest texts in the book, "Ce qu'il y a" [What there is] (Paris 1938), Adamov writes that man is always "un étranger à lui–même" [a stranger to himself] (28). The speaker of *L'aveu*, based on Adamov explains that this is due to a mutilation and a separation at the center of himself. The first mention of the word *absurd* appears in the 1939–1940 entry of the "Journal terrible" [Terrible diary], a diary at the center of *L'aveu*: "il est absurde de vouloir ce qui ne vous est pas destiné car il est alors impossible de vouloir en vérité" [it is absurd to want that which you are not destined to have for it is then impossible truly to want] (122). You cannot truly want anything because you are destined to lose it; you may attempt to regain it, only to lose it again. Already in the 1939–1940 entry, Adamov created a Sisyphean image,

---

8   Adamov began *L'aveu* in 1938, and altered it throughout the war, especially after his internment, publishing different versions of excerpts in *Fontaine* (1942) and *La Nouvelle Revue Française* (1943). Quotes here refer to the version of the text published in *Je, ils* (Gallimard, 1969). For the purposes of this article, this version does not contain significant changes from the other editions.

predating Albert Camus's *Myth of Sisyphus* by two years. Man reaches the summit only to fall: everything gained is lost and must be regained.

In this text Adamov further elaborates the separation that he read in Rilke's poem. In a section dated 1939, "L'humiliation sans fin" [Unending humiliation], Adamov writes that the misfortune of existence is expressed in the very structure of the word *existence*; the prefix *ex* implies a movement of going outside. By merely existing, man is already in exile and expelled (cf. 73). In section 7 of the "Journal terrible," which he wrote after his liberation from the camp and dates to November 1941, he links this separation to his historical moment as he does in the introduction to the Rilke translations. Adamov states that his internment truly made him aware of his historical position: "Jusqu'à présent je ne m'étais pas tout entier plongé dans l'époque. Elle ne me submergeait pas" [Up until the present I had not entirely plunged into the era. It did not submerge me] (141). This realization had much to do with understanding the sense of separation he experienced in the camps: "Séparé littéralement du reste du monde dans un camp de prisonniers, je devais prendre enfin conscience que je vivais séparé de tout au temps où tout est séparé de tout" [Separated literally from the rest of the world in a prison camp, I finally had to become aware that I was living separated from everything at a time when everything is separated from everything] (141).

Later in the Occupation, in the introduction to *L'aveu* dated 1943, Adamov designates the degradation of language as the essential problem of existence in his time (cf. 23, 37, 108). Like in his translations of Rilke's poem and in his introduction to the translations, here he writes of his era as one that is marked by death. But now the measure of the indignity (*ignominie*) of death is the decline of language, in which words have become phantoms of themselves. He repeats this idea later in the text, writing that words have become carcasses of words, phantoms that speakers keep trotting out of their jaws (cf. 113). Even his expression to describe his time, *ignominie*, means that this is a world without a name or a word that is unnamable for words have lost their meaning (cf. 105). This notion of empty or debased language as a sign of the irrationality of the world would later become a hallmark of the postwar Theater of the Absurd.

Adamov never addresses head on that the language in which he is writing, French, is his adopted language of the country that had imprisoned him as a stateless man. Nor does he reflect on the fact that the language from which he translates Rilke, German, is the language of the occupying force. Hannah Arendt would famously declare that "After all, it wasn't the German language that went crazy" to explain how she continued to write in German even after the horrors of the Second World War (quoted in Young-Bruehl 1). She maintained

German as her mother tongue, for it was a connection to a particular mode of thought, or even formed a *Heimat* [homeland] itself (cf. Rosen 103; Young-Bruehl 3). In fact, the journal that published excerpts of Adamov's translations, *Fontaine*, actually folded Rilke in to a story of the democratic Europe it was celebrating even under the Occupation (cf. Vignale 95). Two issues after he published Adamov's translations, Max-Pol Fouchet edited a special issue devoted to "L'Europe française" (French Europe), that is, a Europe influenced by French ideals of liberty (cf. Vignale 93). In his introduction to this special issue, Fouchet cites Rilke as a participant in this idea of Europe and of France ("Deux ans de vie"), and Lanza del Vasto penned the poem "Portrait de Rilke" that echoes some major themes of *Das Buch von der Armut und vom Tode*. In this context, Rilke as a German-language poet was far from representative of the occupying forces.

As such, Rilke and the German language themselves did not stand in as a sign of Adamov's new exile in France. Rather he was able to use language through the tools of translation to express his new entry into an early stage of exile in the war. He conceived of language in *L'aveu* not necessarily in terms of national language but rather as the idea of language. And language is degraded but not crazy nor irreparably destroyed. Words are the only hope, for they still hold within them, hidden, more profound meaning (cf. 37). It is the role of the poet to use words to uncover their sense and deliver to the reader what is hidden in their silence (cf. 23). A word is silent, but the poet makes it speak. Adamov imagines the uncovering of meaning lying dormant in words as digging without stopping at the tree of lost language; this is a tree with its roots growing not *deep* in the ground but rather up to the sky (cf. 23). This upward motion presents a new contrast to Rilke's depths.

In his essay on Adamov's postwar theater in *Mythologies*, Roland Barthes describes Adamov's writing: "Le langage d'Adamov a ses racines à l'air" [Adamov's language has its roots in the open air] (91). For Barthes, Adamov's postwar theater takes everyday speech and turns it into situations of language that put pressure onto our assumptions. He lays language bare, as if he were displaying the roots of a tree. Barthes provides us with an image for talking about Adamov—it is not that language is rootless but rather through uncovering the hidden significance of words, meaning through language can be created. Adamov achieved this in transposing Rilke's poetry onto his present moment, finding meaning in French and German under the Occupation while still elaborating the sense of exile and alienation in occupied France. It is at the beginnings of his new stage of exile in his adopted country and language that he uncovered meaning through the act of translation.

Works Cited

"ADAMIAN Arthur dit ADAMOV." 22 Sept. 1939. Archives of the Prefecture of Police, Paris, series 1W, 1W0153, folder 45855.

Adamov, Arthur. *Je, ils*. Éditions Gallimard, 1969.

Adamov, Arthur. "La politique des restes – Mon théâtre : évolution." N.D. Institut Mémoires de l'Édition Contemporaine, ADM 1.2.1.

Adamov, Arthur. "Avertissement." *Le livre de la pauvreté et de la mort*. Éditions Charlot, 1941, pp. 9–17.

Adamov, Arthur. "Translator's Note." *Le livre de la pauvreté et de la mort*. Éditions Charlot, 1941, p. 18.

Barthes, Roland. *Mythologies*. Éditions du Seuil, 1957.

Caron, Vicki. *Uneasy Asylum: France and the Jewish Refugee Crisis, 1933–1942*. Stanford Studies in Jewish History and Culture. Stanford University Press, 1999.

Champenois, Jean-Jacques. "Letter." 22 July 1941. Archives of the American Friends Service Committee, box 5, folder 77.

"Décret-loi du 2 mai 1938 Police des étrangers." *Journal officiel République française*, 3 May 1938, p. 4967.

"Document 1." N.D. Departmental Archives of Pyrénées-Orientales, Centre d'hébergement d'Argelès-sur-Mer.

"Document 2." 28 Oct. 1941. Departmental Archives of Pyrénées-Orientales, Centre d'hébergement de Rivesaltes, file 11867.

Esslin, Martin. *The Theatre of the Absurd*. Vintage Books, 2001.

Fouchet, Max-Pol. "Deux ans de vie," *Fontaine*, vol. 2, no. 4 (April-May 1941), pp. 281–282.

Greaney, Patrick. *Untimely Beggar: Poverty and Power from Baudelaire to Benjamin*. University of Minnesota Press, 2008.

Masson, André. *Mythologie d'André Masson*. Edited by Jean-Paul Clébert. Éditions Pierre Cailler, 1971.

Rilke, Rainer Maria. *The Book of Hours: Prayers to a Lowly God*. Translation by Annemarie S. Kidder. A bilingual ed, Northwestern University Press, 2001.

Rilke, Rainer Maria. *The Book of Hours in a New Translation*. Translation by Stevie Krayer. Institut für Anglistik und Amerikanistik, Universität Salzburg, 1995.

Rilke, Rainer Maria. *Le livre de la pauvreté et de la mort*. Translation by Arthur Adamov. Éditions Charlot, 1941.

Rilke, Rainer Maria. "Le livre de la pauvreté et de la mort." Translation by Arthur Adamov. *Fontaine*, vol. 2, no. 12, Dec./Jan. 1941, pp. 153–165.

Rilke, Rainer Maria. "Le livre de la pauvreté et de la mort." Translation by Arthur Adamov. *Esprit*, vol. 1, no. 3, 1 Dec. 1932, pp. 388–395.

Rosen, Alan. *Sounds of Defiance: The Holocaust, Multilingualism, and the Problem of English*. University of Nebraska Press, 2005.

Vasto, Lanza del. "Portrait de Rilke," *Fontaine*, vol. 2, no. 14 (April–May 1941), pp. 305–306.

Vignale, François. *La revue* Fontaine: *poésie, résistance, engagement: Alger 1938–Paris 1947*. Presses Universitaires de Rennes, 2012.

Young-Bruehl, Elisabeth. *Hannah Arendt: For Love of the World*. Yale University Press, 1982.

„May God Protect Austria!": der „Anschluss" und seine Folgen im Leben und Werk von Stella Hershan

Olena Komarnicka

Abstract

The "Anschluss" (annexation) and its immediate consequences were early stages of exile for many Jews in Austria and contributed to making flight the only rescue possible. The following article first presents the life of the Austrian-Jewish writer Stella Hershan before exile. After the "Anschluss" the financial situation and the living conditions of the young Austrian and her family dramatically changed. Social alienation and persecution became part of the family's everyday life until they left Vienna in 1939. The writer did not begin to write until arriving in exile, but in her texts she often returned to the time before emigration and chose her home country as the scene of action. Using Hershan's unpublished novel "March 11th 1938" as an example, the early stages of exile are explained in greater detail.

∴

> I was born in Austria, I was Austrian, and I loved my country,
> I loved the beautiful city of Vienna, the mountains surrounding it,
> the lovely lakes where we spent vacations in the summer.
> HERSHAN, *Erinnerungen* 19

∴

Biographische Forschung macht die Geschichte eines Lebens zu einem darstellungswürdigen Phänomen.[1] Es gibt eine Vielfalt von Materialien, die über eine Lebensgeschichte Auskunft geben können. Dazu gehören u.a. biographische Darstellungen, autobiographische Zeugnisse, wie Briefe, Tagebücher oder

---

1   Das Zitat im Titel, „May God protect Austria", ist genommen aus: Hershan, „March 11th 1938". Folder 1, MS 258.

sonstige Texte, Fotografien und historische Dokumente. Zu der wichtigsten Aufgabe der Biographieforschung gehört die Zusammenfassung der verschiedenen Schichten und Aspekte zu einer „die wesentlichen menschlichen und geistigen Bezüge umgreifenden Ganzheit" (Strelka 242). Sie eröffnet den Blick auf den Erfahrungshorizont, d.h. welche Erfahrungen das Individuum macht, wie es daraus lernt und sich im Leben bewährt. In diesem Sinne soll im Folgenden der Versuch der Biographieforschung am Leben der österreichischen Schriftstellerin jüdischer Herkunft Stella Hershan unternommen werden, besonders in Bezug auf die Vorstufen ihres Exils nach dem „Anschluss". Davon finden sich viele Spuren in ihrem Werk und sonstigen Lebenszeugnissen und Dokumenten. Solche Biographieforschung ist schon immer Teil der Grundlagenforschung in Exilstudien gewesen. In den Ausführungen hier soll sie mit den folgenden Fragen verbunden werden: Wie änderte sich ihr Leben und das Leben ihrer Familie nach dem „Anschluss" im Sinne der Vorstufen des Exils? Wie bereitete sich die junge Schriftstellerin auf das Exil vor? Wie schnell wurde der Familie klar, dass die Flucht die einzige Rettung war?

1 Biographisches

Stella Hershan (geb. Kreidl) wurde am 07.02.1915 während des Ersten Weltkrieges in Wien als Kind jüdisch assimilierter Eltern geboren. Ihr Vater Felix Kreidl kam aus St. Pölten und die Mutter Lucy aus Prag. Hershan war keine besonders gute Schülerin. Sie besuchte zuerst die „Freie Schule" und danach ging sie ins Hietzinger Gymnasium, das sie später verließ. Ihre Familie war der Meinung, dass sie keine Ambitionen hatte, die Matura zu machen, geschweige denn zu studieren. Die Autorin besuchte stattdessen eine Sprachschule und lernte dort die Sprachen und Literatur, die in ihrer Zukunft so wichtig sein sollten. Für das literarische Schreiben begeisterte sie sich schon damals.

Als achtzehnjährige junge Frau hat die Autorin den neun Jahre älteren Ingenieur Rudolf Hershan geheiratet. Die Flitterwochen verbrachte das junge Paar in Italien: „Das einzige, das mir zu dieser Zeit wichtig war, war mein neuer Mann Rudi, in den ich ganz schrecklich verliebt war. Ich fand es wunderbar, verheiratet zu sein, und meine Freundinnen waren neidisch. Bald hatten wir auch eine kleine Tochter, die wir Lisa nannten, und waren sehr glücklich" (Hershan, *Erinnerungen* 53). Die Hershans gehörten zu den wohlhabenden Familien Wiens. Als Rudolfs Eltern starben, hat er mit seinen Brüdern die Firma des Vaters, in der Eisenkonstruktionen hergestellt wurden, übernommen. Auch Stellas Vater war ein erfolgreicher Kaufmann. Die Autorin musste sich nie ums Geld kümmern: „Money was something that was given to me, first by my father and later by my husband. You need money? Again? I gave you some

only yesterday! You can only spend it, you don't know how hard it is to earn it"
(Hershan, *Erinnerungen* 63).

Das junge Paar interessierte sich nicht für Politik, und die nationalsozialistische Machtübernahme in Deutschland hatte für sie keine Bedeutung. Die Autorin äußerte sich darüber folgendermaßen: „The fact that in neighboring Germany, that same year, a man named Adolf Hitler became chancellor hardly
made an impact on us" (Hershan, *A memoir* 182). Im Jahre 1934, als der Bürgerkrieg in Wien ausbrach, begann die politische Situation für Hershan an Bedeutung zu gewinnen. Die Schriftstellerin konnte sich aber damals nicht vorstel-
len, das Heimatland zu verlassen: „Leave? Our city? Our home? Why should we
do that? What was happening in Germany could not possibly happen in Austria. Hitler? That clown? Who used to be a housepainter in Vienna? A vagrant?
How in the world could the Germans be afraid of him? Those Germans! They
never were liked in Austria" (Hershan, *A memoir* 182).

2   März 1938

Der Zeitraum vom Berchtesgadener Abkommen am 12. Februar 1938[2] bis zur
Volksabstimmung am 10. April 1938 war einer der ereignisreichsten und fol-
genschwersten Abschnitte der österreichischen Geschichte. Ab Herbst 1937
begann sich der nationalsozialistische Druck auf Österreich sowohl in politischer als auch in wirtschaftlicher Hinsicht zu verstärken. Am 12. März 1938
besetzte die deutsche Wehrmacht Österreich; der „Anschluss" Österreichs an
das Deutsche Reich wurde verkündet, der mit großer Freude und Begeisterung
von der Bevölkerung aufgenommen wurde.[3] Viele empfanden diese Ereignisse

---

2   Abkommen zwischen dem Deutschen Reich und dem Bundesstaat Österreich, durch das den
    österreichischen Nationalsozialisten weitreichende politische Entfaltungsmöglichkeiten zu-
    gesichert werden sollten. Näheres dazu vgl. http://www.oesta.gv.at/site/cob_27099/5164/
    default.aspx.

3   So beschrieb eine andere österreichische Dichterin Mimi Grossberg den „Anschluss": „Am 24.
    Februar 1938 hielt Bundeskanzler Dr. Schuschnigg jene Rede, in der er alle österreichischen
    Bürger, auch die nichtarischen, des ganz besonderen staatlichen Schutzes ihrer Rechte und
    ihres Lebens versicherte. Und gerne glaubten das alle jene, denen ein Verlassen der Heimat
    unmöglich schien! Schon am nächsten Morgen trugen viele das rotweißrote Bändchen der
    Vaterländischen Front' im Knopfloch. Noch am Sonntag vor dem Einmarsch der Hitler-
    Truppen in Österreich gab es im Theater in der Josephstadt in Wien unter der Leitung von
    Ernst Lothar eine Matinee, in der berühmte Schauspieler Dichtungen von Beer-Hofmann,
    Broch, Polgar, Stefan Zweig, Werfel und Weinheber vortrugen. Eine Woche später waren diese
    Dichter – mit Ausnahme Josef Weinhebers – Österreich verfemt. Am 9. März, dem
    dieser Matinee folgenden Mittwoch, verkündeten große Plakate, dass am 13. März eine

als seelische Erleichterung, ohne sich Gedanken darüber zu machen, was nun kommen würde. Manche schwelgten in dem Gefühl, wieder unter dem Schutz einer Großmacht zu stehen, wie zur Zeit der Donaumonarchie. Es zeigte sich sehr schnell, welche Pläne Hitler gegenüber Österreich hatte, und die Begeisterung schlug bald in Entsetzen um. Die Ereignisse im März 1938 übten auch einen großen Einfluss auf das Leben der jüdischen Bevölkerung Österreichs aus. Zunächst war aber die jüdische Bevölkerung davon überzeugt, dass Hitler und die Nationalsozialisten nicht lange an der Macht bleiben würden. Eine andere Emigrantin kommentierte die Vorkommnisse folgendermaßen: "Wir haben immer gedacht, es ist unmöglich, die Welt wird das nicht zulassen [...]" (Hartenstein 158).

Die Eltern von Hershan waren zu dieser Zeit wie eigentlich jedes Jahr im Frühling in Nizza. Sie kamen nicht mehr zurück. Die Ereignisse in dieser Zeit haben dazu beigetragen, dass auch für Hershan Exil die einzige Möglichkeit der Rettung zu sein schien. Verfolgung als Juden, die Beschlagnahme des Vermögens, Flucht und Vertreibung waren die Vorstufen ihres Exils, wie nun gezeigt werden soll.

3   Judentum und jüdische Identität

Wie für viele andere Emigranten war Judentum eine Religion wie jede andere. Hershan wusste nicht viel über den Judaismus: „Ich finde es nach wie vor eine Ungerechtigkeit, dass man als Jude klassifiziert wird und nicht in erster Linie als Deutscher oder Österreicher" (Hartenstein 162). Ihr Mann wusste schon mehr darüber, weil seine Mutter religiös war. Die Emigrantin erfuhr vor dem „Anschluss" keinen Antisemitismus am eigenen Leib, weder von Freunden und Bekannten, noch von Nachbarn. Sie wusste auch nicht, wer in ihrem Umkreis Jude war, und um diese Tatsache hat sie auch gar nicht gekümmert. In ihrer Autobiographie schrieb sie:

Volksabstimmung über die Zugehörigkeit zu Deutschland stattfinden wird; dazu kam es aber nicht mehr. Schon am 11. März musste der Bundeskanzler den Schutz der Heimat und ihrer arischen und nichtarischen Bürger einem Höheren übertragen, denn mit den Worten ‚Gott schütze Österreich!' dankte er ab, zwischen bewaffneten SA-Männern stehend. Seit dem 11. März 1938 gab es in Österreich nur noch zwei Parteien: Die mit und die ohne Hakenkreuz. Nun begann, wie schon 1933 in Deutschland, der Leidensweg der Künstler und der Intellektuellen, deren Mehrzahl zur hakenkreuzlosen Partei gehörte – oder sich ihr freiwillig zugesellte" (*Geschichte* 10).

Religion did not mean anything to me when I grew up in Vienna, Austria, during the early Thirties. Though I was born into a Jewish family, organized religion was not practiced in my home. Mostly I did not even know whether my friends were Jewish or Christian. At that time, long before the State of Israel was established, Judaism to me was only a religion.

HERSHAN, *Erinnerungen* 68

Doch nach dem „Anschluss" sah die Lage anders aus. Nachdem das Judentum der Hershans bestätigt wurde, beschlagnahmten die Nationalsozialisten dem Ehepaar das Auto und später den Betrieb. Danach fing die Zugehörigkeit zu einer Glaubensgemeinschaft an Bedeutung zu gewinnen. In der Autobiografie schrieb Hershan: „The years passed and March 1938 rolled around. The time when Hitler and his Nazis troops marched into Vienna. Suddenly I was Jewish" (*Erinnerungen* 70). Es wurde auch den Christen nicht erlaubt, bei den Juden zu arbeiten. Das Leben und der Lebensstandard veränderten sich rasant. Die Hershans lebten in ständiger Angst.

4   Verlust des Vermögens

Der „Anschluss" bedeutete für die Familie Hershan finanzielle Schwierigkeiten und letztendlich den Verlust des Vermögens. Mehrere Beweise und Dokumente, die sich im Leo Baeck Institute befinden, stellen die finanzielle Situation der beiden Familien Hershan und Kreidl dar (vgl. Stella Hershan Collection, AR 11178).

– *Verzeichnis über das Vermögen von Juden nach dem Stand vom 27. April 1938*

In diesem Dokument berichtet der Vater: „Da ich Jude deutscher Staatsangehörigkeit bin, habe ich in dem nachstehenden Vermögensverzeichnis mein gesamtes inländisches und ausländisches Vermögen angegeben und bewertet." In dem Verzeichnis werden nicht nur Bankguthaben, Zahlungsmittel, Spareinlagen, sondern auch alle wertvollen Sachen wie Schmuckstücke, Teppiche, Silber, sogar jährliche Zuwendungen des Vaters angeführt. In dem Dokument ist auch die Rede von dem am 16. März 1938 requirierten Auto, das nie zurückgegeben wurde.

– *Reichsfluchtssteuerbescheid vom 23. November 1939*

Laut diesem Dokument wurde das Ehepaar Kreidl gezwungen, eine Reichsfluchtsteuer, die ein Viertel des Vermögens betraf, zu bezahlen. Diese Steuer war für diejenigen zu begleichen, die ihren „gewöhnlichen Aufenthalt im Land Österreich oder im übrigen Reichsgebiet aufgegeben haben."

– *Beschlagnahmeverfügung vom 25. Juli 1941*

In diesem Dokument lesen wir: „Das gesamte stehende und liegende Vermögen sowie alle Rechte und Ansprüche des Felix und Lucy Kreidl [...] wird aus Gründen der öffentlichen Sicherheit und Ordnung mit dem Ziele der späteren Einziehung zu Gunsten des Deutschen Reichs beschlagnahmt." Mit diesem Dokument hat die Familie Kreidl ihr ganzes Vermögen verloren.

5 Ausreise und weiteres Leben

Hershans Schwägerin und Schwager hatten Bekannte in den USA und konnten schnell auswandern; sie haben sich dann um ein Affidavit auch für die Hershans gekümmert. Es wurde Januar 1939, bis alle Genehmigungen erteilt wurden und die junge Familie mit der kleinen Tochter Wien verlassen konnten. Sie reisten durch die Schweiz nach Nizza, nahmen Abschied von den Eltern, fuhren dann über Paris nach Cherbourg und setzten von dort mit dem Schiff nach New York über. Die ersten drei Jahre lebten Hershans in Philadelphia. Danach zogen sie sich nach New York, wo bereits ihre Eltern wohnten. Bis zu ihrem Lebensende hat Hershan in dieser Stadt ohne Gedanken an Rückkehr gelebt: „Aber trotzdem hat man nie daran gedacht, daß man zurückgehen würde, um sich wiederzuholen, was einem weggenommen wurde. Man war auch so verletzt, dass das Heimatland einen nicht mehr will. [...] In unserem ganzen Bekanntenkreis war niemand, der zurückgegangen ist. Unserer Meinung nach wäre es charakterlos gewesen" (Hartenstein 162).

Was ihre jüdische Herkunft betraf, hat sich die Schriftstellerin die Fragen gestellt, wie ihr Leben gewesen wäre, wenn sie nicht jüdisch wäre:

> Was wäre geschehen, wenn ich nicht in einer jüdischen Familie in Wien geboren wäre? Wenn ich eine der „anderen" gewesen wäre? Was hätte ich getan? Hätte ich den Mut gehabt, verfolgten Menschen zu helfen? Kinder zu verstecken? Auch wenn mein eigenes Leben gefährdet gewesen wäre? Oder das meiner Familie? Meines Kindes?
>
> HERSHAN, *Erinnerungen* 18

Sie hätte die gestellten Fragen sehr gerne mit „ja" beantwortet, sicher war sie sich aber dessen nicht. Als die Emigrantin im fortgeschrittenen Alter in einem Interview für die *Austrian Heritage Collection* gefragt wurde, ob sie eine Mitteilung für die jüngere Generation hätte, sagte sie nur: „Interessiert euch für die politische Situation in eurem Land. Ihr könnt nicht erlauben, dass noch ein Hitler zur Macht kommt."[4] Hershan verstarb am 22. August 2014 in New York.

---

4 Die Aufnahme des Interviews befindet sich im Leo Baeck Institute.

ILLUSTRATION 16.1   Foto von Stella Hershan in späteren Jahren

6   Literarische Tätigkeit

Angefangen zu schreiben hat die Schriftstellerin erst richtig im Exil. Mehrere
Jahre unterrichtete Hershan Deutsch an der Berlitz-Schule in New York, gleichzeitig besuchte sie auch mehrere Kurse an der Universität und an der New
School. Anfang der 50er Jahre entdeckte sie kreatives Schreiben, und ab dem
Zeitpunkt wurde es ihr Hobby. Damals in Wien hatte sie nicht geahnt, dass sie
einmal in Amerika eine Schriftstellerin werden würde. Dank der Emigration ist
der Traum der Autorin in Erfüllung gegangen: Schreiben.

Während ihres Lebens wurden folgende Werken publiziert:

- *A Woman of Quality* (Crown, 1970)
- *The Naked Angel* (Robert Hale, 1973), deutsche Übersetzung von Ursula
  Heim: *Der nackte Engel* (Molden, 1984)
- *Daughter of Revolution*, deutsche Übersetzung von Ursula Heim: *Ein Kind
  der Revolution* (Universitas Verlag, 1989)
- *In Freundschaft, Elisabeth. Briefroman* (Gryphon Verlag, 1992)
- *The Maiden of Kosovo. Novel* (Gryphon Verlag, 2003)

– *Emigration: Ein Buch für den Frieden. Exilgeschichten* (Gryphon Verlag, 2004)
– *Erinnerungen zwischen zwei Welten / Memories between two Worlds. Exilerzählungen* (Gryphon Verlag, 2006)
Über ihre literarische Tätigkeit berichtete die Autorin insgesamt:

> Durch mein Schreiben habe ich mich viel mit der Vergangenheit beschäftigt und auch mit dem Leben der nächsten Generationen Österreicher und Deutscher. Es ist mir klar geworden, dass auch sie eine schwere Zeit haben mit der Vergangenheit fertig zu werden. Und langsam, langsam, ist der schwere Stein, welchen ich so lange in mir herumgetragen habe, leichter geworden.
>
> HERSHAN, *Erinnerungen* 18

Dies ist auch der Fall in ihrem autobiographischen Werk *Erinnerungen zwischen zwei Welten,* die die Schriftstellerin ihrer Tochter Lisa und Herrn Dr. Robert Streibel in Dankbarkeit dafür widmete, dass „er für mich Wien wieder ein wenig zu meiner Heimat gemacht hat" (Hershan, *Erinnerungen* 3). In dieser zweisprachig gedruckten Autobiografie beschreibt Hershan mit ein wenig Wehmut, aber voll von neuen Eindrücken und Begegnungen mit anderen Menschen ihr Leben zwischen zwei Stühlen bei der Wiederbegegnung mit Wien:

> Ich fühlte mich wie ein Geist, jemand der gestorben war und plötzlich wieder zurück kam. Eine fremde Stadt? Wo ich jede Straße kannte, jeden Stein, wo ich mit geschlossenen Augen meinen Weg finden konnte. Ich wollte auf die Strassen spucken, aber ich wollte mich auch bücken und sie küssen. Die Menschen? Der Klang ihrer Sprache, die auch meine war. Jetzt waren sie mir näher als meine amerikanische Familie. Ich war ein Mensch, der in zwei Teile geteilt war. Der Hass, welcher mir durch die Jahre, die ich fort war, Stärke gab, begann zu schmelzen. Ich wollte rasch wieder fortfahren, aber ich wollte auch bleiben.
>
> HERSHAN, *Erinnerungen* 80

Allerdings fängt die Autobiografie mit dem Elternhaus in Wien an und endet mit der Geschichte über den Besuch in der Heimatstadt. Auf diese Art und Weise hebt die Schriftstellerin hervor, wie wichtig die österreichische Identität für sie geblieben war. Ganz klar ist das auch der Fall in einem Romanmanuskript, das im Folgenden in Bezug auf die Vorstufen des Exils besprochen werden soll.

7   **Typoskript: March 11th 1938. A novel of reorientation** (vgl. Stella K.
     Hershan Collection. Folder 1, MS 258)

Die Handlung dieses unpublizierten Romans beginnt am 31. Dezember 1937
kurz vor dem Neujahr. Das 530-seitige Typoskript beschreibt das Leben einer
adligen Familie bis Ende der 50er Jahre, wobei viel Aufmerksamkeit der Zeit
bis zum Exil gewidmet und deshalb im Kontext der Vorstufen des Exils von
Interesse ist. Die Hauptpersonen Robert von Hochmeyer, Rechtsanwalt und
Sohn eines Rechtsanwaltes und einer christlichen Mutter, und seine Frau Ruth
von Hochmeyer, Tochter eines jüdischen Journalisten, haben vor, Neujahr im
Bekanntenkreis zu verbringen. Das sind nur einige Monate vor dem „Anschluss", aber die Bürger spüren keine Gefahr und plaudern über Uraufführun-
gen im Theater, die Karnevalssaison, sie trinken viel, die Frauen flirten mit den
Männern. Sie sind alle fest davon überzeugt, dass sich Hitler nicht trauen wird,
Österreich zu besetzen: „The German will never dare to attack Austria. They
know the whole world would protest, go to war at once" (17). Es sind aber schon
die ersten Stimmen zu hören, die vor den Nazis und Hitler warnen. In einem
Gespräch mit der Hauptheldin äußert sich ein deutscher Gast über die Situation in Deutschland folgendermaßen: „It is impossible to describe life in Nazi
Germany. You must experience it to understand. Gnaedige Frau. I besiege you,
leave Vienna as long as you are able to—" (23).
      Mit der Zeit fängt man an, den Judenhass überall zu spüren. Es kommt auch
zu einer Auseinandersetzung zwischen dem Dienstmädchen und der Köchin:
„It won't be long before you'll find out what it is like to live in an efficient country with a strong leader... How dare you make fun of the *Fuehrer*? [...] You just
wait, [...], within a short time you won't laugh..." (42). Das Dienstmädchen Else
sieht im Führer eine Befreiung von Juden. Wenn Hitler zur Macht kommt, ver-
schwindet die Ungerechtigkeit in Österreich. Er wird den Juden das Geld beschlagnahmen. Ihrer Meinung nach haben die Juden jahrzehntelang die deutsche Bevölkerung ausgenutzt und ungerecht behandelt. Sie beschuldigt die
Juden, den Krieg angefangen zu haben, in dem ihr Mann starb. Nur weil ihre
Situation ausweglos ist, arbeitet sie in einer jüdischen Familie. Hershan zeigt
in ihrem Roman auch die Unmenschlichkeit zwischen den Leuten oder genauer gesagt: ihren Neid. Das Dienstmädchen träumt davon, dass ihre Arbeitge-
berin von den Nazis verhaftet wird; danach werden diese vielleicht ihr alle Sachen und Kleidung ihrer Arbeitsgeberin zukommen lassen.
      Der Roman zeigt auch, wie viele Österreicher fest davon überzeugt waren,
dass das Bündnis mit Deutschland nur Vorteile mit sich bringen würde. Sogar
der Rechtsanwalt Robert von Hochmeyer ist zunächst eher ein „Anschluss"-
Befürworter. Doch an dem Tag, an dem Bundeskanzler Schuschnigg zurück-
tritt, wird Robert, als er mit Ruth den Vater zum Zug nach Nizza begleitet hat,

auf dem Bahnhof verhaftet. Diese Ereignisse verschärfen nur den Konflikt zwischen der Schwiegertochter und Schwiegermutter. Sie beschuldigt Ruth und ihre jüdische Herkunft für das ganze Unglück und Pech. Um den Mann aus dem Gefängnis zu retten, fängt Ruth eine Liebesbeziehung mit einem Rechtsanwalt an, der Bekannte unter den Nazis hat. Die Befreiung des Ehemannes kostet Ruth nicht nur ihre Ehre, sondern sie wird auch gezwungen, ihm ihren ganzen Schmuck zu geben.

Von Tag zu Tag verschlechtert sich die Situation der Juden in Wien. Immer häufiger kommt es zu Beschlagnahmen und Verhaftungen. Eines Tages wird das Geld und der Schmuck von Ruths Schwiegermutter von der Gestapo konfisziert, von der sie erfährt, dass ihre Großmutter jüdischer Herkunft war. Das wird für sie zu einer unerträglichen Nachricht; vor ihrer Schwiegertochter begeht sie Selbstmord, indem sie aus dem Fenster springt.

Die Kinder des Ehepaares erleben unterdessen den Judenhass am eigenen Leib. Niemand will im Park mit der kleinen Tochter Eva spielen, und der Sohn Hansi wird in der Schule ausgelacht und als jüdischer Bastard bezeichnet.

Trotz des Widerwillens des Vaters entscheidet sich die Familie von Hochmeyer zur Emigration in die USA. Es ist aber nicht einfach, ein Visum zu bekommen; lange Schlangen vor dem Konsulat und die vielen nötigen Dokumente entmutigen sie aber nicht. Sie sehen in Amerika die einzige Rettung. Bei anderen ist die Rettung beliebiger. Eine Frau mit Kind, die in der Schlange steht, ist so verzweifelt, dass sie sagt, sie würde in irgendein beliebiges Land emigrieren, sogar nach Afrika. Wichtig ist nur, dass sie weg von hier kommt.

Die Familie fängt an zu sparen. Ruth erlernt einen für das Exil nützlichen Beruf, indem sie Kurse als Friseuse besucht und von der Köchin lernt, wie man Speisen vorbereitet. Robert leidet stattdessen unter Depressionen, weil er als Rechtsanwalt nur in Österreich arbeiten kann. Dank den gekauften und gefälschten Dokumenten und dem Affidavit von der Familie in den USA gelingt es ihnen, Wien zu verlassen und nach Amerika zu fliehen. Die größere Hälfte des Romans beschäftigt sich dann mit dem Leben und der Anpassung im Exil. Deswegen könnte man ihn letztendlich als Exilroman einordnen.

In dem Werk merkt man viele autobiographische Züge, z.B. gehörte Hershan auch zu einer wohlhabenden Familie, musste nicht arbeiten, und um den Haushalt kümmerten sich die Hausangestellten. Erst im Exil wurde sie gezwungen zu arbeiten. Genauso wie Ruth im Roman fand sie eine Stelle in einem Kosmetik-Geschäft. Das war das erste selbstverdiente Geld. In dem Manuskript wird auch eine Situation beschrieben, wie es Ruth vermeidet, Pflastersteine nach dem „Anschluss" zu putzen. Das verlief sehr ähnlich in Hershans Leben. Ein weiteres Beispiel ist die Nizza-Reise des Vaters im Roman und der Eltern der Schriftstellerin. Die Gestapo war fest davon überzeugt, dass die Eltern der Autorin viel Geld ins Ausland schmuggelten, und wollte dieses

Geld zurückhaben. Im Roman wird Robert von Hochmeyer verhaftet, weil die
Gestapo ihn zwingen will zu verraten, in welchem Land der Vater die großen
Summen versteckt hat. Wie Ruth verbrachte Hershan mit ihrem Mann Neujahr 1938 im exklusiven Imperial Hotel mit Bekannten. Auch der Selbstmord
der Schwiegermutter hat seine Widerspiegelung im realen Leben. Die Mutter
von Hershans Freundin beging auf solche Art und Weise Suizid.

Die erste Hälfte des Romans bringt treffend viele Vorstufen des Exils zum
Ausdruck. Angefangen von den ersten Gerüchten einige Monate vor dem „Anschluss" bis zur Flucht ins Exil. Schon Anfang des Jahres 1938 hört man überall
die unruhigen Stimmen und die Ankündigung großer Änderungen. Nach dem
„Anschluss" verschlechtert sich sowohl die finanzielle als auch die gesellschaftliche die Situation der jüdischen Bevölkerung. Ereignisse vom März 1938 bringen soziale Ausgrenzung, Gehänsel, Verfolgung, Beschlagnahmen des Vermögens und letztendlich Vertreibung mit sich.

Genauso wie ihre Helden in „March 11th 1938" hat sich die Schriftstellerin
mit ihrer Familie trotz aller Schwierigkeiten im neuen Alltag im Exil wieder-
gefunden. Der Untertitel dieses Romans, „A novel of reorientation", fasst passend das Leben der Schriftstellerin nach dem Verlassen der Heimat zusammen. Alle Erfahrungen, die Exil und seine Vorstufen mit sich brachten, haben
dazu beigetragen, dass die damals noch junge Autorin eine starke Persönlichkeit wurde. Nach der Machtübernahme von Nationalsozialisten war Hershan
auf einmal dazu gezwungen, mit ihrer jüdischen Identität und daraus resul-
tierten Folgen zurecht zu kommen. Sehr schnell ist der Familie Hershan klar
geworden, dass die Flucht die einzige Rettungsmöglichkeit zu sein schien. Von
einem sorgenlosen Leben im Heimatland konnte nicht mehr die Rede sein,
angefangen mit der ständigen Angst um das eigene Leben und das der Famili-
enangehörigen bis hin zu finanziellen Schwierigkeiten, die nicht mehr erlaubt
haben, ein gesichertes Leben zu führen. Nicht zu bezweifeln ist auch, dass diese Vorstufen des Exils in jeder Hinsicht eine unauslöschbare Spur in ihrem Leben hinterlassen haben, sodass sie eine Widerspiegelung in ihrem Werk gefunden hat. Mit der literarischen Verarbeitung ihrer Erfahrungen versuchte die
Autorin, eine Identität und sich selbst wiederzufinden.

Zitierte Literatur

Grossberg, Mimi (Hrsg.). *Geschichte im Gedicht. Das politische Gedicht der austro-
    amerikanischen Exilautoren des Schicksalsjahres 1938.* Austrian Institute, 1982.
Hartenstein, Elfi. *Heimat wider Willen. Emigranten in New York – Begegnungen.* Verlag-
    Gemeinschaft Berg, 1991.

Hershan, Stella. „March 11th 1938. A novel of reorientation." Leo Baeck Institute, Stella
    K. Hershan Collection. Folder 1, MS 258.

Hershan, Stella. *Erinnerungen zwischen zwei Welten*. Gryphon Verlag, 2006.

Hershan, Stella. Leo Baeck Institute, Stella Hershan Collection, AR 11178.

Hershan, Stella. *A memoir of Nazi Austria and the Jewish Refugee Experience in America*.
    Leo Baeck Institute, Stella K. Hershan Collection. ME 1055.

Neck, Rudolf und Wandruszka, Adam (Hrsg.). *Anschluss 1938*. Verlag für Geschichte
    und Politik, 1981.

Österreichisches Staatsarchiv. http://www.oesta.gv.at/site/cob__27099/5164/default
    .aspx, Zugriff 25. September 2018.

Strelka, Joseph. *Methodologie der Literaturwissenschaft*. Niemeyer, 1978.

Die Vorstufen des Exils in Thomas Bernhards *Heldenplatz*: die innere Emigration im Spannungsfeld zwischen Utopie und Falle

Krisztina Kaltenecker

Abstract

From the perspective of cultural history, Thomas Bernhard's *Heldenplatz* (1988) represents a new interpretation of the medieval folk tales surrounding the "Wandering Jew," the shoemaker Ahasver. Using the Josef Schuster family as an example, the theater piece delineates not only the external causes that perpetuated the restlessness and homelessness of the Jews who returned to post-war Austria, namely, the denial of the historical trauma as a national consensus, as well as the insidious animosities of the Viennese. In addition, it shines a light on the adjustment of Jewish re-emigrants to an inner exile in Vienna as the early stages of a renewed exile with all its complexity and contradictions in the field of tension between utopia and trap. Regarding the internal forces of segregation, the author's attention is directed to the interrelationships between the traditional culture of repression and isolation, the psychoses determined by trauma, and the Schusters' ambiguous marital games. They make the desperate situation of the couple inalterable and lead to a tragic *exitus*, Josef's suicide and subsequently the probable death of his wife Hedwig.

Im Verlauf der Annexion Österreichs durch das nationalsozialistische Deutschland hielt Adolf Hitler am 15. März 1938 eine Rede auf dem Heldenplatz in Wien. Er verkündete unter „brausender, tobender Zustimmung" sowie „brausende[n] Sieg-Heil-Rufe[n]" von der Neuen Burg aus „die Eingliederung" der „Ostmark" in das Deutsche Reich (Hitler-Rede 140). Im Zuge dessen wurde der Heldenplatz als bewährte Raum-Metapher des habsburgischen bzw. österreichisch-republikanischen historischen Gedächtnisses von den Nationalsozialisten entwertet, entfremdet und für ihre Zwecke vereinnahmt. Für die österreichischen Juden wurde der Gedächtnisort Heldenplatz dadurch zur geographischen Metapher der Aberkennung ihrer Mitbürgerschaft, zum „traumatischen Ort" (Assmann, *Schatten* 221). Thomas Bernhard benützte den Heldenplatz wiederum als literarischen Ort für den titelgebenden Schauplatz seines Bühnenstückes, mit einer weiteren Funktion als Gedächtnisort.

Heldenplatz entstand im Auftrag von Claus Peymann als Beitrag zum 100-jährigen Bestehen des Wiener Burgtheaters 1988. Das Bühnenstück zeigt komplexe Konsequenzen der lange Zeit beschwiegenen nationalsozialistischen Verstrickung Österreichs exemplarisch, und zwar anhand einer Wiener Familiengeschichte auf (vgl. Götz von Olenhusen, Klesse und van Ingen 23). Aus der Sicht einer 1958 aus dem englischen Exil nach Wien zurückgekehrten jüdischen Bildungsbürgerfamilie beantwortet es aktuelle Fragen zum Leben in der inneren Emigration (vgl. van Ingen 22). Es stellt dar, inwiefern der sogenannten Opfergeneration sowie deren Kindern die (Re-)Integration in ihrem Vaterland, bzw. dem Vaterland die Integration der jüdischen (Re-)Migranten misslang, was tragischerweise zu einer erneuten Situation des Exils, bzw. dessen Vorstufen führte.

Als Thomas Bernhard die Segregation der remigrierten Juden in Wien als Vorstufen eines erneuten Exils definierte, provozierte er einen skandalträchtigen Tabubruch mit einer politischen und medialen Öffentlichkeit, die das Thema jahrzehntelang verschwiegen hatte (vgl. Huber, Judex 138–139, van Ingen 55). Bei einem ehemaligen KZ-Häftling, dem ungarischen Schriftsteller und Nobelpreisträger Imre Kertész, löste das Werk hingegen einen schlagartigen Moment des Wiedererkennens aus: „Die Dialoge in Heldenplatz habe ich so von Juden in Budapest gehört." Diesen Moment erklärte er sich damit, dass sich Bernhard „mit den Juden identifiziert" habe (zit. nach Phillip und Zintzen 160). Ausgehend von dem Aha-Erlebnis von Kertész möchte ich nun die innere Emigration der Familie Schuster in Wien 1958–1988, bzw. die Vorstufen eines sich wiederholenden Exils in dem vorliegenden Beitrag kulturwissenschaftlich beleuchten.

1 Die externen Ursachen des Einrichtens in der inneren Emigration und erneute Vorstufen des Exils

1.1 *Eine vorgetäuschte Amnesie und das große Beschweigen*

Der Politologe Tony Judt schreibt, dass die nationalen Gedächtnisse Europas während des Kalten Krieges eingefroren waren, um die neuen Allianzen diesseits und jenseits des Eisernen Vorhangs zu stützen (vgl. Assman, *Unbehagen* 184). Indem „alle Verantwortung für den Krieg den Deutschen zufiel", wurden laut dem Historiker Martin Sabrow z.B. jene Verbrechen, die während des Zweiten Weltkrieges unmittelbar davor oder danach von anderen verübt wurden, „passenderweise vergessen" (zit. nach Assmann, *Unbehagen* 185). Damit vollzog sich die politische Konsolidierung in Nachkriegseuropa auf der gemeinsamen Grundlage eines „Vergessens" der Opfer (Assmann, *Unbehagen* 184–185).

Auch im Österreich der Nachkriegszeit war die eigene antisemitische und nationalsozialistische Vergangenheit lange Zeit kein Thema. Die bewusste selektive Amnesie im nationalen Gedächtnis führte zur Aberkennung der Leiden der Opfer des NS-Systems. Sie marginalisierte die Verfolgung und die Ermordung der österreichischen Juden vor und im Zweiten Weltkrieg als Elemente der österreichischen Vergangenheit (vgl. Safrian-Witek sowie Moser 296–297). Die Shoah galt daher in ihrer Eigenschaft als Menschheitsverbrechen als relativ irrelevant für das österreichische Selbstbild.

Es ist davon auszugehen, dass die „Verdrängungskultur" (Klesse), d.h. das Beschweigen der Verstrickung zehntausender Österreicher mit dem NS-Regime und somit der Ausschluss dieser Verstrickung aus dem nationalen Selbstbild und dem öffentlichen Diskurs, von einem kühlen Pragmatismus diktiert war. Er strebte in erster Linie eine funktionelle Anpassung der politischen Kultur an die neue Zeit, den Kalten Krieg, an (vgl. Assmann, *Unbehagen* 45). Hinzu kam, dass die traumatisierten Remigranten der 1950er Jahre auf ein repressives politisches Klima trafen. Die allmähliche demokratische Veränderung des offiziellen Werterahmens in Österreich hatte zunächst kaum Konsequenzen für die etablierten Machtstrukturen, die sich im Alltag fortsetzten – zur Frustration, Kränkung und Verzweiflung vieler Opfer (vgl. Assmann, *Schatten* 46).

1.2   Die kollektive Opferidentität als „nationale Deckerinnerung"

Das nationale Selbstbild zeigte Österreich bis Ende der 1980er Jahre als erstes Opfer Hitlers. In diesem Zusammenhang funktionieren „nationale Deckerinnerungen" bei der Bildung kollektiver Identitäten folgenderweise: Passende partielle Erinnerungen, die durch Erfahrung gedeckt sind, werden als einheitliche und ausschließliche Erinnerung für das gesamte Kollektiv in Anspruch genommen, womit die unpassenden Elemente aus dem nationalen Diskurs und Selbstbild ausgeschlossen bleiben, so die Literatur- und Kulturwissenschaftlerin Aleida Assmann (vgl. *Schatten* 261). Das heißt, wer sich kollektiv in der Opferrolle sieht, ist z.B. kaum bereit, in dieses Narrativ auch Episoden eigener Verbrechen, der Kollaboration mit der nationalsozialistischen deutschen Besatzung und der Beteiligung an der Judenverfolgung und dem Judenmord zu integrieren (vgl. Assmann, *Schatten* 147). Durch die Selbstviktimisierung waren die Österreicher unwillig und unfähig, eine „Politik der Reue" zu entwickeln, die eine empathische Beziehung zu den Opfern der eigenen Politik und die Anerkennung verschiedener Opfer- und Täterkonstellationen ermöglicht hätte (vgl. Assmann, *Schatten* 148).

Jahrzehntelang wurde den österreichischen Juden der ihnen zustehende historische Opferstatus verwehrt, der Shoah der ihr gebührende Platz im nationalen Gedächtnis verweigert (vgl. Assmann, *Schatten* 113 und *Unbehagen* 151).

Das historische Trauma, das die Opfer erlitten hatten, hätte allerdings der Anerkennung durch Aufnahme in das nationale Gedächtnis bedurft, um zu einem Heilungsprozess zu führen. Es umgab die Überlebenden jedoch nur das große Beschweigen, und zwar als nationaler Konsens.

2   Die internen Ursachen des Einrichtens in der inneren Emigration und erneute Vorstufen des Exils

2.1   *Das Leben in der Falle und für eine Utopie*

Rückblickend kann das Exil der Schusters in England 1938–1958 als Erfolgsgeschichte bezeichnet werden: Josef machte in Oxford als Professor der Mathematik Karriere, Robert in Cambridge als Professor der Philosophie. Sie gaben die englische Staatsbürgerschaft schließlich trotzdem zurück. Verschiedene Gründe und Ziele spielten bei der Rückkehr nach Österreich eine Rolle. Josef hörte auf die Bitte des Wiener Bürgermeisters, der ihm damals auch einen Lehrstuhl anbot, wobei er den heftigen Protest seiner Frau Hedwig gegen die Rückkehr ignorierte. Beide Brüder hatten Sehnsucht nach der Wiener Musik, und speziell Josef wollte auch seine Kindheit wiederhaben. Allerdings war ihr eigentliches, gemeinsames, aber stillschweigendes Motiv die feste Überzeugung, dass sie wieder bzw. noch immer ein Vaterland hätten (vgl. Bernhard 163).

Einmal in Österreich angekommen, zieht sich Robert aufs Land nach Neuhaus, in die alte Sommerfrische der Familie, zurück. Sich auf seinen stets schlechten Gesundheitszustand berufend, unternimmt er keinen Versuch, sich den realen gesellschaftlichen und politischen Begebenheiten zu stellen (vgl. Bernhard 90). Josef hingegen geht bei der Aneignung der Heimat scheinbar offensiv vor und kauft sich in der Hauptstadt ausgerechnet gegenüber dem Heldenplatz eine Wohnung. Er nimmt wohl an, dass sich die Zeit und der Ort vom Nationalsozialismus vollständig erholt hätten und im idyllischen Vorkriegszustand befinden würden, ohne modernen Antisemitismus. Eine familiäre Utopie will er im Wien der auslaufenden 1950er Jahre verwirklicht vorfinden. Unvermeidlich führt sein absurder Voluntarismus zu einer persönlichen Krise (vgl. Bernhard 111–112).

Um diese Kränkung mit einem Gedankenspiel zu überwinden, versucht Josef, sich einer falschen Nostalgie hinzugeben. Als Projektionsfläche verschiedener Sehnsüchte bietet sich logischerweise in erster Linie die vormalige österreichisch-ungarische Doppelmonarchie an (vgl. Bernhard 144). Doch der Mathematikprofessor, der Geistesmensch, kann das nostalgisch-sentimental verklärte Bild der Habsburgermonarchie nur als Ablenkung benutzen, nicht aber als brauchbares Hilfsmittel, Zeit und Ort im Dienste der eigenen Integration zurechtzurücken.

Auf die Ignoranz, Ausgrenzung und Gewalt seitens der Wiener reagieren die Schusters öffentlich lediglich sporadisch und üblicherweise nur mit längst überholten politischen Mitteln des einstigen Obrigkeitsstaates Österreich-Ungarn: mit Protestbriefen an vermeintlich einflussreiche Honoratioren (vgl. Bernhard 76–79, 86–87) oder mit Einladung der Kommunalpolitiker zum Abendessen (vgl. Bernhard 142). Anstatt einer pro-aktiven und emanzipierten Teilnahme am öffentlichen und politischen Leben ziehen sie sich strikt ins Private zurück.

Die Utopie Wien, deren süßen Verlockungen die Schusters immer wieder erliegen und deren zuliebe sie sich mit einem Leben im Provisorium, in mittelbaren Vorstufen eines erneuten Exils, opportun abfinden, steht für sie für eine flüchtige, verführerische und vor allem durch sie immer wieder aufs Neue erzeugbare Sinnestäuschung, es hätte schon irgendwann mal ein perfektes Wien existiert. Damit wird ein Wien ohne antisemitische Ressentiments gemeint, ein Wien, wo die Juden mit Empathie und Solidarität aufgenommen worden wären:

> Wir wollen alle nur in der Vergangenheit leben
> die haben wir uns so schön eingerichtet die Vergangenheit
> wie wir wollen.
> BERNHARD 144

Oder es wird eine Erwartungshaltung formuliert, es sollte endlich einmal und ohne ihr aktives persönliches Zutun eine solche Heimat Wien zustande kommen.

Die Kinder der Schusters reagieren auf die Segregation ihrer Eltern von der Wiener Gesellschaft mit Solidarität: Das Weltbild und Verhaltensmuster des Vaters übernimmt Anna aus Überzeugung, Olga aus Gehorsam. Lukas identifiziert sich mit den Rollenspielen seiner Mutter: Spielt die Frau Professor eine „Theatralikerin" (Bernhard 138), benimmt er sich wie ein leichtsinniger Bohème. Die gesamte Familie Schuster fühlt sich zu Hause, in der Heimat, heimatlos, fremd und bedroht (vgl. Bernhard 163). Dabei verfestigt die Realitätsverweigerung ihre Heimatlosigkeit im Laufe der Zeit und macht ihnen das dauerhafte Einrichten in dem inneren Exil alternativlos (vgl. Bernhard 111). Die familieninterne Bezeichnung der inneren Emigration, der Begriff „Wiener Falle" bzw. „Österreichfalle" (Bernhard 163), belegt, dass sie irrtümlicherweise ausschließlich externe Kräfte für ihre Segregation verantwortlich machen. Sie sind nicht imstande zu erkennen, dass ihr Festhalten an der althergebrachten familiären

Utopie Wien, der Phantasie, der Einbildung, dem Gegenentwurf zum realen Wien jegliche Ankunft im Realraum von vornherein verhindert. Durchaus vermögen es manche Requisiten der bürgerlichen Existenz aus der Zeit Österreich-Ungarns, wie das Theater, der Musikverein, die Gasthäuser mit ihren Köstlichkeiten, die Kaffeehäuser mit ihren gepflegten Kaffees, die Innenstadt, die Klinik Steinhof und der Friedhof in Döbling usw., Professor Josef und seine Familie zu kleinen Momenten des Glücklichseins zu verhelfen (vgl. Bernhard 178). Doch „Illusionsräume" (Foucault 45) des Wunschdenkens und der Ablenkung können bei der tatsächlichen Ankunft der Remigrierten *hic et nunc* auch nicht helfen:

> Ich gehe auf die Mariahilferstraße
> und suche die Mariahilferstraße
> und ich bin auf der Mariahilferstraße
> und finde sie nicht.
>
> BERNHARD 111

Laut dem Philosophen Michel Foucault werden diese Räume oft zum Zwecke erschaffen, damit der gesamte Realraum als noch illusorischer bloßgestellt wird (45). Tatsächlich entlarven die Schusters untereinander Österreich immer wieder sehr gern als Welttheater des Irrsinns und der Unterwerfung, in dem ein neuer Hitler herbeigesehnt wird:

> Österreich selbst ist nichts als eine Bühne
> auf der alles verlottert und vermodert und verkommen ist
> eine in sich selber verhaßte Statisterie
> von sechseinhalb Millionen Alleingelassenen
> sechseinhalb Millionen Debile und Tobsüchtige
> die ununterbrochen aus vollem Hals nach einem Regisseur schreien
> Der Regisseur wird kommen
> und sie endgültig in den Abgrund hinunterstoßen.
>
> BERNHARD 89

2.2   *Das Lebensspiel der Familie Schuster*

Zum Selbstschutz nehmen sich die Schusters vor, das historisch Zerstörerische und Zersetzende noch rechtzeitig, sozusagen noch vor der zweiten Machtergreifung, zu enthüllen (vgl. Bernhard 42). Die Familie und deren engste Freunde entwickeln sich dabei einen antifaschistischen Zeitvertreib (vgl. Assmann, *Unbehagen* 50), ein „Spiel" (Bernhard 67–70) im Sinne der Theorie des Psychiaters

Eric Berne. Die Spieler berichten im Familien- und Freundeskreis immer wieder über Elemente der nationalsozialistischen Vergangenheit Österreichs, denen sie wiederbegegnet sind oder die sie sogar erneut erleiden mussten, gewissermaßen als bewusste Auseinandersetzung mit sich wiederholenden Vorstufen eines Exils in ihrem Schicksal. Im Widerstandsspiel können sie gegen die erneut registrierten Missstände mit ihrer ganzen Sprachgewalt vorgehen. Dadurch lässt es die historischen Traumata der Opfer zur Sprache kommen. Sie offenbaren sich dann in Form von maßlosen Übertreibungen, apokalyptischen Weltuntergangsprophezeiungen sowie endlosen, brutalen Schimpftiraden usw. (vgl. Bernhard 89). Die Opfergeneration als primäre Zeugen der nationalsozialistischen Gräueltaten beansprucht der zweiten Generation gegenüber eine Deutungshoheit in Bezug auf die Gegenwart und dominiert somit das Spiel. Der Vorfall zum Beispiel, als Olga in der Schottergasse bespuckt worden ist, kann laut Onkel Robert, der die Shoah als Erwachsener erlitten hat, ausschließlich von ihm selbst im historisch richtigen Kontext gedeutet werden:

> Irrtümlich irrtümlich glaubt ihr
> das war nicht irrtümlich
> natürlich wenn man es nicht erlebt hat
> aber wenn man es tatsächlich erlebt hat.
> BERNHARD 113

Der Zeitvertreib der Familie bewährt sich als Ventil, um aufgestaute negative Gefühlskomplexe in Bewusstseinsströmungen abzulassen. Schleichend entwickelt er sich jedoch geradezu zu ihrem Universalmittel gegen beliebige Problemlagen, d.h. zum „Lebensspiel" (Berne 103) der Familie. Dieses Allheilmittel benutzen sie sogar als Trauerritual und zur Ursachensuche sowohl im Volksgarten nach der Beerdigung Josefs als auch in der Wiener Wohnung beim Trauerschmaus. Doch das Lebensspiel der Familie Schuster geht von vornherein mit einer verhängnisvollen Einschränkung der Wahrnehmung einher: Die Spieler schließen die Kräfte des Demokratisierungsprozesses in Österreich als irrelevant aus. Folgerichtig macht das „Allheilmittel" die Vorstufen einer zweiten Flucht aus Wien in ihrem Bewusstsein allgegenwärtig. Ein weiteres Problem entsteht aus der Ausblendung insofern, als es zwei Spielern mit der Zeit gar nicht mehr gelingt, zwischen der Wahrheit im Spielrahmen und derjenigen außerhalb des Spielrahmens zu differenzieren: Sowohl Josef als auch seine Frau leiden immer mehr unter Verfolgungswahn (vgl. Bernhard 81), der auch zur Zementierung der Vorstufen eines erneuten Exils im Bewusstsein der beiden Figuren beiträgt.

Es kann vermutet werden, dass sich das oben beschriebene Aha-Erlebnis des Holocaust-Überlebenden Imre Kertész genau auf das Lebensspiel bezog. Der ungarische Nobelpreisträger kann es nach dem Zweiten Weltkrieg im Kreise der Budapester Juden sehr wohl kennengelernt haben. Somit ist davon auszugehen, dass es sowohl in Österreich als auch in Ungarn eine typische Reaktion der in der inneren Emigration lebenden Opfergeneration auf das repressive politische Klima im Vaterland gewesen sein muss.

3 Die internen Ursachen des tragischen Exitus

3.1 Psychosen und Wahrnehmungsverluste des Ehepaars

Josef geht beim geistigen Kampf gegen die drohende neue Naziherrschaft in Österreich am Weitesten: Er muss ununterbrochen alles sehen, alles hören, um die „Zeichen der Zeit" wahrnehmen, dokumentieren und richtig deuten zu können. Eigentlich beabsichtigt er, die Erkenntnisse in drei Bänden unter demselben Titel auch herauszugeben. Doch aus seiner leidenschaftlichen präventiven Forschungsarbeit wird langsam Besessenheit und Manie. Er übertreibt maßlos und begeht den denkbar größten Fehler als Ehemann: Der Arbeit zuliebe verzichtet er bereitwillig auf sein Intimleben, seine Liebesbeziehung zu seiner Frau. Sowohl verschiedene etablierte Ehespiele als auch sein „Geschöpf", Frau Zittel, und ihre Rolle in seinem Leben als Mittelpunkt (Bernhard 72–73) deuten darauf hin, dass Josef mit der Liebe immer größere Schwierigkeiten hat. Er entwickelt gleichzeitig verschiedene neue Zwänge und Marotten. Anstatt diese Symptome der psychischen Erkrankung wahrzunehmen, belügt er sich, als würde sein ausgeprägtes Zwangsverhalten aus lobenswerten Tugenden bestehen, die ihn sogar berechtigt hätten, seine Familie aus Fürsorge und Liebe zu „kujonieren" (Bernhard 42–43).

Wie es der Name des Projektes „Zeichen der Zeit" verrät, sieht sich Josef Schuster den arglosen oder etablierten Intelligenzlern gegenüber überlegen, weil nur er aus der Naziherrschaft die richtige Lehre ziehen und beherzigen würde: Einem jeden Wissenschaftler obliegt die Pflicht, sich mit dem Offensichtlichen bedingungslos auseinanderzusetzen. Allerdings funktioniert seine Forschungsarbeit wegen der oben bereits genannten Einschränkung der Wahrnehmung als eine selbsterfüllende Prophezeiung. Die Konklusion, „dass die Österreicher nach dem Krieg / viel gehässiger und noch viel judenfeindlicher" (Bernhard 112) als vor dem Krieg geworden sind, ist daher vorprogrammiert, bestätigt seine schlimmsten Befürchtungen und schleudert ihn auf die unmittelbaren Vorstufen eines erneuten Exils. Nun lebt er nämlich in der „Wiener

Falle" in ständiger *und* steigender Furcht, und es vergehen ihm dabei der Ta-
tendurst und die Lebenslust. Seinem abschließenden Forschungsergebnis
nach sei in Österreich alles in „Auflösung" begriffen (Bernhard 99, 132). Von da
an gibt es für ihn keinen trostspendenden Illusionsraum mehr (vgl. Bernhard
69–70).

Es ist davon auszugehen, dass Hedwig die Wiener Rede Hitlers 1938 an Ort
und Stelle persönlich erleben musste und diesen historischen Schock in einer
traumatischen Erinnerung bewahrt hatte (vgl. Bernhard 139). Obwohl sie ihren
Mann 1958 anbettelte, auf eine Wohnung direkt am Heldenplatz in Wien als
Wohnsitz der Familie zu verzichten, war Josef nicht bereit, über eine Alternative nachzudenken. Der psychische Zustand Hedwigs verschlechtert sich daraufhin fortwährend (vgl. Bernhard 138). Sie fängt in ihrer neuen Wohnung an,
das Geschrei vom Heldenplatz 1938 zu hören. Der Heldenplatz als Sitz der
Familie wird für sie zum Auslöser lebhafter und detailgenauer Flashback-
Erinnerungen an die früheren traumatisierenden Erfahrungen, die damals die
Vorstufen des ersten Exils der Familie dominierten. Doch Josef gibt die Woh-
nung nicht einmal angesichts der Leiden seiner Ehefrau auf. Er nimmt dadurch
Hedwig die Chance, in Wien je wieder beheimatet zu werden. Das unbedingte
Festhalten am Wohnsitz Heldenplatz begründet Josef mit dem unnachgiebig
zu führenden Kampf gegen den Nationalsozialismus. Er müsste nämlich den
Auszug als eine neue Niederlage gegenüber Hitler auffassen (vgl. Bernhard 21).

3.2 *Verhängnisvolle Ehespiele*

Es war ein doppelbödiges, unaufrichtiges Spiel, das die Ehe der Schusters zu-
sammenhält. Hedwig hatte Josef zum Gatten gewählt, um sich von ihm ver-
bieten zu lassen, was sie im Leben eigentlich fürchtete: Selbständig handeln
und für die Taten Verantwortung übernehmen zu müssen. Diesen guten Dienst
aber dankt sie ihrem Ehemann schlecht: Ständig hält sie ihm vor, dass sie alles grundsätzlich anders machen würde. Josef hingegen ist seinerseits auf
die Schwächen seiner Ehefrau angewiesen. Er kann nämlich nur mit einer
entscheidungsschwachen Frau zusammenleben, die ihm seinen Führungs-
anspruch in der Ehe ausleben lässt. Im Leben fürchtet er am meisten den
Kontrollverlust.

Wie der aus mittelalterlichen Volkssagen bekannte Wandernde Jude, der
Schuhmacher Ahasver (vgl. *Lexikonartikel*), war Professor *Schuster* nun ein Leben lang rastlos. 1938 musste er vor dem nationalsozialistischen Regime aus
Wien ins Exil nach England flüchten. In Oxford angekommen, fühlte er sich
auch nicht geborgen: Ihm schien die englische Universitätsstadt zu kleinka-
riert. Wieder in Österreich ab 1958 befindet er sich kontinuierlich in einem
„nach dem Exil ist vor dem Exil"-Zustand. Zunächst kommt er mit der Tatsache

nicht klar, dass das Wien seiner Jugend nicht zurückzubringen ist. Zudem hat er eigentlich die ganze Zeit nicht nach dem realen Ort seiner Kindheit Sehnsucht, sondern nach einer Utopie. In den darauffolgenden drei Jahrzehnten findet er als Remigrant das repressive politische Klima in der Hauptstadt schlimmer als dasjenige nach dem „Anschluss" durch das Deutsche Reich. Graz oder Linz als Sitz der Familie wären ihm auch ein Graus wegen deren nationalsozialistischer Vergangenheit. Nicht einmal nach Neuhaus kann er ausweichen, weil ihm die Ortschaft zu öde ist.

Es kommt für ihn noch erschwerend dazu, dass sich Hedwig immer „entgegengesetzt" zu seiner Meinung äußert (Bernhard 161). 1938 wollte sie nicht nach England fliehen. 1958 wäre sie lieber in Oxford geblieben. Nachdem sich ihr Mann eine Wohnung trotz ihrer heftigen Proteste gerade am Wiener Heldenplatz gefunden hatte, verschlechtert sich ihr psychischer Zustand dramatisch. Hedwig kann sich in Neuhaus auch nicht einleben; dort ist sie auch immer gesundheitlich angeschlagen.

Die stets kontroversen Stellungnahmen in Bezug auf den gewünschten Wohnort beweisen, dass die permanente Unruhe des Ehepaars nicht einseitig in den externen Umständen wurzelt, wie die Schusters das irrtümlicherweise meinen, sondern auch auf interne Ursachen zurückgeht, worüber sich das Paar allerdings nicht im Klaren wird. Somit ist ihr Unglück in der „Wiener Falle" durch die Interaktion von (verborgenen) internen und (offensichtlichen) externen Faktoren motiviert. Offensichtlich sind für die Schusters die Auswirkungen der Verdrängungskultur in Österreich; verborgen bleiben für sie die Folgen der eigenen politischen Kultur, ihrer psychischen Erkrankungen und des eigenen Liebeslebens.

Schließlich drei Jahrzehnte nach der Rückkehr nach Österreich, erklärt Josef den Versuch, die Utopie Wien durch die innere Emigration aufrechtzuerhalten, für endgültig gescheitert, und entscheidet sich für eine zweite Flucht mit seiner Familie nach Oxford (vgl. Bernhard 13). Ein für Josef lange nicht mehr üblicher Tatendrang und die Schaffung von Tatsachen charakterisieren daraufhin diese letzten Vorstufen des erneuten Exils: Die gemeinsame Wohnung am Heldenplatz wird auf der Stelle verkauft und gleichzeitig eine neue Immobilie in Oxford für die Familie erworben. Allerdings spricht sich Hedwig gegen das Exil und für einen Umzug innerhalb der Innenstadt aus. Josef muss jedoch unbedingt und unverzüglich weg, da er es in Wien, zum einem aus politischen Gründen und zum anderen wegen seiner schweren Paranoia, nicht mehr aushält. Doch er kann eigentlich auch nicht mehr ins Exil nach Oxford:

> Daß Wien mein Tod ist
> habe ich immer gewußt

hat der Professor gesagt
In Oxford bin ich genauso wenig zuhause
wie in Wien.

Seine absolute und unabänderliche Heimatlosigkeit ist also letztendlich die
ganze Wahrheit. Josefs Selbstmord am 15. März auf dem Heldenplatz ist daher
ein letztes, endgültiges Aufbegehren gegen das persönliche Schicksal, vertrieben von Nationalsozialismus und Antisemitismus, sowie getrieben von Illusionen, Traumata und falschen Ehespielen, verflucht zur ewigen Rast- und
Heimatlosigkeit.

Josefs Freitod zerstört das System, das Hedwigs Leben bis jetzt ordnete und
ihr Halt gab. Sie muss und kann sich dann nicht mehr gegen ihren tyranni-
schen Ehemann und dessen Edikte wehren. Wie beängstigend muss die Tatsache auf sie wirken, dass niemand sie nunmehr davon abhält zu tun, was sie
will. Folglich brechen alte Phobien drastisch auf: Hedwig verzweifelt und fällt
beim Trauerschmaus (wahrscheinlich) tot um. Zudem ist ihr Trauma ein genauso relevanter direkter Auslöser des tragischen Ereignisses am Ende des
Theaterstücks: Sie hört wieder seit Minuten das unerträgliche Menschenge-
schrei vom Heldenplatz 1938, als sie mit dem Gesicht voraus auf die Tischplatte
fällt (vgl. Bernhard 165).

4   Fazit

Thomas Bernhards *Heldenplatz* widerspiegelt mit geradezu dokumentarischer
Authentizität, welche Segregationserscheinungen die Demokratisierungsdefi-
zite der österreichischen Gesellschaft bei den aus dem Exil zurückgekehrten,
traumatisierten Juden verursachten, Segregationserscheinungen, die sich die
Vorstufen des Exils wiederholen ließen. Die durch diesen Tabubruch bloßge-
stellte Öffentlichkeit protestierte gegen das Bühnenstück zu Lebzeiten des Au-
tors aufs schärfste, auch um jede Art der historischen Verantwortung von sich
zu weisen.

Was den sich hysterisch benehmenden Zeitgenossen 1988 komplett ent-
ging, ist die Tatsache, dass *Heldenplatz* einen Mangel an politischer Kultur als
eine relevante, tradierte interne Segregationskraft bewertet. Das Stück zeigt
eine ausgeprägte Verdrängungs- und Abschottungskultur auf, die die jüdischen Remigranten ihrerseits an der gelungenen Integration hindert. Sie führt
(in Wechselwirkung mit anderen Faktoren) zu erneuten Vorstufen des Exils
und macht die zweite Emigration alternativlos: Die Schusters schaffen es aus

eigener Kraft nicht, sich der ihnen fremden und nicht von ihnen (mit)be-
stimmten Realität zu stellen und von der Utopie Wien sowie deren Illusions-
räumen loszulösen. Sie ziehen sich opportun ins Private zurück, anstatt an
einem pro-aktiven, emanzipierten und verbindlichen Leben teilzunehmen.
Das Einrichten in der inneren Emigration nennen sie untereinander „Wiener
Falle" bzw. „Österreichfalle" (Bernhard 163), weil sie ihre stete Rast- und Heimatlosigkeit irrtümlicherweise einseitig und ausschließlich auf externe Faktoren zurückführen. Im Dienste einer familiären Utopie in der „Falle", d.h. hier
in mittelbaren Vorstufen eines erneuten Exils, ausharrend, sedieren sie sich
mit der Entwicklung eines antifaschistischen Widerstandsspiels. Der Zeitvertreib bewährt sich als ihr Ventil, um die alltägliche politische Erfahrung der
Segregation seitens der Wiener untereinander abzureagieren. Sie verwenden
ihn allerdings im Laufe der Jahrzehnte immer öfter generell als Universalmittel, als Lebensspiel, obzwar er im Grunde genommen wie eine selbsterfüllende Prophezeiung funktioniert. Exakt dieser Denkfehler ist verantwortlich dafür, dass die Schusters in die unmittelbaren Vorstufen eines zweiten Exils
schlittern, ohne je als agile Persönlichkeiten an die politische Öffentlichkeit
herangetreten zu sein.

Es blieb der zeitgenössischen Skandalpresse ebenfalls verborgen, dass im
Heldenplatz die Interaktion zwischen internen Segregationskräften, nämlich
der Verdrängungs- und Abschottungskultur, den traumabedingten psychischen Erkrankungen und den fatalen Ehespielen, als der direkte Auslöser bestimmt wird, der schlussendlich formell zum Ausbruch aus der „Wiener Falle",
zum Überschreiten der Grenze zwischen den Vorstufen eines Exils und end-
gültigem „Exil", faktisch allerdings zum tragischen Exitus führt: zum Selbstmord von Josef und darauffolgend zum wahrscheinlichen Tod von Hedwig
Schuster.

Zitierte Literatur

Assmann, Aleida. *Das neue Unbehagen an der Erinnerungskultur. Eine Intervention.*
    C.H. Beck, 2013.
Assmann, Aleida. *Der lange Schatten der Vergangenheit. Erinnerungskultur und Ge-
    schichtspolitik.* C.H. Beck, 2006.
Berne, Eric. *Spiele der Erwachsenen: Psychologie der menschlichen Beziehungen.*
    Rowohlt Taschenbuch, 2007.
Bernhard, Thomas. *Heldenplatz.* Suhrkamp, 1995.
Die Hitler-Rede auf dem Heldenplatz in Wien im März 1938. www.doew.at/cms/
    download/78t22/maerz38_heldenplatz.pdf.

„Ewiger Jude, Ahasver, *Lexikonartikel*". *Homepage der GRA Stiftung gegen Rassismus und Antisemitismus, 2015.* www.gra.ch/bildung/gra-glossar/begriffe/judentum/ewiger-jude.

Foucault, Michel. „Andere Räume". *Aisthesis. Wahrnehmungen heute oder Perspektiven einer anderen Ästhetik. Essais.* Hrg. Karlheinz Barck, Peter Gente, Heidi Paris und Stefan Richter. Reclam, 1992, S. 34–46.

Götz von Olenhusen, Albrecht und Irmtraud. *Nazisuppe oder: Pathologien der Erinnerung. Thomas Bernhards Dramen und die Geschichtskultur.* www.literaturkritik.de/public/rezension.php?rez_id=18202.

Huber, Martin. *Der Heldenplatz-Skandal. Eine Rekonstruktion von Martin Huber.* www.thomasbernhard.at/index.php?id=190%20.

Ingen, Ferdinand van. *Thomas Bernhard: Heldenplatz. Grundlagen und Gedanken zum Verständnis des Dramas.* Moritz Diesterweg, 1996.

Judex, Bernhard. *Thomas Bernhard. Epoche – Werk – Wirkung.* C.H. Beck, 2010.

Klesse, Marc. „Verdrängungskultur. Thomas Bernhards Heldenplatz und das Tätertrauma Österreichs". *Parapluie. Elektronische Zeitschrift für Kulturen, Künste, Literaturen,* Nr. 22, Zeugenschaft, Winter 2005/2006, www.parapluie.de/archiv/zeugenschaft.

Moser, Jonny. „Die Apokalypse der Wiener Juden". *Wien 1938. Ausstellungskatalog. 110. Sonderausstellung.* Hrg. Historisches Museum der Stadt Wien, 1988, S. 286–297.

Reichensperger, Richard [*rire*]. *Literaturkritik | Kulturkritik.* Hrg. Claus Philipp und Christiane Zintzen. Springer, 2005.

Safrian, Hans und Hans Witek. *Und keiner war dabei. Dokumente des alltäglichen Antisemitismus in Wien 1938.* Picus, 1988.

Thomas Bernhard. TEXT+KRITIK. *Zeitschrift für Literatur.* Hrg. Heinz Ludwig Arnold. Heft 43, November 1991.

Namensverzeichnis / Index of Names